GOD AND MAN

LOVE ON THE ROCKS

STEVEN ROSNER

COVER DESIGN
AUDREY ROSNER

The opinions expressed in this manuscript are solely the opinions of the author and do not represent the opinions or thoughts of the publisher. The author has represented and warranted full ownership and/or legal right to publish all the materials in this book.

God and Man: Love on the Rocks
All Rights Reserved.
Copyright © 2018 Steven Rosner
v1.0

Author Contact: 347-304-0068
Email: smrosner@optonline.net

Cover © 2018 Audrey Rosner. All rights reserved - used with permission.

This book may not be reproduced, transmitted, or stored in whole or in part by any means, including graphic, electronic, or mechanical without the express written consent of the publisher except in the case of brief quotations embodied in critical articles and reviews.

Outskirts Press, Inc.
http://www.outskirtspress.com

ISBN: 978-1-4787-9632-9

Outskirts Press and the "OP" logo are trademarks belonging to Outskirts Press, Inc.

PRINTED IN THE UNITED STATES OF AMERICA

Preface

Love on the Rocks, ain't no surprise.
Just pour me a drink, and I'll tell you some lies. . . .
Gave you my heart, gave you my soul,
You left me alone there, with nothing to hold.
Neil Diamond[1]

Neil Diamond is, of course, referring to his relationship with a woman. But nothing could be a better metaphor to describe God's relationship with man—hence the title of this book. In our case, however, we don't need lies, but *truth*. For God created us with love and gave us *His* heart and soul:

And God created Man in His Own Likeness;
In God's image created He him; both male and female.[2]

We need to understand why God is estranged from us, and more importantly, how to repair our relationship and gain His many blessings.

To gain this understanding, we need to know something about God, something about ourselves, something about religion, and something about history. Most importantly, we need to know why His love for us is on the rocks and what specifically—not just abstractly—we can do about it!

This book takes on that enormous task, and, if you forgive me, that enormous responsibility!

Steven Rosner
April, 2018

---

[1] *Love on the Rocks*, by Neil Diamond and Gilbert Bécaud, in *The Jazz Singer*. Dir. Richard Fleisher. Singer: Neil Diamond. EMI Films, 1980.
[2] Genesis 1:27

ALSO BY STEVEN ROSNER

Books
A Guide to the Psalms of David
God is Good
[Available at Amazon]

Short Stories
Through Your Thick Skull
The "Get."
Only Their Names Were Different.
Sherlock Holmes and the Case of the Disappearing God
Sherlock Holmes: A Question of Motive
Sherlock Holmes: A Needle in a Haystack

Plays
Charles Grodin x Three

Essays
Ten Lessons from the Story of Creation
Messiah Now?
Who Has It Better—Man or Woman?
Three Little Words
An Irresistible Force vs. an Immovable Object
The Mystery of Suffering

Compilations
The Rebbe's Perspective

Reports
Leading the Lambs to Slaughter:
(Kings County Housing Court:
Solutions for a Dysfunctional System)
A Guide to Mental Health and Developmental Disability in Iowa

Citations

Following are the major sources used in the creation of this work. They and any other source are credited in the footnotes. Upon information and belief, no citation requires express permission for inclusion, for one of several reasons, including "being in the public domain," allowable under the "fair use" provision of copyright law, being a previous work by the author, or in the case of "Wikipedia," under its license, giving permission to use any text, for any purpose, provided the source is cited.

1. Citations of all psalms are taken directly from the author's translation, in his book, *A Guide to the Psalms of David*, 2nd Edition. (Colorado: Outskirts Press, 2015).

2. All other Old Testament citations have been extracted from various sources and/or translated or edited by the author. All citations are referenced with Chapter, and the Verse of the beginning of the citation. Note: quotes are not always literal. The author has, at times, taken poetic license and liberally construed, modified, shortened, or reworked Scripture for readability, so as to provide the reader with as much clarity as possible.

3. Several chapters in Part II and Part III have made substantial use of H. G. Wells' *An Outline of History*, whether through direct citations with footnotes, or the paraphrasing of content—the work being in the public domain.

4. Similarly, Flavius Josephus' *Wars of the Jews* and *Jewish Antiquity* in Chapter 16, are cited relating to intra-religious conflicts and wars within Judaism.

5. Direct quotes from other sources are footnoted appropriately, and/or covered under the *fair use* of copyright law.

6. Wikipedia articles are covered by the Creative Commons Attribution-Sharealike Unported License (CC-BY-SA), or the GNU Free Documentation License (GFDL), which allow unlimited use for any purpose, as long as the source is noted. See *https://creativecommons.org/licenses/by-sa/3.0/legalcode*

7. Citations whose sources are directly from the internet are footnoted, but there can be no guarantee that those links will still be valid after publication.

CONTENTS

	Page
Preface	iii
Citations	v
Chapter 1: Introduction	1
• Book Outline	5

Part I. God and Man

Chapter 2: Proving God Exists	11
Chapter 3: Biblical Creation vs. the Big Bang Theory	15
• Biblical Creation	15
• The Big Bang Theory	17
• Creation and the Big Bang	20
• Other Theories of Creation	21
Chapter 4: Scripture and Science	23
• Introduction	23
• Dinosaurs	24
• Carbon Dating	26
• Scripture and Science	31
Chapter 5: God	35
• God's Attributes	35
o Loving and Merciful	39
o The "Most Moved of Movers"	40
o Gracious and Forgiving	43
Chapter 6: Man	46
• Free Will	46
• The Soul	50
• Mind and Body	53

	Page
Chapter 7: Good and Evil	55
• Introduction	55
• Theories of Evil	56
• The Nature of Evil	59
• Praising Evil	62
• What is Good	64
• Satan	65
• Summary	68

Part II: Ethical Systems and Religion

Chapter 8: Ethical Systems	71
• Introduction	71
• Ethical Systems	72
o Stoicism	72
o Hedonism	73
o Consequentialism	75
o Deontology	75
• Problems	77
Chapter 9: Religion	80
• Introduction	80
• Religious Systems	82
Chapter 10: Judaism	87
• Introduction	87
• History	89
• Laws	93
o Laws Relating to Animals	94
o Laws of Slavery	96
o Laws of the Judiciary	97
o Criminal Law	98
o Civil and Business Law	100
o Laws of Compassion	102
o Laws of Personal Relationships	103

	Page
Chapter 11: Christianity	105
• History	105
• The Reformation	108
• Creed and Beliefs	110
○ Roman Catholicism	110
○ Protestantism	111
Chapter 12: Islam	113
• History	113
• Creed and Beliefs	117
Chapter 13: Buddhism	121
• History	121
• Creed	123
Chapter 14: Confucianism and Hinduism	128
• Confucianism	128
• Hinduism	131
• Summary	135

Part III: Love on the Rocks

Chapter 15: Love on the Rocks	137
• Our Laboratory	138
Chapter 16: *Intra*-Religious Conflicts and Wars	141
• Introduction	141
• Judaism	142
• Christianity	150
○ Early Crusades	150
○ The Inquisition	153
▪ The Inquisition - Not Very Jesus Like	159
○ Catholics vs. Protestants	161
▪ St. Bartholomew's Day Massacre–France: 1572	163
▪ The Siege of Alkmaar–The Netherlands: 1573	166

	Page
• Islam	168
o Sunnis vs. Shiites	168

Chapter 17: *Inter*-Religious Wars and Conflicts — 171
- Christian vs. Moslem — 171
  - The Crusades — 171
  - The Black Death — 174
- Moslem vs. Hindu — 178
  - Timurlane — 179

Chapter 18: War and Evil: 3000 BCE-350 BCE — 184
- Biblical History — 184
  - The Flood — 184
  - Tower of Babel — 186
  - Sodom and Gomorrah — 187
    - What if there was One Righteous — 189
  - Egypt — 190
  - Canaanite Nations — 192
  - The Kingdom of Israel — 193
  - Assyria — 194
  - The Kingdom of Judea — 195
  - Babylon — 196
    - Nebuchadnezzar Learns his Lesson — 198
  - Other Mid-Eastern Nations — 199
    - Moab — 199
    - Ammon — 200
    - Edom — 200
    - The Philistines — 201
  - Summary — 201

Chapter 19: War and Evil: 350 BCE-1900 AD — 203
- The Roman Republic/Empire (350 BCE-575AD) — 203
  - The Punic Wars — 203
  - Gladiator Games — 205
- The Mongols (1200-1400) — 207
- The Spanish Empire (1525-1825) — 212
- Napoleon (1790-1815) — 217

		Page
○ Whether an Individual or a Nation		222

Chapter 20: War and Evil: 1900-1950 — 223
- World War I — 223
- The Russian Civil War — 225
- Communism and The Soviet Union — 229
- World War II, the Nazis, and the Holocaust — 232

Chapter 21: War and Evil: 1950-Present — 236
- India and Pakistan — 236
- Genocide — 237
  - Cambodia — 237
  - Bosnia — 240
  - Rwanda — 242
- Summary — 244

Part IV: The Road Back

Chapter 22: Engaging God — 247
- Introduction — 247
- Divine Providence — 248
- Righteousness — 251
- A Relationship with Man — 254
- Engaging God — 256
- Faith — 258
- Loss of Faith — 266
- Summary — 268
  - How God Communicates with *You* Real-time — 269

Chapter 23: Suffering — 270
- Introduction — 270
- Causes of Suffering — 272
  - Death — 272
  - Accidents — 273
  - Illness — 277
    - The Most Serious Life-Threatening Diseases — 278

	Page
○ Man Inflicted Suffering	279
▪ War	279
▪ Exploitation	279
▪ Death of Children	280
○ Acts of God	284
○ Summary	286
• Reasons for Suffering	287
○ *Punishment* for sins	287
○ As a Preventive *before* one will Sin	288
○ Self-Inflicted	289
○ As a Sacrifice/Substitute for Another's Sins	290
○ To Test our Character	291
○ As a Prophylactic/Preventive Measure	291
○ To Teach Us Wisdom	292
○ As God's Emissary	293
○ To Identify with God	295
• A Final Word	296
Chapter 24: The Meaning of Life	297
• A Question of *Will*	297
• Saving the World	300
Epilogue	303

Appendices

Appendix I: The Ten Commandments	304
Appendix II: FAQs about God	305
Appendix III: Ten Ways to Connect to God	307
Appendix IV: Psalms for Special Situations	309
Appendix V: An Irresistible Force vs. an Immovable Object	311
Appendix VI: Ten Truisms about God	314
Appendix VII: Psalm 37 – by David	315

Chapter 1
Introduction

We live in an unprecedented time . . . The world is in disarray. The threat of a nuclear war is the greatest since the mid-1960s . . . Truth is an endangered species . . . Privacy no longer exists. The powerful and wealthy are heartless, while the poor are exploited. Our leaders are arrogant, and if not overtly corrupt, have no wisdom—and too many follow their lead. One's word is virtually meaningless. The United States has not been this divisive since the Viet Nam War. For decades the media has been no longer content with reporting the news, but making it—with a virtual disregard for truth. And now with the internet, every Tom, Dick, and Cathy has a forum for his/her venom—disturbed individuals who love to hate.

Terrorism is more frequent and more dangerous. Within a little over a month, beginning in October of 2017, 58 people were killed at a Las Vegas concert and another 26 at a church—no less—not to mention the hundreds who were injured. All by a lone gunman! No one is safe anymore; no one—no country—is immune!

Iran and North Korea have demonstrated they have nuclear capability. Even as I write these words, the latter is provoking the United States weekly by its rhetoric, while launching missiles over allies of this country. Yet the U.S., which could destroy North Korea in an instant, is incredibly foolish by escalating the war of words, oblivious to the fact that the "pen is mightier than the sword," for there is no telling what Kim Jong Un might do, if provoked enough, to save face. Alas, Theodore Roosevelt's admonition to "speak softly but carry a big stick," has been totally ignored by our leadership.

No one seems safe anymore. Yet if we ignore what is happening, events will soon catch up with us.

Fortunately, there is a God Who cares and Who has given us guidance over the centuries, through individuals as disparate as Moses and Jesus, Buddha and Mohammed, Confucius and the Beatles—yes, the Beatles—in a world in which hardship and suffering is the norm rather than the exception.

Indeed, not only was this country founded upon the belief in God, but George Washington had such certainty in Divine Providence that he even required his army to attend church!

> The General most earnestly requires and expects . . . of all Officers and Soldiers, not engaged in actual duty, a punctual attendance of divine Service, to implore the blessings of heaven upon the means used for our safety and defense.[3]

Unfortunately, these days in America, God is mostly ignored, while too often abused, disparaged, and forsaken—not necessarily by most of its citizens, but by foolish and self-righteous—often evil—individuals; to get attention for their

---

[3] Washington, George, *General Orders*: July 4, 1773, in *George Washington: A Collection,* edited by W. B. Allen (Indianapolis, Liberty Fund, 1988) p. 43.

agenda of the destruction of a society in which they are misfits. But far worse, our leadership fears them, the courts pander to them out of a misguided belief that freedom means anything goes, while celebrities and sports icons, who have nothing to recommend them except a certain talent that we foolishly value, instead of counting their blessings, add to the chaos by acting as if they are statesmen, when, in fact, they are more like ostriches who are so dumb they forget they have just laid eggs, if not actually crushing them inadvertently.

But as we intend to show, *you* can choose to do something to get the greatest protection of all—God!

> A thousand may fall at your side
> And ten thousand by your right hand,
> But it shall not approach you.
> For He shall dispatch His angels in your behalf;
> They shall transport you in their hands
> Lest you stub your toe against a stone.
> "Because he yearns for Me, I will deliver him."[4]

This book presumes that there is *One* God Who created our universe, a God Who goes by the Name of "Allah" for Moslems, "Hashem" for Jews, "The Father" for Christians, "Jehovah" for Jehovah Witnesses, or whatever name in whatever language denotes Monotheism. Presumes, actually understates the author's conviction of the truth of this statement. To him, that is not a mere assumption, but a certainty, and Chapter 2 proves God's existence by pure reason.

---

[4] Psalm 91

Now if we accept God as a reality, and as He cannot be deceitful, it must be axiomatic that the Bible is factual, in that everything stated therein of a historical nature actually occurred. This does not mean everything must be taken literally. Clearly metaphors and similes abound. But they are easily distinguished. For example, before giving the Ten Commandments, God says to the Children of Israel, "You have seen how I have borne you on the wings of an eagle."[5] Obviously, that is not to be taken literally. Likewise, when God states Israel is His first born son, He is speaking metaphorically, not that He has physically given birth to them.

This book, however, is not only about God, but *about you and me*. It is about our failure to heed God's word and His advice. Historically, the wisdom of Scripture that God has given us through His prophets has been ignored at best, but mostly mocked, while the world has been fraught with evil, danger, and suffering at every level. Yet God created the world and human beings out of *love*, and required very little of us. But since the eating of the fruit in the Garden of Eden, we have, as a species, totally failed to act in accordance with His relatively few wishes, have continually let Him down, and as a result, have brought unrelenting havoc to our lives.

But everything is subject to change. We—you and I—can start to repair the world—one person and one day at a time. For God

---

[5] Exodus 19:4

appreciates one who searches for truth and who lives a life of integrity. He will forgive that individual much more readily than those who strictly conform to ritual—whatever their religion—but have deceit in their hearts!

Book Outline

The book is divided into four parts entitled (1) *God and Man* (2) *Ethics and Religion* (3) *Love on the Rocks* and (4) *The Road Back*.

Part I begins with Chapter 2, proving that God exists using pure *reason*, with a unique but powerful argument. Chapter 3 discusses the Big Bang Theory vs. Creation as described in Genesis, and demonstrates, at the very least, they are absolutely and positively *mutually exclusive*—regardless of the number of books that state they are compatible; books that exploit the naivety of the public, so the authors can gain wealth and fame.

Chapter 4 discusses Scripture and Science, and maintains the two *must* be compatible. When they do not seem to be, as in Darwin's theory of evolution, we easily can show how such theories cannot be proven and, therefore, are *not* science. We discuss *Carbon Dating* and the flaws inherent in trying to extrapolate the age of animal and plant samples. We also show how the existence of dinosaurs is not only factual, but referred to in the *Book of Job*. And if we accept that the Bible is God's word, there are some amazing facts that can be *deduced*, such as: This is *not* the first universe!

Chapter 5 discusses God: His nature and attributes, such as His Love, Goodness, Graciousness, and Compassion—always ready to forgive us. And contrary to the assertions of some Cabalists, we demonstrate that God has feelings, and suffers greatly when we humans act abominably.

Chapter 6 is about Man, our nature, and the fact that we have a *body and soul*. And most importantly, that we were given the great gift of *Free Will*!

Chapter 7 explores *good* and *evil*. It reviews several theories of evil and answers the question whether evil has an independent existence, and if so, how it came about. It also discusses what "good" is and what "righteousness" means. Finally, it addresses *Satan* and clarifies what his functions, powers and limits are; i.e., whether he can turn into a scantily clad woman to tempt us into sin. We also answer the question whether Satan is, in fact, evil.

Part II is about ethics and religion. Chapter 8 is an introduction to ethics and reviews systems such as Stoicism, Hedonism, and Utilitarianism, and the problems with each. Chapter 9 is an introduction to Religion, and Chapters 10-14 review the history and major tenets of six major religions: Judaism, Christianity, Islam, Buddhism, Hinduism, and Confucianism. We will discover that the core of each is basically the same, but all have been changed drastically by those that came after its founder.

Part III describes why "Love" between God and Man is "On the Rocks," and provides numerous examples of Man's evil—as a result of greed, lust for power, arrogance, and pride. Chapter 16 details the *Intra-Faith* wars within Judaism, Christianity, and Islam, while Chapter 17 describes the major *Inter-Faith* wars, including those between Christians and Moslems, and Moslems and Hindus.

Chapter 18 through 21 review the history of the world from its creation until the present, demonstrating repeatedly how man's evil ultimately results in God punishing or destroying the perpetuator(s)—whether nation or individual. Chapter 18 covers Biblical times onwards to the 4th Century BCE, while Chapter 19 covers the period 350 BCE through 1900, with numerous examples, such as the destruction of Sodom and Gomorrah, the Roman Empire, the Mongols, and the Spanish Empire. Chapter 20 covers 1900 through 1950; fifty years of the worst monstrosity in the history of man, including World War I, the Russian Civil War, World War II, Communism, Nazism, and the Holocaust. Chapter 21 takes us from 1950 to the present, and includes the genocides in Rwanda, Cambodia, and Bosnia.

Part IV, *The Road Back,* shows how to improve our relationship with God, and begin to repair the damage we have caused—which, by so doing, allows us to regain His blessings.

Chapter 22 is about engaging God and identifying what He desires from His Creatures. That includes *righteousness*, a *relationship* with Him, and having *faith*. Chapter 23 is about *suffering*—the reasons and causes—and why God cannot be held responsible in the overwhelming majority of cases in which we suffer. Finally, Chapter 24 asks the question, "What is the meaning of life?" It suggests an answer, and reiterates the book's basic conclusions. It considers Divine Providence; whether God is involved in our world, or simply just watches us from afar without intervening in our daily lives. It also reviews how to gain God's blessings, and discusses whether we are only here to do God's *Will*, or whether, in fact, God very much wants to do *our* Will.

An Epilogue follows, and several Appendices add to the utility of the book. Appendix 1 contains the Ten Commandments, Appendix II contains FAQs about God, while Appendix III suggests ten practical and easy ways to connect to Him. Appendix IV suggests psalms to recite for 20 common life situations, such as when seriously ill, to find a husband or wife, before surgery, and during a divorce or break-up. Appendix V contains the inspirational essay, *An Irresistible Force vs. an Immovable Object*. Appendix VI summarizes ten truisms about God. Finally, Appendix VII contains the inspirational Psalm 37, by David,

Will this book change your life? No! Only you can change your life! But it will give you ample guidance and you will see how incredibly easy it is to make your life better—whatever your religion, if any! In all events, I hope not only to challenge but to delight, not only to educate—as painful as that will be at times—but console.

I hope and pray this book will give you new insight about God, and more importantly, motivate you to change your behavior in some small, but significant, way so you can take part in the goodness that life has to offer, and make your life more fulfilling. It will take some work, perhaps a leap of faith, and, most of all, courage. But the rewards are incalculable!

I might add that I am under no illusions that this book will inspire leaders of nations, or inspire even one executive to reconsider corporate policy and treat his employees better. But if only one act of kindness is a result of this book, it will have been worth the year-long effort—for every good deed, no matter how small, makes God feel just a trifle better, and by so doing, makes our world a better place!

Part I:

God and Man

Chapter 2
Proving God Exists

Between Moslems, Jews, and Christians, billions of people all over the world believe in a Being known in the English world as *God*. And billions more believe in His existence who do not ascribe to any particular religion. It also seems fair to say the overwhelming majority believe in God on *faith*. That certainly is not a bad thing, but in truth, the existence of God can easily be proven through pure reason. We will do so here, because His existence is a prerequisite for answering major questions of life: Where did we come from? Why are we here? Do we serve a purpose? Do we have any intrinsic value? What does God expect from us? To these, and many other questions relating to ethics and morality, the existence of God is fundamental.

Now there are several means of arriving at the knowledge of God—through faith, revelation, or experience—but all are valid only for the individual so inclined. Adding to the above is science. For example, advances in molecular biology have revealed enormous amounts of information encoded in every living cell—thousands upon thousands of what may be termed "exquisitely designed machines" at the molecular level. But information requires intelligence and design requires a *designer*. Biochemists and mathematicians have calculated that the odds against life arising from non-life via *unintelligent* processes are astronomical—if, in fact, scientifically possible. But if life did not arise by chance, how did it arise? Clearly, natural laws order the universe. Where did these laws come from, and what purpose do they serve? The answer, of course, is from God.

Yet the above proofs don't convince everyone. For example, no amount of evidence could change the mind of an atheist, already dedicated to the philosophical idea that nothing can exist outside of the natural realm. Asking him whether God exists would be pointless. His answer would always be "no." He would simply state anything that God might have done (that is, any supernatural act which might serve as evidence for His existence) can be explained in terms of natural causes, not because he knows what those natural causes are, but simply because a supernatural God is not *allowed* to exist!

Accordingly, it is knowledge through pure reason alone that allows God's existence to be proven *for all humans for all time*!

And, in fact, the proof of the existence of God is incredibly simple, and should be understandable to all readers—provided one keeps an open mind and is willing to think outside the box. We begin with the following premises:

Postulate 1: Consider the inanimate objects in the universe, either in nature or man-made: the sun, moon, Empire State Building, automobiles, baseballs, pebbles on the beach, the chair you are sitting on. I think you will agree none can create itself, let alone any other object that comes to mind.

Postulate 2: Now consider all plant life, such as trees, flowers, and shrubs. Again, I think you will agree that none could create itself nor create any other living or non-living object.

Postulate 3: Now consider animals and man. Again, it should be obvious that *none can create itself* (although most could be the source of an offspring), nor could any create another living entity—except that man can create certain non-living objects here on earth.

It should be manifest, therefore, that as every material object—inanimate or alive—on the face of this earth or in heaven above does *not* have the ability to create itself, we can only conclude they must have been created by a being with the power to do so—a being we designate as *God*!

But, you may reasonably ask, "Who created God?"

"Oh, that is easy," I tell you. "Albert Einstein."

"Albert Einstein?" you respond, humoring me. "Well, who created Albert Einstein?"

"Why I thought you knew. Sigmund Freud."

Figuring I have totally gone off my rocker, you try once more. "Okay, then who created Sigmund?"

"What, you don't know that either? Why, Attila the Hun, of course."

Now God doesn't mind a laugh or three, but in truth, no matter how far you take this absurd path, no matter how many regressions you go through, you can never logically satisfy the proposition that *God was created*. Accordingly, there is no other choice but to conclude *God was not created*! Or in other words, *God always existed*!

Granted, this is extremely difficult for a human being to comprehend. Our mind is programmed to believe in cause and effect. Everything must have a cause, our mind tells us. But we have just proven logically—without doubt—*that* is not possible! Go over our reasoning. Can you find a flaw?

Accordingly, we need to reprogram ourselves and accept the fact that true *reality is* that *cause and effect* are secondary within our universe; that is, it is only based upon the laws of nature that God created, while *God has no cause other than His own.* Put another way, *God's essence is His existence, while our existence is based upon His gift of grace.*

I realize this proposition will take some getting used to, and, as I indicated earlier, it requires thinking out of the box. However, review the proof once or twice and you should have no difficulty realizing *there is no other possibility*!

Given the above, it is a simple matter to deduce that the Bible is, in fact, God's word. Furthermore, any miracles reported therein must be assumed to have actually occurred. One cannot believe in God while denying He is incapable of miracles.

Chapter 3
Biblical Creation vs. the Big Bang Theory

Biblical Creation

According to Scripture, our world was created by *design*—by an ineffable Being we call *God.*

In the beginning, God created the heavens and the earth![6]

Those ten words are a lesson *revealed* for all time. It was God, the ultimate *Source* Who created our universe. Clear, concise, powerful. Darwin and other evolutionists, as well as modern scholars who believe that man evolved over hundreds of thousands of years, and that this world is billions of years old, are absolutely contradicted by the Bible. There can be no splitting of hairs despite recent books that claim the Big Bang theory and Scripture are compatible. One can be in either camp—*but not in both*!

A brief review of Scripture, therefore, which elegantly and succinctly describes the creation of our universe, is in order. Note it depicts *what* God did, not *how*. Each act was a *miracle*. Creation took place in *six days*, and "on the seventh day, God rested."[7]

Prior to creation, the earth was formless and empty, darkness was over the surface of the deep, and the Spirit of God hovered over the waters.

---

[6] Genesis 1:1
[7] Genesis 2:1

On Day One, God created light and separated the light from the darkness.

On Day Two, God created a firmament between the waters and separated them. And He called the firmament "Heaven."

On Day Three, God gathered the waters under the firmament into various seas, and caused dry ground to appear. He called the dry ground "Earth." Additionally, God caused the earth to produce vegetation: seed-bearing plants and trees that would bear fruit.

On Day Four, God created the sun, the moon, and the stars—to separate day from night, and to serve as signs for calculating months, years, and the seasons.

On Day Five, God created fish, birds, creatures of the sea, and every living thing in which the water teems.

On Day Six, God created the land animals, livestock, beasts, and creeping things He also created us, humans, stating, "Let us make mankind in Our likeness, so that they may rule over the fish in the sea, the birds in the sky, the livestock and all the wild animals, and over all the creatures that move along the ground."[8]

Scripture then tells us God rested on the seventh day (the Sabbath), and hallowed it because He had completed His work.

Now there are those who believe each "day" was not 24 hours—which is the obvious meaning of Scripture—but lasted billions of years to conform to *science*. They would like to make Scripture and science compatible at any price. Truthfully however, there is no basis to accept that. If one believes in God, then one must believe He could have created our universe in six 24-hour days.

---

[8] Genesis 1:1-31

But even some adherents of Scripture wish to change the meaning of the verses to suit their scientific bent. This is most evident in the "Big Bang" theory of creation, which is the dominant—but far from only—theory of the origin of the universe. Books have been written purporting to show how the Big Bang and the Bible are compatible. But that is pure nonsense! Those authors are simply exploiting the naivety of the public for their own agenda and to sell books. Accordingly, we will review the essence of the Big Bang theory and show how both views are, and must be, *mutually exclusive*!

Parenthetically, we might mention that Scripture also contradicts the major Kabalistic theory of creation, which states that the transformation of the "spirit" of God to the "material" was accomplished through "vessels" that shattered, and we, humans, must repair the damage. While I personally believe there is no reason to consider *how* God created this universe, the theory that postulates a shattering of vessels is both false to the Bible and demeans God by stating what He did was flawed.

Au contraire: "And God saw everything that He had made, and behold it was *very good*. And there was evening and morning: the sixth day."[9]

The Big Bang Theory

According to the Big Bang theory, our universe sprang into existence around 13.7 billion years ago. It began as an

---

[9] Genesis 1:31

infinitesimally miniscule, infinitely hot, infinitely dense object, known as a "singularity." Where it came from and why it appeared, science doesn't tell us.

Regardless, the singularity presumably inflated, expanded, and cooled, evolving from the very, very small and the very, very hot, to the size and temperature of our current universe. It continues to expand and cool to this day.

Note that the expansion is not viewed as conventional explosion, but rather an event filling all of *space* with the particles of the embryonic universe rushing away from each other. That is, the Big Bang postulates an inflating of *space* within itself—not one of matter. Unlike a balloon popping and releasing its contents, scientists imagine an infinitesimally small balloon expanding to the size of our current universe—and we are in it.

In fact, scientists believe space did not exist prior to the Big Bang. According to the theory, time and space had a finite beginning that corresponded to the origin of matter and energy. The *singularity* did not reside in space; rather, space was born inside the singularity. Prior to the singularity, nothing existed: neither space, time, matter, nor energy.

The process in which the universe was formed, according to the Big Bang—the steps number over a dozen—is beyond the scope of this book. It is enough to relate that as the universe continued growing in size and the temperature dropped, there existed an almost equal amount of matter and antimatter,[10] which collided and was transformed into pure energy. But as matter was fractionally more numerous than anti-matter, the universe matured in a way favorable for matter to persist. Slowly, the discrepancy grew larger and matter began to dominate. Further evolution resulted in the slightly denser regions of the distributed matter gravitationally attracting other nearby matter and growing even denser, forming gas clouds, stars, galaxies, and planets.

Theory suggests that the first galaxies[11] formed about a billion years after the Big Bang, and since then, larger structures evolved, such as galaxy clusters and super clusters. Groups of stars have been aging and evolving, so that galaxies that formed relatively recently appear markedly different from galaxies formed at similar distances shortly after the Big Bang. Scientists believe this based upon a phenomenon known as the *red shift*,[12] in which as light from distant galaxies approaches earth, its wavelength becomes stretched.

Georges Lemaître, in 1927, was the first to propose the Big Bang theory, after observing a red shift in distant nebulae. He

---

[10] Theory states antimatter are particles identical to matter (i.e. have the same mass) but have the opposite electrical charge.

[11] Galaxies are composed mainly of stars, interstellar gas, and dust that are gravitationally bound together.

[12] Red shift describes how light changes as objects in space, such as stars or galaxies, move farther away from us. Visible light is a spectrum of colors, as seen in a rainbow. When an object moves away from earth, the light is shifted to the red end of the spectrum, as its wavelength becomes longer.

found that distant galaxies in every direction were traveling away from us at enormous speeds. As seen from Earth, light from other galaxies is red-shifted in direct proportion to their distance. That is, galaxies that are twice as far from us are moving twice as fast.

Creation and the Big Bang

We now are in a position to analyze the so-called compatibility of the Big Bang and Scripture. What should be obvious is that the Big Bang requires the stars to be created *prior* to the earth, which needed billions of years of cooling before it could be formed. But as we saw earlier, the sun, moon, and stars were created on the fourth day—*after* the earth! Even more telling is the fact that the Bible begins with, "In the beginning God created the heavens and the earth. Now the earth was formless and empty, darkness was over the surface of the deep, and the Spirit of God hovered over the waters."[13] Incredibly, even *before* Day One, *water* existed! That fact alone should put to bed any consideration of compatibility between the Big Bang and Scripture.

Although we need no other evidence than the above, we might mention that *vegetation* was created on the third day—*prior to the creation of the sun and moon*. Unless temperatures were about what they are today, vegetation would be impossible. Yet there is nothing remotely in the Big Bang theory that would allow vegetation to be created before the sun, unless it was a miracle!

---

[13] Genesis 1:1

Accordingly, the two points of view are mutually exclusive!

We have gone into considerable depth, and will do so again in the next chapter relating to Scripture and science. It is not to prove the validity of Scripture's account, but to show the fallacy of the untenable—indeed, ludicrous—claims that are often made in the name of science, as well as to strengthen people of faith who might be influenced by a theory which rejects what their heart longs for.

Other Theories of Creation

Of course, the Big Bang is not the only plausible cosmological theory which exists. Many physicists have devised models operating within a biblical framework, which—to-date—have withstood criticism from the most vehement of opponents.

One such theory is based upon two laws of thermodynamics which are recognized as fundamental to science—that everything in the universe is some form of energy, and every process is a form of energy conversion. The First Law of Thermodynamics—known as the Law of the Conservation of Energy—states energy can be neither be created nor destroyed. While it can be transferred from place to place or transformed from one form to another, the total quantity of energy in the universe is constant.

The Second Law states that every transformation of energy is accompanied by a loss in the availability of energy for the future performance of work. This idea can be expressed quantitatively by the term *entropy*, which is the amount of energy in a conversion process which becomes unavailable for further work.

In short, no process can be 100 percent efficient. Some energy must be used to overcome friction, and will eventually be radiated into space and dispersed.

Based upon these two laws, at some point all energy in the universe becomes unavailable, as it will have been gradually converted into uniformly dispersed heat. All will be at the same low temperature, no more work can be done, and the universe will reach equilibrium, or what physicists call, "heat death."

Now if the universe was eternal,[14] the amount of usable energy available for work would have already been exhausted; its thermal energy would have been evenly distributed throughout the cosmos, leaving each region at a uniform temperature close to absolute zero. But that is not the case. Clearly, therefore, the universe must have been created—when the entropy value would have been absolute zero; increasing from then on.

In short, the universe had to have a beginning; it could have not begun itself. As total energy is constant, but available energy decreases over time, as we go backward, the available energy would have been progressively greater until the point where it equaled total energy. Time could go back no further. At that point, not only energy, but time, had to come into existence. And since energy could not create itself, the most scientific and logical conclusion is that: "In the beginning, God created the heaven and the earth."

---

[14] Eternal is defined as an event with no beginning and no end.

Chapter 4
Scripture and Science

Introduction

Millions of individuals who do not know Scripture assume that science and the Bible are incompatible. On the other hand, some very devout people of all religions disdain and distrust science, believing only that the Bible is correct.

But, in fact, God created this universe with certain laws that we can rely on—*science*—otherwise we'd be living in chaos. Does the sun not come up every day, and until recently, did not sailors need the stars to steer by?

> The heavens testify to the Glory of God
> And the firmament proclaims His handiwork.
> Day after day reveals His word
> And night after night reveals His wisdom.
> Yet there is no speech; there is no language.
> Their voice is not audible.
> Rather, His Grandeur emerges throughout all the world.
> Their words are manifestations to the ends of the earth.
> In their midst He has set a tent for the sun. . . .
> Rising from one end of heaven
> And traversing the sky to the other end.
> Nothing is hidden from its warmth.[15]

Accordingly, Scripture and science *must* agree. And while, over the centuries, God has allowed us to discover many scientific laws, it has not all been straightforward. Virtually every scientific advance has been subject to an untold number of errors, until it reached the point that truly may be called *science*.

---
[15] Psalm 19

Therefore, the major question we must consider is whether a *theory*—such as relativity—can be called science. As theories have been shown to be incorrect—such as the causes of disease, or that the sun revolved around the earth—it only proved they were *never* science. What is science, then? The fact that one can take two-parts hydrogen gas and one-part oxygen gas, mix them under a specified temperature and pressure, and always get water.

Indeed, if a so-called scientific theory is incompatible with Scripture, *it must be both wrong <u>and</u> not science*! True science/technology is not only *not* a threat to God's word; it can often explain certain mysteries in Scripture that have stymied our scholars for millennia.

Two topics that many believe are incompatible with Scripture are dinosaurs and carbon dating. Both seem to imply that the earth has been in existence far longer than the almost 6000 years that Scripture asserts. Let us examine both and see if we can find a resolution to the seeming incompatibility.

Dinosaurs

The existence of humongous animals such as the Dinosaur, the Tyrannosaurus rex, and the Spinosaurus is factual enough, but the idea that they had to be roaming the earth millions of years earlier can easily be refuted. But first, let us look into Scripture, which describes such animals in great detail!

We turn to the *Book of Job*, in which he bitterly complains about his fate, and demands to speak to God. And indeed, Job gets his wish:

Gird your loins like a warrior! I will question you, and you shall answer me. Do you have an arm like the Lord's? Can your voice, like His, evoke thunder? See now the Behemoth, which I created along with man and who chews grass like cattle. What strength it has in its thighs; what force in the midst of its belly! Its tail is akin to a cedar; the sinews of its thighs cannot be separated. Its bones are fashioned as bronze; its limbs, rods of iron. It ranks first among the works of God, yet only its Creator can approach it with His sword. A raging torrent does not frighten it. Can anyone capture it or pierce its nose?

Can you reel in the Leviathan with a fishhook or secure him with a rope? Can you put a tether through his nostrils? Can you adopt him as a pet like a bird or place a leash upon him for your maidens? Can you fill his hide with harpoons or his head with fishing spears? If you place a hand upon him, your end will be instantaneous! Any hope of subduing him is a fantasy; the mere sight of him evokes terror. No one is rash enough to arouse him.

Who dares breach the portals of his face, surrounded by teeth of destruction. His spine has rows of shields sealed together that cannot be parted. No air can pass between them. His snorting emits flashes of light; from his mouth sparks of fire are expelled! Smoke spews from his nostrils; his breath sets coals aflame!

His might resides in his neck. His heart is firm as rock; hard as a millstone. When he rises, even the mighty are terrified. Swords have no effect; neither does the spear or javelin. He treats iron like straw and copper like rotten wood. Arrows are like dust particles; slingshot stones are like pollen. He laughs at harpoons.

His undersides are jagged shards; he reclines on boulders as if they were a bed made of down. He makes the depths of the sea boil over like a caldron, leaving a glistening wake as white as the ancients. Nothing on earth can compare to him—a creature without fear. He looks down on all that are haughty. He is king over the insolent.[16]

Clearly, the above describes the dinosaur or the Spinosaurus—one living on land and one in the sea—not remotely like any animal that is alive today. Yet what happened to them? Can we find a solution to this dilemma? Most likely and most reasonable is that they were destroyed—for whatever reason God determined—in the great flood during the time of Noah. Their bones would eventually come to the fore, and so they can now be seen in museums.

Yet we must also consider that they may still exist in remote corners of the world, but God has kept them hidden. While this is not an assertion, it is not beyond the realm of possibility that they reside in the Bermuda Triangle, and are the cause of the unexplained disappearance, over the centuries, of a number of ships in that part of the world. Probably, most readers would be skeptical of this explanation, believing with our modern technology and hundreds of satellites circling the globe, that dinosaurs would surely have been seen if still extant. But if God wishes to hide them, He certainly can accomplish that.

Carbon Dating

Second, and more challenging, is *carbon dating*. It was developed in the 1940s as a standard tool for archeologists, and they claim dates have been measured of up to 50,000 years ago—far greater than the Bible would allow for.

---

[16] Job 40:7

For our purposes, a simplified review of the nature of an *atom*—the smallest stable unit of matter—is called for. Composed of three particles, a *proton, neutron,* and *electron,* the last has a negative charge and a negligible weight—technically, known as *mass.* A proton has a positive charge whose mass is about 1850 times that of an electron, while a neutron has no charge, but whose mass is slightly more than that of a proton. The number of electrons in an atom determines its physical properties, defined by the term *element.* Thus, hydrogen has one electron, carbon six electrons, and oxygen eight electrons. When atoms collide with one another, they form molecules, or in some cases transpose into different elements.

Although the number of protons and electrons are always equal, most atoms have two or three variations of mass, based on the number of *neutrons.* Each variation is known as an *isotope.*

Carbon, our focus here, has three naturally occurring isotopes: C^{12}, C^{13}, and C^{14}. C^{12} and C^{13} are stable, but C^{14} is *radioactive* and is constantly being created in the atmosphere by the interaction of cosmic rays with atmospheric nitrogen. It then combines with oxygen to form carbon dioxide, which is incorporated into plants by photosynthesis, and is passed on to animals that eat the plants.

When the animal or plant dies, the radioactive carbon that decays is no longer replenished by the environment. Measuring the amount in a sample from wood, a dead plant, or an animal provides information that can be used to calculate how long ago the animal or plant lived. The older a sample, the less C^{14} there is to be detected, because the half-life—or period for half of the radioactive carbon to decay—is about 5,700 years.

Let us first assume carbon dating *is* science and it *can* measure samples up to 50,000 years. That would not be incompatible with Scripture, if we posit that *this is not the first universe*! If so, the destruction of earth would have remnants—bones, wood from plants, etc., of creatures and fauna existing *before* our current universe, which could easily result in the 50,000-year calculation—except that scientists would never consider that their samples came from a *previous* universe.

Is this mere fantasy? Not at all. If one accepts the truth of the Bible, we can deduce that this, in fact, is *not* the first universe!

> In the beginning God created the heavens and the earth. Now the earth was formless and empty, darkness encapsulated the surface of the deep, and the *Spirit of God hovered above the waters.* Then God said, "Let there be light," and there was light. And God saw that the light was good; and He separated the light from the darkness. And God called the light "day," and the darkness "night." And there was evening and there was morning; the first day.[17]

---

[17] Genesis 1:1

Astoundingly, before God did anything such as creating light (Day One), separating the waters (Day Two), planting seeds (Day Three), and creating the sun, moon, and stars (Day Four), *water already existed*! Where did it come from? Clearly, one cannot hold that God and water existed simultaneously. Rather God must have created water—in a previous universe! In fact, many universes might have been created and destroyed before ours. But even one previous universe can easily explain the carbon dating findings.

Nevertheless, I suspect this extremely simple solution will make most readers uncomfortable. Accordingly, let us examine why carbon dating is *not* yet scientific, and why it grossly overestimates the age of a sample.

As stated above, once a *living* thing dies, C^{14} is no longer replenished but decays, while C^{12} remains constant. Therefore, if we know the ratio of C^{14} to C^{12} for *living* entities, and can measure the amount of C^{14} in the remains—knowing that its half-life is 5,730 years—simple arithmetic should tell us how old the sample is.

Now in the atmosphere, the ratio of C^{14} to C^{12} turns out to be one C^{14} atom for a trillion C^{12} atoms. Assuming the ratio in a living plant or animal is the same, when it dies the ratio will begin decreasing, as C^{14} decays but is no longer replenished.

Accordingly, the smaller the ratio, the longer the sample has been dead.[18]

Two critical assumptions must be true, however, for the dating to be accurate. First, the ratio of C^{14} to C^{12} in the atmosphere must be constant. That is, it must *always* have been 1 to 1 trillion. Second, the C^{14} ingested by plants must equal the C^{14} that undergoes decay. If either or both assumptions are false, then the calculation of the starting amount of C^{14} would be impossible to determine.

As it turns out, neither assumption holds. Ironically, the discoverer of carbon dating himself, Dr. Willard Libby's very own calculations showed that if the earth began with no C^{14} in the atmosphere, it would take 30,000 years to get to the point in which the Production Rate (SPR) of C^{14} and the Decay Rate (SDR) were equal—i.e. in *equilibrium*.

However in 2017, SPR is 18.8 atoms per gram of carbon per minute, while SDR is only 16.1 atoms per gram per minute. Clearly, if it takes 30,000 years to reach *equilibrium*, but that has yet to occur, even 30,000 years, already 20,000 years less than

---

[18] For example, if the remains were found to have one C^{14} atom for every two trillion C^{12} atoms, the sample would be dated 5730 years ago—since it would take that long for the C^{14} to decay in half. Similarly, if the sample was found to have one C^{14} atom for 4 trillion C^{12} atoms, it would be dated 11,460 years ago. (Assume there were 10,000 C^{14} atoms in a bone fragment at the time an animal died. After 5730 years, half the C^{14} would decay leaving 5,000 left. Then 5730 years later, half of that would decay leaving 2,500, or one-quarter of the starting amount.)

that claimed by carbon dating, would be much too early a date for any given sample.

Second, one must consider the earth's magnetic field. Continually decaying, it is currently about 10 percent weaker than when first measured in 1845, less than 200 years ago. But as the stronger the magnetic field, the fewer cosmic rays reach the atmosphere, there had to be much smaller production of C^{14} in prior millennia. Accordingly, the C^{14} in any remains would be incorrectly thought to have undergone much more decay than in actuality, resulting in significantly overestimating its age.

Last, but not necessarily least, the Genesis flood had to have buried huge amounts of carbon from living organisms to form today's fossil fuels. Those vastly larger quantities of vegetation than exist currently is evidence that the biosphere prior to the flood had hundreds of times more carbon in living organisms than it does today. As a result, the C^{14}/C^{12} ratio could have been up to 1/500 less than today's level and estimates of samples prior to the flood could wrongly be dated ten times greater than its *true* age.

For all these reasons, *carbon dating* cannot be relied upon. While it may be sexy, it is yet to be proven that it is *science*!

Scripture and Science

Not only is science compatible with Scripture, it can often explain puzzling events or episodes, such as when Elijah died and was taken to heaven in a chariot of fire:

> Now when the Lord was about to take up Elijah by a whirlwind to heaven. . . . Elisha went with him to the Jordan River. And Elijah took his mantle, folded it, struck the waters, and they parted. Then both crossed over on the dry ground. Upon reaching the other shore, Elijah said to Elisha, "What may I do for you before I am taken?"
>
> And Elisha said, "May twice as much spirit as yours be placed upon me."
>
> Elijah responded, "Your request is difficult. Yet if you see me when I take leave of you, it shall be so; but if not, it shall not be so." Then, behold, a chariot of fire appeared with horses of fire separating the two. And Elijah went up by a whirlwind to heaven.
>
> Elisha saw it and exclaimed, "My father, my father, the chariot of Israel and its horseman!" He took hold of his garment and tore it in two. He then retrieved the mantle of Elijah that fell from him, stood by the bank of the Jordan, and declared, "Where is the Lord, the God of Elijah?" And when he struck the waters, they separated, and Elisha crossed over.[19]

As it turned out, Elisha produced the most miracles of any prophet in the Old Testament. But isn't it a bit odd that only if Elisha saw Elijah going to heaven would he have that power? What is that supposed to signify? Here, science can provide an answer. We now understand that light is largely a wave, and humans can only see a portion of the spectrum—based upon the wave's *length*—from red at the low end to violet at the high end. But higher and lower wave lengths exist, including ultra-violet rays, x-rays, infra-red rays, and gamma rays. All are part of light, but invisible to man. Accordingly, Elijah knew that if Elisha could see him taken up to heaven, God would provide him with

---

[19] II Kings 2:1

the ability to see *infra-red*—invisible to other humans—which would give him great power.

This manifested itself later when the king of Aram sent troops to Elisha's home to capture him, because, through prophesy, he was constantly revealing to the King of Israel when and where Aram deployed its troops to attack her.

> Now the king of Aram sent horses, chariots and a large army to Elisha's city. They arrived at night and surrounded it. When the servant of the man of God had risen and gone out, behold, he saw the army encircling the city. So he said to Elisha, "Alas, my master! What shall we do?"
> Elisha answered, "Be not afraid, for those who are with us are more numerous than those who are opposed to us." Then Elisha prayed, "Oh Lord, I pray Thee, open his eyes that he may see." And the Lord opened the servant's eyes, and behold, the mountain was full of horses and chariots of fire all around Elisha.[20]

Temporarily, Elisha's servant was also given the ability to see infra-red light.

Aside from science explaining Scripture, the above demonstrates unequivocally that there are indeed spiritual forces we cannot see, and if we are righteous, God will place them around us for protection!

> He who dwells within the abode of the Most High
> Shall rest securely under the shadow of the Almighty.
> You will not fear the terror by night,
> Nor the arrows launched by day;
> Neither the pestilence that treads in the darkness,
> Nor the destruction that ravages at noon.
> A thousand may fall at your side
> And ten thousand by your right hand,

---

[20] II Kings 6:14

> But it shall not approach you.
> *For He shall dispatch His angels in your behalf;*
> *To watch over you in all you do.*
> They shall transport you in their hands
> Lest you stub your toe against a stone.
> "Because he yearns for Me, I will deliver him.
> I will elevate him, because he knows My Name.
> When he calls upon Me, I will answer him.
> I will fulfill him with long life.
> And make known to him My salvation."[21]

To conclude, there is nothing incompatible between Scripture and science.

---

[21] Psalm 91

Chapter 5

God

He is God alone; the Eternal. There is none like unto Him.
   The Koran: Sura 112

God's Attributes

Having proved the existence of God and demonstrated there is every reason to believe the Five Books of Moses are God's word and thus factual, we are now in a position to ascertain His nature. The Bible, of course, is the first and most comprehensive source of information about God—but it is far from the only means of understanding Him. Other sources, including the Koran, history, and our own experiences will be cited during the course of this book.

If there is one word that describes God's nature, *beneficent* would be a good choice. While *evil* does exist in the world, and the age-old question—which we will examine in Part IV—why it seems the wicked thrive and the righteous suffer is still not entirely answered, we will temporarily put that aside.

Now if you asked people for one or two words to describe God, most would probably use such terms as Infinite, All-Powerful, Omniscient, Perfect, Omnipotent, Eternal, and Awesome—qualities no human is capable of. Yet in Exodus 34:6, when Moses requests that God reveal His Glory, He states nothing about His perfection, His power, His wisdom, or His knowledge.

God's answer? וַיִּקְרָא יְיָ ׀ יְיָ אֵל רַחוּם וְחַנּוּן אֶרֶךְ אַפַּיִם וְרַב חֶסֶד וֶאֱמֶת transliterated as "Hashem, Hashem, El rachum vchanun, erech apayim, vrav chesed, vemes—or *"The Lord, the Lord, merciful, and gracious, slow to anger, and abundant in goodness and truth."*

Analyzing what God stated, we find the Hebrew "rachum" means *compassionate*, by which we can be sure God goes out of His way to help our physical, spiritual, and emotional hurts or pains. Now "compassion" comes from the Latin *compati* "to feel pity," evolving from *com* "together" + *pate* "to suffer." Thus, we can state without fear of contradiction, *when we suffer, God suffers*. Also, we should note that this attribute of God *does not* involve any judgment of the individual, whatsoever.

The Hebrew "chanun" on the other hand means "graciousness" or "favor," which does have a *moral* or judgment component, yet is still granted freely by God if He desires—even though we might not deserve it. Conversely, we can add "mercy" to our definition in the sense of forgiveness, so that it should be clear God is always—or at least almost always—ready to forgive us for our follies—provided we are sincere in regretting them.

Now "erech apayim" usually is translated "slow to anger," but literally "erech" means "lengthy" or "prolonged," and "apayim" comes from the root "panim" which means "face" or "countenance." In effect then, we can derive its meaning as "long-suffering." More precisely, God holds His anger in when we evoke His wrath by our abominations, but He suffers for it.

"Chesed," which we define as "kindness," is somewhat different than both "compassionate" and "gracious." The former two describes the *character* of God, whereas the latter, together with the word "rav" meaning "much" or "abundant," speak more about God's desires and deeds. In other words, God wishes to bestow goodness or *blessings* upon mankind. *That* is His basic nature, and why He created this universe. However, being good or kind is behavior marked by ethical characteristics and unlike "graciousness," God blesses only those who deserve it.

Finally, "emes" means "truth" which needs no adjective, such as "abundant." Something is either true or not. And it is important to recognize that "truth" not only means that God's word can be depended on absolutely, but He is *faithful* as well. Unlike humans, God keeps His promises!

It should be also noted that at the beginning of the verse, God states His Name, the four Hebrew letters yud, hey, vov, hey, which translates to "the Lord." Yet names are only used to distinguish between multiples of one species, while it is—or should be—obvious there is only One of Him. Therefore, one might understandably think that stating His Name or even having a name is superfluous. But although subtle, God, by stating "the Lord" twice, is instructing us that "names" or more precisely, *reputations,* are extremely important. Indeed, its importance is brought out vividly in the *Book of Job*, while our own laws of slander and libel testify to that, as well. We can be sure therefore, God gets quite angry when we gossip, especially when we talk about someone behind his/her back—which is also denoted by the commandment, "Do not curse the deaf."[22] Incidentally, as one's name is an abstract concept and belongs in the realm of the *spiritual*, we have evidence, even if indirect, that the spirit or soul remains after the body passes away.

In summary, amazingly—and significantly—God clearly states that the most important godly qualities *are those that humans can emulate and attain*—Compassion, graciousness, integrity, forgiveness. For God would like us to emulate Him—or as Scripture states, "walk in His ways."

Looking at God from a broader and historical perspective, we again see His beneficence. As described in my book, *God is Good*,[23] there are 155 instances recorded in the Old Testament in which an individual, a group, or a nation prayed to God for something specific. And God's response? *In 139 cases, or 90 percent of the time, He assented to the request*!

Now if growing up, our father acceded to our wishes 50 percent of the time, would we not think we had the best father in the world? Accordingly, despite all the suffering we see around us, including that which we ourselves might be subject to, we can only conclude God is in fact good, and only wishes the best for us!

---

[22] Leviticus 19:14
[23] Rosner, Steven, *God is Good* (Colorado: Outskirts Press, 2016) available at Amazon, Barnes & Nobel, or can be ordered from your local bookstore.

Loving and Merciful

God is even willing to undergo pain, by creating a world that He knew would largely be corrupt, for the sake of showering His blessings at least upon some of us (as few as we may be), and sharing even an infinitesimal part of His goodness.

> And the Lord God took the man, and put him into the Garden of Eden to cultivate it and to keep it. And the Lord God commanded the man, saying, "Of every tree of the garden you may freely eat: but of the Tree of the Knowledge of Good and Evil, you shall not eat of it: for in the day that you eat thereof you shall surely die!"[24]

Is it not true that because of God's benevolence and love, initially man was placed in a most beautiful garden that had everything? There was no pollution, the weather was perfect, the food was all-natural and delicious. Animals were tame, and there was no suffering. Adam and Eve had only one prohibition—any other choice they made was acceptable.

Although fiction, this idea could hardly be expressed better than by the character of Sherlock Holmes in one of Arthur Conan Doyle's stories. Holmes is investigating the disappearance of a document detailing a secret treaty between England and Italy, which, if leaked, would have immense repercussions.

> *Holmes*: "What a lovely thing a rose is!"
> *Dr. Watson*: Holmes walked past the couch to the open window, and held up the drooping stalk of a moss rose, looking down at the dainty blend of crimson and green. It was a new phase of his character to me, for I have never before seen him show any keen interest in natural objects.

---

[24] Genesis 2:15

> *Holmes:* "There is nothing in which deduction is so necessary as in religion," said he, leaning with his back against the shutters. "It can be built up as an exact science by the reasoner. Our highest assurance of the *goodness* of Providence seems to me to rest in the flowers. All other things, our powers, our desires, our food, are really necessary for our existence in the first instance. But this rose is an extra. Its smell and its color are an embellishment of life, not a condition of it. It is only goodness which gives extras, and so I say again that we have much to hope from the flowers!"[25]

The Most Moved of Movers

Many theologians believe that God is neither changeable nor has feelings. Their reasoning is that as God is "perfect," He cannot have emotions nor change His mind—for both indicate lack of perfection. The problem with that point of view is that *perfect* is a human concept and applying it to God truly makes no sense. Looking at it from a different angle, if God was incapable of changing His mind, would that not be considered a *lack* of omnipotence? Likewise, is there any reason *a priori* to assume that having feelings is an imperfection? Quite the contrary. Having no feelings would indicate God's power is limited.

Rather, as we alluded to earlier, God *suffers* when mankind does evil.

> Now when men began to multiply on the face of the earth, and daughters were born unto them, the sons of God saw that they were fair, and they took themselves wives of whoever they chose. And the Lord said, "My Spirit shall not always contend with man, for he is of flesh; yet his days shall be a

---

[25] Doyle, Arthur Conan, *The Naval Treaty*, as reproduced in: eastoftheweb.com/short-stories/UBooks/NavaTrea.shtml, p. 15.

hundred and twenty years." And God saw that the wickedness of man was great, and that every imagination of his heart was only for evil. And the Lord regretted that He had created mankind, and *He suffered heartfelt grief.*[26]

According to Abraham Joshua Heschel:

If we put aside the categories and logic of Greek philosophy and try to understand biblical religion in its own terms, we will soon discover that the God of the bible is not Aristotle's impassive, unmoved mover at all; He can only be described as *"the Most Moved Mover."*

According to the Bible, the single most important thing about God is not His perfection, but *His concern for the world.* . . . The God of the Bible is not aloof but involved, not distant but near, not immune from, but vulnerable to what happens in His world and what His creatures do. In a word, God seeks intimacy. He is especially "in search of man," desiring a relationship and cherishing the hope that, out of this relationship will come proper human actions and just societies. God has a stake in our behavior. Thus, He cries when we fail and rejoices when we succeed. He weeps when we ignore widows, exploit orphans, and abuse strangers; and when we violate the norms He has taken pains to communicate to us, He angrily sends prophets to chastise and warn us. What all this means is that God is filled with feeling, with pathos. Strange as this might be to Aristotle, it is the very essence of Biblical religion and of the Judaism that arose from it.[27]

An even more poignant example can be found in Jeremiah. God has contended with the Children of Israel for centuries, and

---

[26] Genesis 6:1
[27] The Philosophy of Abraham Joshua Heschel, in *An Introduction to Modern Jewish Thinkers: From Spinoza to Soloveitchik*, Alan T. Levenson, (Lanham, MA, Roman and Littlefield, 2006), p. 215., citing Fritz A. Rothchild, "Architect and Herald of a New Theology," *Conservative Judaism* (Fall 1973) p. 58. "Chapter Thirteen: Abraham Joshua Heschel," p. 21.

despite everything He did for them, they continually rebel and commit all sorts of abominations. God is both angry and saddened by the above, and can no longer abide by their evil. He causes an extended drought in Judea. Jeremiah thus exclaims:

> Judea is filled with anguish. Her cities are wasted away. Weeping is heard in Jerusalem. The nobles send their servants to get water, but they do not find any. Everyone is terrified. They have no hope. There has been no rain in the land. The ground is parched. The farmers are trembling.
>
> "Oh Lord, although our sins are a witness against us; although we have completely turned away from You; act now for the honor of Your Name. You are our only hope. You have always rescued us in time of trouble. Why are You like a stranger to us? Lord, You are among us. And we are Your people. Please don't desert us!"[28]

But God is too angry and hurt by centuries of abuse.

> "These people do not desire Me. Their feet traverse the path of iniquity. I will not accept them. I will only remember the evil they have done and punish them for their sins. Do not pray for them, Jeremiah. For even if they go without food and put on sack cloth, I will not listen to their cries. Rather I will destroy them with war, hunger and the plague. Their own evil will return upon their heads."[29]

This prophesy devastates Jeremiah, but he loved his people far too much to remain silent. He cannot help, therefore, but ask for mercy:

> "The tears flow from my eyes day and night. The people of my nation have been devastated. If I go to the fields, I see

---

[28] Jeremiah 14:2
[29] Jeremiah 14:10

people who have been killed by the sword. And if I enter a city, I see corpses who have died of hunger.[30]

"Lord, have You turned Your back on Judea completely? Do You so loathe us? Why have You stricken us so we can't be healed? We hoped for peace, but there is only war. We hoped for healing; but there is only disease. We hoped for redemption, but there is only terror. We know, Oh Lord, of our evil. We also confess the iniquity of our forefathers. For it is true that we've sinned against You. So for the sake of Your Name, do not turn Your back on us. Remember the covenant You made with us. Please don't annul it. For can any of the worthless gods of the other nations produce rain? Is it not You and You alone, the Lord, God? So we put our hope in You."[31]

But enough is enough! God has suffered too much to relent!

"Even if *Moses and Samuel were standing in front of Me praying on behalf of these people, My heart would have no desire for them.* Send them away from Me!"[32]

Clearly, Scripture does not hold the view that God has no feelings. Rather, multiple times it states God has exceptionally strong feelings, affected greatly by what we, His creatures, do. Can there be any doubt that the anger and pathos expressed in His dialogue with Jeremiah, can only be the result of the great love God has for us, which, through the centuries, we have scorned?

Gracious and Forgiving.

The above, it should be noted, is an extreme case. But consider this: Not once . . . not twice . . . not three times . . . but seven separate times, God was ready to destroy the Children of Israel, but forgave them because of the intercession of Moses.

---

[30] Jeremiah 14:17
[31] Jeremiah 14:19
[32] Jeremiah 15:1

Of course, God explicitly states He is ready to forgive us numerous times. For example, in Ezekiel:

> "If a wicked person turns away from the sins that he has committed and does what is just and righteous, he shall surely live; he shall not die. None of the transgressions that he has committed shall be remembered; but for his righteousness he shall live. Have I any pleasure in the death of the wicked," declares the Lord, "rather that he should turn from his evil ways and live."
>
> "Repent and turn away from sin lest it be your ruin. Cast away the evil you have committed and create for yourself a new heart and a new spirit! Why should you die? For I take no pleasure in the death of anyone," declares the Lord, "so turn away from sin and live."[33]

As another example, God was ready to destroy the city of Nineveh—the capital of Assyria—and tells Jonah to go to the city and relay His word that unless they cease their evil, in 30 days the city will be razed. Jonah eventually does so, and Nineveh repents. Yet Jonah is upset about the situation.

> But it greatly displeased Jonah, so he left Nineveh and made a shelter for himself. He sat under it to see what would become of the city. Now God appointed a plant and directed that it cover Jonah and be a shade over his head, to keep him from discomfort. So Jonah exceedingly relished the plant. But at dawn the next day, God directed a worm to attack the plant, so that it withered. Then a scorching east wind and the sun beat down on Jonah so that he became faint.
>
> And he asked that his life be taken, stating, "It is better for me to die than to live."
>
> So God said to Jonah, "Are you grieving on behalf of the plant? You pity the plant, for which you did not labor nor make grow; which came into being in one day and perished in

---

[33] Ezekiel 18:21

one night. Should I, therefore, not have compassion on Nineveh—that great city, in which there are over 120,000 people who do not know their right hand from their left?"[34]

Although we too do not know our right hand from our left, God still watches over us.

For a fitting end to this chapter, let us cite George Washington's sentiments at the end of the Revolutionary War:

> The Commander in Chief orders the Cessation of Hostilities between the United States of America and the king of Great Britain to be publicly proclaimed tomorrow at 12 o'clock. . . . After which the Chaplains with the several Brigades will render thanks to almighty God, for all His mercies, particularly for His overruling the wrath of man to His own glory, and causing the rage of war to cease amongst the nations.[35]

---

[34] Jonah 4:1
[35] Washington, George, *General Orders*: April 18, 1783, in *George Washington: A Collection,* p. 236.

Chapter 6

Man

And Man was created in God's image . . . in His likeness.
Genesis 1:27

Free Will

The above citation does not, of course, mean that God has a physical presence. Rather, man was given various attributes that God has, such as the ability to think and to feel. But of all the gifts God gave man, by far the most crucial was *Free Will;* the liberty to choose; to decide which road to take. Angels do not have that ability, but are constrained to do what God commands.

This gift cannot be overemphasized, since the overwhelming majority of evil in the world stems from it. In this chapter, we will look at some of the proofs of man's free will, beginning with, arguably, the most important section in all of Scripture.

> And it came to pass, that Cain brought the fruit of the earth for an offering to the Lord. And Abel, as well, brought of the first of his flock and of the fat thereof. And the Lord accepted Abel's offering, but as for Cain and his offering, He desired not.
> So Cain became exceedingly wroth and his countenance fell. And the Lord said to Cain, "Why are you so wroth? And why has your countenance fallen? When you do well, shall it not be lifted up? Although, be advised should you not do well, sin crouches at your door and you shall be tempted by its desire. *But you may rule over it!*"[36]

---

[36] Genesis 4:3

Here, God is making a statement to humans *for all time*! We absolutely have *free will*! *We always have a choice*! The idea that we can overcome sin—better temptation—is stated clearly! Of course, with this gift, comes *responsibility*. When we make the wrong choice, God will hold us responsible.

Naturally, when things go badly and we become desperate, it is much easier to go astray. Easier, but not mandatory! Temptations can be overcome! Indeed, not only does one have a choice of doing what is right and good; one also has a choice *not to be a victim of others*!

The implications of the above are profound and need to be stated clearly. For when we look at our world today, sensitive humans are appalled by our values and morality in virtually every sphere of endeavor: politics, business, medicine, law, sports and academia. We constantly make excuses and say we could not have done otherwise or everybody does it. We are told by a corrupt medical establishment—who only wish to gouge us out of our money controlled by drug and insurance companies—that alcoholism, for example, is an illness; that it is in our genes; that "substance abuse" is a disease and should be treated as such, say like mental illness. Hogwash! The Bible—as we have just seen—says *not so*; which is also attested to by common sense.

Rather, in moral issues we need to think more in terms of black and white. Being too liberal in allowing destructive behavior by others in our society is not wise. An important example relates to alcoholism. Surely one has a choice: "to drink or not to drink," as Shakespeare might have put it—and how much. Indeed, if we do *not* make that distinction, we may as well absolve all crimes committed in that state as "unavoidable illness," and throw out the *Driving Under Intoxication* laws, for in that scenario, drunks who maim and kill others while driving, have a disease, and therefore no moral responsibility for their action.

God's statement to Cain is only one of many examples of this imperative in the Bible. Let us look at three additional examples. Consider the very first day when God created light.

> And God said, "Let there be light." And there was light. And God saw the light and it was good, and God separated the light from the darkness.[37]

I believe God was making an initial statement confirmed by the rest of Scripture—that in the *moral* sphere, there are *no* gray areas! Behavior is either black or white, smart or foolish, good or evil!

Especially noteworthy is when God commanded Adam and Eve not to eat from the Tree of Knowledge of Good and Evil. Clearly He could have easily restricted their access to it, or not have planted it in the first place. Yet, that one *and only one* commandment was sufficient to tell us for all time that God desired that humans *have a choice*. So, even before we knew—or were tempted by—evil, *Free Will* was in effect.

---

[37] Genesis 1:3

Then there is the charge Moses gave to the Children of Israel, shortly before they were to cross the Jordan River into Canaan.

"See, I have set before you today, life and prosperity; death and adversity; in that I charge you this very day to love the Lord your God, to walk in His ways and to keep His statutes, so that He may bless you in the land He has promised. But should your heart turn away and you rebel by worshipping and serving other gods, I declare to you that you shall surely perish. Your days will be cut off in the land across the Jordan.

"I now call heaven and earth to bear witness against you; that I have set before you *life and death, good and evil, a blessing and a curse. Choose life,* in order that you may live—you and your children—by loving the Lord, obeying His voice, and cleaving to Him. For through Him is your life and the length of your days."[38]

In fact, not only do we have *Free Will*, but it is perfect as such! That is, while our knowledge is far inferior to God's knowledge, our *Will* has no such boundaries, but is equivalent to God's own Will. Rene Descartes has expressed this idea as follows:

"Considering what my errors are, I observe that these depend on the occurrence of two causes; viz., the faculty of cognition that I possess, and the election or power of free choice—in other words, the *understanding* and the *will*. . . .

"Nor can I complain that God has not given me freedom of choice or a will sufficiently ample and perfect, since I am conscious of a will so ample and extended to be superior to all limits.

"And what appears to me to be highly remarkable is that of all the other properties I possess, *there is none so great and perfect that I do not clearly discern could be even greater and more perfect*. . . . For although the faculty of the Will is

---

[38] Deuteronomy 30:15

incomparably greater in God than in myself, as in respect of the knowledge and power that are conjoined with it, and that render it stronger and more efficacious. . . . It does not nevertheless seem to me greater, considered in itself formally and precisely; for the power of Will consists only in this, that we are able to do or not do a thing . . . [and] *are not conscious of being determined to a particular action by any external force.*"[39]

Alas, the real tragedy is that most people are totally unaware that whenever we do what is difficult and take the morally right road, even when it seems to our disadvantage, things will work out for our benefit—although not necessarily immediately. At the very least, we are earning future points for our "retirement." It is fair to say for each spiritual dollar we put in our IRA or 401K account in heaven by acting morally and doing what is right, God contributes twice as much, if not more. But when we act wrongly, it is like prematurely taking money out of our heavenly IRA, and incurring severe penalties.

The Soul

Besides free will, man was also given a *soul*. Virtually all monotheistic religions agree to that idea, and posit some sort of after-life and ultimate resurrection, although it is not clear whether it will be of a physical or purely spiritual nature. There is also disagreement about the criteria for the above—whether it is based upon works, faith, or some combination. In Part II, we will consider what the various religions believe, but for now let

---

[39] Descartes, Rene, *Discourse on Method*, Meditation IV, trans. E. Nicole Meyer (New York, Barnes & Nobel, 2004) pp. 112-113.

us provide several examples proving that, indeed, the soul lives on after we die.

The first is indirect, yet quite powerful. Taking the Pentateuch at face value and accepting it as the word of God, the deductions one can make are profound. Thus, Moses commands the Children of Israel:

> When you arrive at the land which the Lord your God has promised you, you shall not follow after the abominations of those nations therein. There shall not be among you any that that makes his son or his daughter pass through fire, practices divination, astrology, or consults with *familiar spirits*. Nor with one who acts as an enchanter, a witch, a charmer, or a *necromancer*.[40]

Aside from the obvious implication that God desires we should not—for our own good—attempt to know the future, the fact that we should not consult *familiar spirits*—that is, someone known to us, or *necromancers*—who bring up the dead—is a strong indication that the soul lives on—or else there would be no need to add both prohibitions to that commandment.

While there are dozens of examples asserting there is life after death, both in the New Testament and in the Koran, we will limit ourselves to three additional from the Old Testament.

Psalm 91 discusses the benefits of being righteous and having faith in God:

> Because you stated, "The Lord is my Refuge,"
> No evil shall befall you,
> Nor shall the plague approach your dwelling.

---

[40] Deuteronomy 18:9

> For He shall dispatch His angels in your behalf;
> To watch over you in all you do.
> They shall transport you in their hands
> Lest you stub your toe against a stone.
> "Because he yearns for Me, I will deliver him.
> I will elevate him, because he knows My Name.
> When he calls upon Me, I will answer him.
> I will be with him in his disquietude.
> I will deliver and honor him.
> I will fulfill him with long life.
> *And make known to him My salvation.*"[41]

The meaning should be clear. Besides long life, a righteous person will see ultimate salvation—and he/she will be resurrected at the appropriate time.

Next is when Saul, the King of Israel, consults a necromancer to bring up the prophet Samuel—who originally anointed him—to find out his fate in the coming battle with the Philistines.

> Then the Necromancer said [to Saul], "Whom shall I bring up for you?"
> "Bring up Samuel for me."
> When the woman saw Samuel, she cried out with a loud voice.
> Saul said to her, "What is his appearance?"
> And she said, "An old man is arising wrapped in a robe."
> And Saul bowed with his face to the ground and paid homage. Then Samuel said to Saul, "Why have you disturbed me by bringing me up?"
> Saul answered, "I am in great distress, for the Philistines are gathered against me, and God has turned away from me and answers me no longer, either by prophets or by dreams. Therefore I have summoned you to tell me what I shall do."

---

[41] Psalm 91

And Samuel said, "Why do you ask me, since the Lord has turned from you and become your enemy? The Lord has done to you as He spoke, and has torn the kingdom out of your hand and given it to David. Moreover, the Lord has given Israel into the hand of the Philistines; tomorrow you and your sons shall be with me."[42]

Finally, Daniel, having prayed to gain an understanding of visions he had seen, is visited by the angel Michael:

> Then I, Daniel, looked, and before me stood two others. One said to the man clothed in linen, "How long will it be before these astonishing things are fulfilled?" and I heard him say "It will be for a time, times, and half a time; when the power of the holy people has been finally broken, all these things will be completed."
> I heard, but I did not understand. So I inquired: "My lord, what will the outcome of all this be?"
> He replied, "Go on your way, Daniel, because the words are obscure and sealed until the time of the end. Many will be purified, but the wicked will continue to do evil. None of the wicked will understand, but those who are wise, will. As for you, go your way. You will rest, but at the end of days *you will rise to receive your allotted inheritance.*"[43]

Mind and Body

If the soul is separate from the body—and lives on after death—how does it relate to the *mind*, which many philosophers believe is also separate from the *body*. Is the mind, then, the same as the soul? And what about our emotions? Are they part of the mind, part of the body, or perhaps they are independent of both?

These are difficult questions to answer, but it appears that the

---

[42] I Samuel 28:11
[43] Daniel 12:5

mind and soul are separate entities, and that the former controls the body—at least in terms of conscious action. The following schematic—overly simplified—describes the sequence of events.

Feeling/Desire/Emotion → Mind → Will → Body → Action.

In other words, our emotions/desires enter the conscious mind, which evaluates what to do, then instructs the Will to provoke the body to action. We will leave out the soul in this scenario, and see how, or whether, it fits in later.

It certainly appears that actions are based primarily upon our feelings or desires. That is, the major cause of doing something—good or bad, right or wrong—stems from our emotions. If we are infatuated with a woman, we will find some excuse to engage her in conversation. If we fear someone who happens to be walking towards us, we will cross the street to avoid him.

Most people would not consider doing something contrary to how they feel. But what if, at times, *our feelings come from God—to test us*? Then we should consider that actions/feelings may be bi-directional. [*Feeling/Desire/Emotion ←→ Action.*]

In other words, if we act first, appropriate feelings will follow!

We end this chapter, by asserting that this is *one of the secrets of the human/divine relationship*. This insight should not be underestimated. Because of Divine Providence, when God sees you act in a certain way—the right way—He changes how you feel—not only emotionally, but physically. When you take a leap of faith, God sees that you land on your feet!

Chapter 7

Good and Evil

Woe to those who call evil "good" and good "evil"; who place darkness for light and light for darkness.
Isaiah 5:20

Introduction

One of the most profound questions about the nature of man and problematic for all religions relates to *good* and *evil*. Specifically, what is good? What is evil? Does evil have an independent existence? Where did it arise from? Why does God allow it—or is He incapable of preventing it? Are "Acts of God" evil? Is there a difference between the fate of the righteous and the wicked? And what, if anything, can *we* do about it?

Many people think of evil as just violence or criminal behavior, but that is hardly sufficient. Old but true, "the pen *is* mightier than the sword." Too often, words hurt more than a slap in the face. In this chapter we will propose a definition of evil and look at some examples. We will find that in many cases evil *is actually praised by our society*! In Chapter 23, we will examine suffering in depth; why it appears good things happen to the wicked and bad things happen to the righteous, and whether we can hold God responsible.

Theories of Evil

By way of comparison, we will briefly review several theories of evil and the reasons they are inadequate. One basic question is whether evil has an independent existence or is simply the *absence of good*. Many philosophers and theologians, in both Judaism and Christianity, believe that evil is the latter.

For example, St. Augustine considered the idea that if God cannot abolish evil, He cannot be all-powerful, while if He chooses not to, He cannot be all-good. But neither was acceptable to Augustine, so he concluded. "Nothing *evil* exists in itself, but can only be part of some actual entity. Where there is no privation of good, there can be no evil."[44] For Augustine, evil is parasitic on the good.

He argues that while God is totally and *absolutely* good, created things are only *relatively* good. That is, they can be diminished—i.e. corrupted—or augmented. Diminishing good things is evil because it results in privation. In other words, as something is being corrupted, the good in it is being removed. Usually, some good remains unless there is total corruption, in which case there is no good left, because the thing no longer exists—and not even the corruption remains, because there is nothing tangible to attach itself to. Therefore, according to Augustine, "there can be no evil where there is no good."

---

[44] Saint Augustine, *Enchiridion On Faith, Hope, and Love*, Translated by Albert C. Outler, Ph.D., D.D., Chapter IV, No. 12, as reproduced in: "www.tertullian.org/fathers/augustine_enchiridion_02_trans.htm"

There are several problems with this point of view. Three that come to mind include the fact that corruption or destruction to Augustine is a "thing," which in the overwhelming majority of cases can hardly be considered evil. If I eat an apple—which is good—the more I eat, the more diminished it becomes, but no one would think my eating it is evil. A second problem, common to many theories of evil, is that Augustine considers evil a noun—that is, something material, when evil, as we shall see, must be a verb—or some sort of action. Finally, whether some things are good cannot be stated *a priori*, but depend upon their use. Thus, there are certain plants of which a little ingested can heal, while too much can kill. Are they good or evil?

For Cabbalists evil is a much thought about topic. According to one tradition, evil has no objective reality, but is only an illusion. In creating the world, God used ten vessels, called *Sefirot*, to manifest His essence. Each vessel contained Godly attributes such as wisdom, power, beauty, and compassion. However, according to this theory, man was unable to receive all the emanations of the *Sefirot* and this lack, is the origin of evil—a "negative" reality separated from its Source.

This is quite unsatisfactory, on the one hand because it is based on the *process* of Creation which is pure speculation. Nothing in Scripture remotely indicates that God uses "vessels" to manifest His Essence, nor is there any reason to think He need do so. Even accepting the Sefirot framework, why would one think God could not make each vessel adequate to hold His emanation.

More reasonable is another Kabalistic view that holds the universe has a duality of sort; that in the *Sefirot*, there must be an actual root of evil and death, balanced by a root of good and life. But the former became separate and substantive while being differentiated. This, at least, posits a separate existence of evil, but it still fails in that it only explains the *potential* for evil, which is far different than its actuality. Nor is it clear what that potential is.

Neuroscientists have recently added to the mix by claiming evil doesn't exist because what society considers evil is actually a malfunction or a malformation of the brain. According to their view, actions that cause someone else to suffer are not made consciously. Autonomous, conscious decision-making is an illusion, so intentional evil is impossible. They would abolish prisons, because man can never be guilty of a crime; even individuals like Hitler and Stalin were not evil *per se*, but compelled to do what they did.

Aside from rejecting *free will*, their viewpoint is ludicrous. We mention this not only because their atheistic theology has no basis, but because we deem those holding this view are themselves evil, as they couldn't care less about the victims, while totally exonerating those whose behavior is monstrous!

The Nature of Evil

To start with, it should be clear that evil is not pain; it is not suffering; it is not death. Nor is it a noun or "thing" as implied by Augustine. If we say John Doe is evil, we are not saying he entered the world that way, but has acted abominably enough times that we judge him to be evil. Our definition supposes that we humans are neither intrinsically good nor bad, but are the product of accumulated forces in our lives which affect our *free will*. Evil, then, is an action of the will and must have an independent existence.

As an example, say you pass a well-dressed man late at night who is lying in an alley. You go to check him out and find he is neither ill nor hurt, but drunk. You remove his wallet to find his name, and discover he has 5000 dollars in cash. If you take it and leave the scene, you have acted evilly. If you wake him up and help him home, you have done good. Or, you may just replace his wallet and walk on, not wishing to get involved. Evil, thus, is not the absence of good, but has its own life. It is *tangible*!

To claim otherwise cannot be sustained by either Scripture or logic. Taking the latter first, we know there are many things in life that are neither good nor evil—i.e., whether one decides to eat at a Chinese or Italian restaurant. But logically, that would not be possible if we accept that the absence of good must be evil.

Scripture is also quite clear on this point. When God told Adam not to eat the fruit of the Tree of the Knowledge of Good and Evil, it should be manifest that evil already existed, else there could be no knowledge of it. More specifically, in a number of places in Scripture, God, through His prophets, talks about punishing certain behavior as destroying *the evil in your midst!* Why would a beneficent God create or, at least, allow evil? The answer to this question has to do with *free will*. If there was no *potential* for evil, *free will* would be meaningless.

We quoted this earlier, but an excerpt is worth repeating:

> "See, I have set before you today *life and goodness; death and evil*, in that I command you today to love the Lord your God and to walk in His ways, so that He may bless you in the land you are entering. But if you will rebel, are drawn away, and worship and serve other gods, I declare to you this very day that you shall surely perish. I have set before you *life and death, a blessing and a curse. Choose life* so that you may live; you and your descendants."[45]

Here, God, Himself, states through Moses that evil exists independently of good.

We also must distinguish between suffering and evil. Evil always has a moral quality. A terrorist who blows up 20 people is evil. The prosecutor, judge and jury who see that he hangs are not. In mathematics, two negatives multiplied make a positive (i.e. $-4 * -6 = +24$). Likewise, God's or man's action in destroying an evil individual or nation, is actually good.

If evil is tangible, what does it consist of? According to Christian theology, there are seven categories of sin: Lust, Gluttony, Greed, Sloth, Wrath, Envy, and Pride.

---

[45] Deuteronomy 30:15

Judaism largely agrees with these categories: It states evil is:

A proud (vain) look.
A lying tongue.
Hands that shed innocent blood.
A heart that devises wicked acts.
Feet that are swift in running to mischief.
A false witness that speaks lies.
He that sows discord among his brothers.[46]

Additionally, during the Day of Atonement (Yom Kippur), Jews ask God to forgive the sins that they may have committed during the previous year. They include:

*Murder, *Robbery, *Violence, *Haughtiness, *Gossip, *Perversion, *Scoffing, *Idolatry, *Deceit, *Contempt, *Bribery, *False Promises, *Extortion, *Brazenness, *Jealousy, *Baseless Hatred.

Note in both Judaism and Christianity, evil is much more than criminal behavior. Indeed, certain acts such as scoffing, gossip, haughtiness, sloth, and envy, while not subject to the modern laws of nations, are evil in God's eyes!

Regarding murder, premeditation is, of course, evil, but killing someone in war/self-defense is not. In the latter instance, the person knows he is in danger and has the right to defend himself. But what about insulting someone, acting pretentiously, treating others with disrespect, or telling tales about someone? What about acts, such as adultery—prevalent among all societies? Is that not evil? As prohibitions of the Old Testament, it certainly is in God's eyes!

---

[46] Proverbs 6:16-19

Praising Evil

Especially difficult to justify is *evil* disguised as *good*. One example is the corporate CEO who is behind a hostile takeover of another corporation. The act itself implies unbelievable arrogance on the part of the CEO to initiate a multi-billion-dollar deal solely because of his/her own ego. In fact, almost 85 percent of corporate takeovers *fail* miserably for a variety of reasons, not the least being that these acts are extremely hateful to God.[47]

The evil, of course, is the fact that for two years or more before the merger is approved and takes place, *hundreds of thousands* of individuals of both companies are placed in no-man's land, not knowing their future in the new corporation. And the unknown is psychologically the worst of all fears! Will their pension be cut or eliminated? What about their health insurance? Will they even have a job? These takeovers wreak havoc upon hundreds of thousands of lives, and cause the families of the employees' tremendous anxiety. The terrible effects have been well-documented. Is this not evil incarnate? All because of one individual who initiated the takeover, concerned only with power, and ruled by greed. Yet, takeovers are usually *praised* by segments of our society, such as the Wall Street Journal and other financial publications, not to mention the investment banks who finance the takeover—making tens of millions in the process—as

---

[47] http://lakeletcapital.com/blog/2017/3/15/success-and-fail-rate-of-acquisitions

a "smart" economic move on the part of the initiating corporation.

Personally, I would not want to be in the shoes of the CEO when he comes before God to be judged! I have no doubt he will suffer exponentially more than the jewel thief, who practiced his avocation for thirty years, but burglarized homes that were always empty, and who never actually hurt anyone.

Another evil that is accepted and praised by most of society are class action suits against corporations and corporate officers for security law violations. They, of course, only occur when the stock price goes down sharply. But they are morally and legally indefensible because (1) corporate officers do not determine the price of a stock, and (2) there is absolutely no proven relationship between the economic soundness of a company and its stock price. Examples proliferate, such as the dotcoms in the late 1990s who were bid up to 100 dollars a share without any economic basis whatsoever, and a year or two later either folded or struggled along at a dollar or less. The fact that many corporate executives are ambitious, egotistical, and greedy does not mean they are criminally dishonest or that they have committed fraud in their corporate news releases by knowingly providing false and over-inflated estimates of earnings and revenue.

Rather, these suits are all about the greed of law firms who earn *billions of dollars* a year in settlements, while the shareholders get a small percentage of what they allegedly lost— even though 95 percent of the time the reasons they bought the stock had nothing to do with the claims of the lawsuit or announcements of the company. For trial lawyers, the winning payouts are staggering. For example, overall class action settlement fees for attorney firms in 2006 was over *16 billion dollars*—while the average return to the shareholders who were presumably defrauded totaled less than 100 dollars.[48]

Can anyone doubt the *evil* of the above two examples whose only basis is incredible greed and arrogance!

What is Good.

If evil has an independent existence, so does *good*. Scripture repeatedly relates what God considers good, which, in essence, is the basis for all the religions we will cover. It is treating your fellow man the way *you* would wish to be treated. To be more specific, a number of psalms summarize characteristics and actions that are good—and attest to their just rewards. Characteristics include integrity, compassion, and sincerity. Behaviors include:

- He who walks uprightly and who acts with righteousness.
- Whose words are heartfelt.
- Who does not slander with his tongue.
- Who has not cast aspersions against his colleagues.
- In whose eyes a contemptible person is repugnant.
- Who honors those that fear the Lord.
- Who keeps his vows, even to his detriment.
- Who clothes the widow.
- Who feeds the orphan.

---

[48] www.instituteforlegalreform.com/uploads/sites/1/Securities_Class_ Actions_Final1.pdf

- Who lends not his money at interest,
- Who does not take a bribe against the innocent.
- He who does all these things "shall never come to ruin."[49]

Satan

Most religions—especially large segments of both Judaism and Christianity—believe in a being known as *Satan*, otherwise known as the devil, and they attribute to him several key attributes that make him the source of evil. But who exactly is Satan and where did he come from?

Scripture first mentions him in the *Book of Job*:

> Now the angels of God came before the Lord, and the Satan, as well, came among them. And the Lord said to the Satan: "Where have you been?"
> And the Satan replied, "From going to and fro upon the earth."
> And the Lord said to the Satan, "Have you observed My servant Job; that there is none like him; whole-hearted and upright; one that fears God, and shuns evil?"
> Then the Satan answered, "Does Job fear God for nothing? Have You not placed a hedge about him; his house, all he owns, and blessed the work of his hands? But put forth Your hand and remove all that he has; surely he will blaspheme You to Your face."
> So the Lord said unto the Satan: "Behold, everything of his is in your power; only upon his person restrain your hand."[50]

In Hebrew, the translation of Satan is "adversary," in the sense of a spiritual prosecutor. Notice that Satan is always prefaced by the word *the* indicating there is only one such being. Accordingly, we may conclude that chief among Satan's duties,

---

[49] Most of the above are derived from Psalm 15.
[50] Job 1:6

is to inform God when those of us on earth have sinned (leaving alone why God needs Satan to do that—doesn't He know everything a man does). Also, it should be manifest that as an angel, Satan has extraordinary powers—evident by all the misfortune he inflicts upon Job.

However, the key issue is whether Satan, or others like him, *tempt* man into sin. In other words, is there a *transcendent* "evil" force outside of our emotions, feelings, and desires that tries to lead us astray? If a man sees a ravishingly, beautiful woman tempting him to sin, is the woman real or rather some spiritual being that is disguised as a human? I would argue the answer must be the former.

First, our own emotional and physical make-up is such that we are constantly struggling to do good; to be righteous and not to sin. That is enough of a challenge without having additional outside forces to deal with. More importantly, as Satan is a spiritual being with extraordinary powers, would it not be unfair of God to make us have to fight him off, in addition to controlling our own emotions and predilections? But God is, above all, fair and righteous. Accordingly, it is inconceivable that He would create beings outside ourselves to try to make us succumb to sin.[51]

We also should point out that Satan cannot formally be considered evil, as claimed by many religious theologies. This is

---

[51] Every rule has an exception, and there are times in which we are constrained to act in a manner determined by God.

because God would not create an evil angel. Significantly, as an angel, Satan does *not* have free will. He can only do what God directs him to. That alone precludes judging him morally by his behavior. Just as district attorneys who prosecute criminals, and policemen who give out parking tickets are feared and not liked very much, they certainly cannot be considered evil. So too, with Satan.

Finally, we need to address the serpent in the Garden of Eden, who tempted Adam and Eve to rebel against God. Many readers might understandably point out that if it was not Satan himself, clearly it *was* transcendent—an outside force—that tempted Eve.

We would agree, except to state it was the one and only time God permitted an outside force to tempt us—necessary to test Adam and Eve. Despite that, they were not at an unfair disadvantage. Weighed against the serpent, was the Garden of Eden—beautiful to look at, with wonderful fragrances; having pure and delicious food and perfect weather, not to mention the ability to engage their Creator. Even more telling, neither Adam nor Eve was born of a human; both were created by God Himself and had a purity and goodness that was at least equal to the evil of the serpent. Should they not have resisted the temptation?

And when they did eat from the tree, keep in mind that it was not a tree only of the knowledge of *evil*, but the knowledge of *good and evil*! As such, each of us has at least a 50/50 chance of doing good, for in all things God is eminently fair!

Finally, as further evidence that the serpent was a one-time deal, we must not forget that God ultimately relegated him to the dust!

Summary

To conclude this chapter, it would be a major step forward for all religions to recognize what Satan can and cannot do, and not blame him for our deficiencies! While he is used as an excuse for all sorts of evil; the cliché, "the devil made me do it" is clearly without merit. Sadly, however, there are still those, including some courts of justice, who give credence to it.

Yet we might ask, "Does the reason for evil really matter?" For whatever excuses we can conjure up, a sensitive reader might understandably be depressed over man's inability to do good. Is there no hope? Are we living in a jungle? Must we all become like animals to survive?

Each reader must answer that question for him/herself. But in the macrocosmic darkness, there have been microcosmic rays of light. God has sent good and righteous people to help us; to inform us what He desires; to assure us He will be with us if we act righteously. We will see in Chapters 10-14, that whatever the specific details of each religion, the founders—Moses, Jesus, Buddha—have given us an uncomplicated road map that is remarkably similar. Was not *Love your neighbor like yourself*, as first taught by Moses,[52] echoed by Mathew, Mark and Luke?[53]

---

[52] Leviticus 19:18

Did not Mohammed teach, *"In the Name of God, the Compassionate, and the Merciful. We guided man to the way; they fulfill their vows; they feed the poor, the orphan and the captive. So Allah will grant them radiance and joy."*[54]

And if most theologies have issues with God, simply because He created evil—which He, Himself, states,[55] one must recognize that God only created the *ability* to act evilly. *He Himself does not commit evil!* There is a profound difference between the creation of a possibility and its manifestation. Fire is neither good nor evil, but depends upon how it is used. When heating a home, it is used for good, when burning it down, it is used for evil. Likewise, nuclear power can heat an entire city or destroy it.

God gave humans *free will*—the ability to choose between *good* and *evil*. But when we choose the latter, *we* are responsible, not God! In Part III, we show many examples where God brings about evil upon an individual or nation. But that is *good*—destroying the "cancer" in the world that has already claimed many victims!

---

[53] Mark 12:31; Matthew 22:39; Luke 10:27
[54] The Koran: Sura 76
[55] "I form light and create darkness; I make peace and create evil. I, the Lord, do all these things." (Isaiah 45:7)

Part II:

Ethical Systems and Religion

Chapter 8
Ethical Systems

Introduction

Ethics is a branch of philosophy that studies and systemizes *morality,* or the difference between good and evil; right and wrong. As such, it investigates the questions: "What is *good, right,* or *virtuous*?" "What is *evil, wrong,* or *vice*?" "What is the best way for people to live." It also asks, "What actions are right or wrong in particular circumstances?"

Although related, it is crucial to understand that religion and ethics are not synonymous and have evolved separately. Scripture starts with a number of laws, which are not directly systemized into a coherent ethical system, and only later did religious philosophers/commentators attempt to do so by asserting general principles. As the basis of this book is that Scripture is God's word, the laws therein are deemed to come from *Him*.

Ethics, on the other hand, begins with general propositions, and was conceived by *man*. Laws or actions, if you will, then can be deduced by the ethical system in question. It should be helpful therefore to briefly review several systems of ethics, show where they agree or differ from Scripture, and identify the inherent weakness of each.

Ethical Systems

There are three major areas of study within ethics:

Meta-ethics studies the meaning of moral propositions, and if and how their truth values can be determined. It asks how we understand, know about, and what we mean when we discuss good and evil. Meta-ethical questions are abstract and do not judge specific behaviors, but rather ask questions such as, "Is it even possible to have knowledge of what is right and wrong, good or evil?"

Normative ethics relates to the practical means of determining a moral course of action. Traditionally, normative ethics is the study of what makes actions right or wrong. These theories offer general principles one may refer to in resolving difficult moral decisions. This is our major concern here.

Applied ethics studies what a person is obligated (or permitted) to do in a specific situation. It investigates how one ought to act under certain circumstances. This is a secondary concern here.

Several ethical systems are reviewed below:

Stoicism

According to *Stoicism*, the greatest good is contentment and peace of mind. Self-mastery over one's desires and emotions leads to spiritual peace. The "unconquerable will" is central to this philosophy. The individual's *will* must be independent and inviolate. Allowing another to disturb one's mental equilibrium is, in essence, offering oneself to slavery. If a person can easily anger you, you have no control over your internal world, and therefore no freedom. Freedom from material attachments is also necessary. If a possession breaks or is lost, one should not be upset, but realize those things happen. Similarly, if someone should die, the serenity of those close to him should be unaffected, because the loved one was made of flesh and blood and ultimately destined for death.

Stoicism states one must accept that which cannot be changed, resigning oneself to existence, and enduring it in a rational fashion. Death is not to be feared. People do not "lose" their life, but instead "return" to God. The Stoic philosopher, Epictetus, stated that difficult problems in life should not be avoided, but embraced. They are necessary exercises for the health of the spirit, just as physical exercise is required for the health of the body. He also held that sexual desire is to be avoided, as it is the greatest threat to the integrity and equilibrium of a man's mind. Abstinence is highly desirable, which, in the face of temptation, is a victory for which man can be proud.

As we shall see, many of these beliefs are similar to that of Confucianism, while the last has echoes of Roman Catholicism.

Hedonism

Hedonism, with its principle of maximizing pleasure and minimizing pain, is radically different from Stoicism. However, there are several schools of thought ranging from those advocating the indulgence of even momentary desires, to those teaching a pursuit of spiritual bliss. Considering the *consequence* of one's action, views range from those advocating self-gratification regardless of the pain or detriment to others, to those stating that the most ethical pursuit maximizes pleasure and happiness for the most people.

The former view, known as *Cyrenicism*, values immediate gratification or pleasure. The familiar "eat, drink and be merry, for tomorrow we die," is its mantra. Even fleeting desires should be indulged, lest the opportunity be forever lost. There is little concern with the future; the *present* is all that matters in the pursuit of pleasure. Cyrenaic hedonism encourages the pursuit of enjoyment and indulgence without hesitation, believing pleasure to be the only good.

Epicureanism, while hedonist, postulates behavior subject to virtue. Epicurus, its founder, rejected Cyrenicism, asserting that there were pleasures which were detrimental, and that indiscriminate indulgence often had negative consequences. Some unpleasant experiences were even to be endured to ensure a better life in the future. To Epicurus, the greatest good was prudence, exercised through moderation. Excessive indulgence was destructive to pleasure and could even lead to pain. Thus, eating a particular food too often would cause a person to lose the taste for it.

Pain and fear were also to be avoided. Living was essentially good, barring pain and illness. Fear was considered the source of unhappiness. Like Stoicism, death was not to be feared. Conquering the fear of death would naturally lead to a happier life, for if there was an afterlife and immortality, the fear was misguided, while if there was no life after death, it would be irrational to worry over that which did not exist.

Consequentialism

Consequentialism asserts that the *result* is the basis for any valid moral judgment about an action. From that standpoint, a morally right action is one that produces a good outcome. This view is often expressed as, "The ends justify the means." Of course, questions arise as to what sort of consequences are deemed *good*. Who are the primary beneficiaries of such action? How are the consequences judged, and who judges them?

The answers include *Utilitarianism*, in which virtue is that which result in the most good for the greatest number of individuals. John Stuart Mill argued that the proper course of action is one that maximizes a positive effect, such as "happiness," "welfare," or the ability to live according to personal preferences. "The best action is the one that results in the greatest happiness of the greatest number of people."[56] What matters is the aggregate positive effect for everyone, not of any one individual.

Deontology

Deontology is an approach popularized by Immanuel Kant that determines goodness or rightness from the examination of the acts, the rules, and the duties one strives to fulfill. Known as the

---

[56] Hutcheson, Francis, *An Inquiry into the Original of Our Ideas of Beauty & Virtue* (1725) https://en.wikipedia.org/wiki/Utilitarianism

moral imperative, an act may be considered good, even if it produces an undesirable consequence, if it follows the rule that "one should do unto others as they would want done unto them." This holds even if the person who does the act lacks virtue and does it out of some self-serving need. According to deontology, people have a duty to act in a way that is inherently good (such as telling the truth), and/or to follow an objectively obligatory rule.

Kant believed that to act morally, people must act from duty. The ends or consequences of one's actions are not important in and of themselves; it is rather the *motives* that are crucial. He argued that the highest good must be both intrinsically good and good without qualification. In order words, pleasure is not good without qualification—for instance, when one takes pleasure in watching someone suffer. Kant concludes that there is only one thing that is truly good: a *Good Will*.

Some deontologists, such as Rene Descartes believe in the "Divine Command" theory, whose essence is that an action is right if God has decreed that it is right. Moral obligations thus arise from God's commands as per Scripture—added to by the various religions. Like Kant, Descartes believed the rightness of any action depends upon it being performed because it is a duty, not because of the likelihood of a particular consequence.

Of extreme significance, however, Kantian deontologism maintains that it is *man*, as a rational being, who makes the moral law universal, whereas, Divine Command theory maintains that it is *God* Who makes the moral law universal.

Ethical Systems 77

Problems

All the above systems except for the Divine Command theory, suffer from one problem or another. *Stoicism,* despite some good ideas, is essentially fatalistic and fails to consider that we have some control over our lives. By accepting everything that occurs, we are not motivated to change. Major branches of *Hedonism* are not only selfish, but foolish, as they do not take into account the consequence of one's behavior—even that detrimental to the self, such as smoking or drinking heavily. *Consequentialism* and *Utilitarianism*, while perhaps satisfying in terms of virtue being what is good for most people, fails to address *who* determines what good consequences are. Equally problematic, it leads to an "end justifies the means" mentality which, by definition, abrogates the ethical foundation. But, in fact, the end does *not* justify the means. Otherwise, Stalin could justify the slaughter of millions as necessary for a Communist utopia. Likewise, the rights of minorities would have no moral value, for slavery in the U.S. during the 17th-19th centuries could now be justified as providing the greatest good for a majority of Americans, regardless of its effects on the slave population.

Kantian *Deontology* suffers from the notion that *man* determines morality, which has no possibility of being universal, since different cultures have differing moralities.

It is our contention *that God is the ultimate determiner of morality, not man*! No individual or nation has the wisdom to promulgate universal moral laws, which will become obvious in

Part III, as we review the evil in the world since Creation. The fact that man believes he has the power to make those determinations is a distortion of truth and a symptom of man's incredible arrogance.

Alas, these days truth is an endangered species, and justice has fled the scene. In the Old Testament, at least, moral principles are black and white—just as in a chess game where there are no grey areas. Indeed, perhaps the greatest chess player of all time, Emanuel Lasker—World Champion for 27 years and a philosopher to boot—stated:

> Oh Principle of justice! Thou art a power effective in history in spite of all that has been done to thee by the army of liars that want to hurt thee, yet have to play the hypocrite, for the people instinctively love thee. . . . On the chessboard lies and hypocrisy do not survive long. The creative combination lays bare the presumption of a lie; the merciless fact, culminating in a checkmate, contradicts the hypocrite. Our little chess is one of the sanctuaries where this principle of justice has occasionally had to hide to gain sustenance and a respite, after the army of mediocrities had driven it from the market place.[57]

In the final analysis, morality must or should be *God's word*, not ours. *Humans have no business determining morality*. We are fallible, and do not have enough wisdom. *Biblical ethics is about fairness, not winning*. And if God's morality seems weird to us; i.e. an eye for an eye, or a tooth for a tooth, imagine how our morality seems to Him. That is why God gave us Scripture.

---

[57] Lasker, Emanuel, *Lasker's Manual of Chess*, (New York, Dover Publications, 1947) p. 235.

His laws are designed to remove evil from our midst, because it is really true that a rotten apple eventually spoils the bunch. If someone is discovered to have cancer, is it not removed at an early stage and no one thinks twice? That is exactly what God intends by the commandment:

> "So shall you do to him, as he had wished to have done to his brother. Thus shall you remove the evil from among you. And those who remain shall hear and fear, and shall no longer commit such evil."[58]

---

[58] Deuteronomy 19:19

Chapter 9

Religion

Introduction

It is customary to blame secular science and anti-religious philosophy for the eclipse of religion in modern society. It would be more honest to blame religion for its own defeats. Religion declined not because it was refuted, but because it became irrelevant, dull, oppressive, and insipid. When faith is completely replaced by creed, worship by discipline, love by habit; when the crisis of today is ignored because of the splendor of the past; when faith becomes an heirloom rather than a living fountain; when religion speaks only in the name of authority rather than with the voice of compassion—its message becomes meaningless.
Abraham Joshua Heschel[59]

There are an untold number of "religions" the world over. In Chapters 10-14, we will describe the major ones: Judaism, Christianity, Islam, Buddhism, Confucianism, and Hinduism. It might surprise you that whatever the rituals, the founders and foundations of each have a lot more in common than one would imagine. As an analogy, one can go to different restaurants and sample hundreds of dishes that seem totally unlike one another. Yet when broken down, each consists of only four components: carbohydrates, proteins, lipids, and nucleic acids—the basic building blocks of life.

So too with religion. We will see how virtually all are based upon similar building blocks, as articulated by its "founder," regardless of the changes, additions, and in some cases corruption

---

[59] Heschel, Abraham Joshua, *God in Search of Man: A Philosophy of Judaism* (New York: Farrar, Straus and Giroux, 1955), p. 3.

by those that came later—for reasons too often other than altruistic. Indeed, it is doubtful whether Jesus, Moses, or Buddha would even recognize what they espoused. And, if religion is supposed to get one close to God—or a "Source"—it has failed spectacularly. Not only are the various rituals so diverse and detailed—one needs a computer to catalogue them all—tragically, as chronicled in Chapters 15-16, the differences within a religion—let alone between religions—are so varied, that the adherents are not content to "live and let live" and debate their point of view rationally, but excommunicate, assault, maim and even kill those who are not in agreement with their views. Over the centuries, nations have gone to war, and have committed all sorts of atrocities in religion's name—causing untold horror and suffering to hundreds of millions of people. Does that honor God? Killing or torturing one another in the name of religion? Indeed, the religious conflicts and wars over the centuries boggle one's mind. Alas, the *conceit* and *arrogance* of man knows no bounds.

In some respects, we might even suggest there is no such thing as a *true* religion; that if we accept God revealed Himself to Moses, Jesus, Mohammed, etc., we must also assume that He gave each laws and decrees *suitable* for the people they were representing at the time; the particular culture they were born into.

Just as children with special needs are treated differently, so humans having different cultures are likewise treated in accordance with their capabilities by God. But the basis of each—*righteousness, compassion, justice, and truth*—remain constant.

Religious Systems

As we have seen in the previous chapter, while ethical systems provide a basis for what is moral, each is devised and promulgated by *man*. This presents a problem *a priori* in that which, if any, can or should we accept as valid. Is any human or group of men, whose ethical systems differ substantially, wiser than another? Indeed, is any human so wise that he/she alone is able to determine the actions that all of us should adhere to? Should we truly "eat, drink and be merry for tomorrow we may die," or should we accept things that cannot be changed, resigning oneself to a miserable existence? Must we *embrace* suffering and repress sexual desire?

We can, of course, rationalize that perfect ethics is only a concept—a goal to be striven for, but never reached in actuality. But that still begs the question.

There is an alternative, however, and for now we will simply give it the name of *religion*. It provides a different way of dealing with moral issues, especially in the monotheistic Judeo-Christian-Islamic tradition in which certain acts are viewed in more specific and absolute terms. Yet even religion is not always positively associated with morality. That is, many religious values diverge from commonly-held contemporary moral positions, such as those relating to the death penalty, marriage, slavery and homosexuality.

And we must contend with Biblical critics, such as Simon Blackburn, who states that the "Bible can be read as giving us a carte blanche for harsh attitudes to children, the mentally handicapped, animals, the environment, the divorced, unbelievers, people with various sexual habits, and elderly women, both in the Old and New Testaments,"[60] and Elizabeth Anderson, who holds that "the Bible contains both good and evil teachings," and is "morally inconsistent."[61]

Adding to the difficulty, unlike ethical systems, Biblical Laws, especially in the Old Testament, are in the hundreds, typically very specific, and cannot be summed up easily, nor are they organized or grouped into a coherent system. Additionally, some seem weird to us here in the 21st century, while others appear far beyond normative ethics, and require the Hebrews, at least, to act "way beyond the call of duty."

Accordingly, we will review the various religions in enough detail so that you can judge for yourself whether criticism by those above and others have merit. Of course, we believe that religious values or morality whose source is Scripture, *comes*

---

[60] Blackburn, Simon, *Ethics: A Very Short Introduction*. (Oxford: Oxford University Press, 2001) p. 12.
Cited in https://en.wikipedia.org/wiki/Ethics_in_the_Bible
[61] Anderson, Elizabeth: "If God is Dead, Is Everything Permitted?" In Hitchens, Christopher , *The Portable Atheist: Essential Readings for the Nonbeliever*. (Philadelphia: Da Capo Press 2007) p. 336.

directly from God! For if we assume otherwise—that the Five Books of Moses say, was written by *humans,* here one minute and gone the next, we have no *root*s to attach ourselves to; nothing to hang on to, and any criticism of morality—then and now—is useless!

Is it truly not God Whose wisdom is—and should be—the source of moral behavior? Consider, Exodus 3:14 when Moses asks God His Name at the Burning Bush. God doesn't answer directly, but states אֶהְיֶה אֲשֶׁר אֶהְיֶה or "I will be, that Who I will be."

Is not God's answer a bit strange? Clearly, His response is *not* His Name, assuming He has—or needs—one. I think therefore, we can deduce the following. He is telling Moses that there is no reason to reveal His Name *at this point in history*! His Name would not be known anyway, as we learn later when Pharaoh states, "Who is this god you Hebrews want to go and pray to? He is not in my list of gods."[62] Instead, it should be manifest God is stating three important principles. First, He will, in the near-term, reveal His Name when appropriate—which occurred later at Mount Sinai. Second, He is stating in the distant future—today in 2018—that *He still will remain the same*! That is, the *morality* that He gave man 3300 years earlier is still in effect. And, I dare say, human morality has changed over time *for the worse*—due to the scientific method, the Industrial Revolution and modern

---

[62] Exodus 5:2

technology. For example, adultery, in some countries is not only condoned, but expected. Yet, God is still outraged by it.

Finally, the sum of the letters; that is, Aleph which is 1, two Hets of 5 each, and Yud which is 10, total 21. Now in the game of blackjack, is not 21 always the best hand? We can therefore deduce that God is stating those that follow Him and observe His commandments will always wind up with 21 *in the game of life!*

In our view, Blackburn's cynicism[63] and Anderson's assertions cannot be but hot air "blowin in the wind"; just one man's/woman's opinion 3300 years after the events and statutes they criticize. Indeed, it is clear they hardly understand it, taking out of context segments here and there for their own purposes. Obviously, they, as well as most modern Biblical scholars, do not believe in the Divine word.

Yet there are humanists, such as Paul Kurtz, who believe that we *can* identify moral values across cultures, even if we do not appeal to a supernatural or universalist understanding of principles—values including integrity, trustworthiness, benevolence, and fairness. These values can be resources for finding common round between believers and nonbelievers. Can we not but construe that laws in the Old Testament showed the evolution of moral standards towards protecting the vulnerable?

---

[63] Blackburn, especially, doesn't know what he is talking about, nor truly comprehends the Pentateuch. When you, the reader, discover the laws of Judaism delineated on pages 94 through 104, you will see for yourself that virtually all of his assertions are patently false.

In the following chapters, we will describe six major religions of the world—review their history, their assertions, creeds, and statutes—so that you can judge for yourself whether the ramblings of Blackburn, Anderson, and others have any basis. We hope to show how, despite what on the surface often seems a most complex series of beliefs, laws, and rituals, the core of each is remarkably similar—particularly as it relates to ethics and morality. As Judaism forms the basis for most other religions, we will concentrate on its laws and statutes, organizing them succinctly and with clarity.

To conclude, we assert that the key to righteousness is the religious values and morality whose source is Scripture—*coming directly from God*! And the consequences of not adhering to His morality is dire.

Chapter 10
Judaism

Love your Neighbor as Yourself!
Leviticus 19:18

Introduction

Although Jews make up less than one percent of the world population, as the first monotheistic religion and the basis of Christianity and Islam, as well its influence on virtually all other religions, its origin and its laws are critical to an understanding of those that follow. Accordingly, we will be more detailed here, than we will in subsequent chapters.

Very few people, even non-believers, would deny that the Bible—consisting of the Old and New Testaments—is the most unique and important document ever produced. Judaism, for those unfamiliar with the basics of religion, only considers the Old Testament, in which the Five Books of Moses, otherwise known as the Pentateuch, form the basis for God's Word, laws, and statutes. They include: Genesis, Exodus, Leviticus, Numbers, and Deuteronomy. While most modern scholars believe these books have been written by several individuals over the course of time, we totally and absolutely reject that view. Like traditional Jews, Moslems, and Christians, we accept the Bible as the Word of God given to Moses, and deem its content factual.

Those of you who do not believe as the author does, I would simply ask you to consider the following with an open mind.[64] Certainly, an omnipotent and omniscient God could easily arrange for the Bible to be His word, and to be passed down and translated for all peoples all over the world—not only to inform them about His nature, but to help them thrive, or at least survive, in a world where too many of us state, "Life's a bitch and then you die!"

If we assume otherwise—that *humans* wrote the Bible—how in good conscience can one rely on anything that is stated? Perhaps it is simply someone's over-active imagination. We also are at liberty to disagree with anything that doesn't meet our own desires, needs, or cultural beliefs. We simply rationalize that a human wrote it, and too often he/she was in error. Only by accepting God as the true and only author, do we have a foundation for deducing other truths by the events and laws that are revealed. On a personal level, if I did not believe the Pentateuch came from God, you would not be reading this book, because I would have no faith that any of my assertions have value—given that I would be depending upon events and laws that a *human* contrived. That being said, let us look into the history and laws of Judaism.

---

[64] Note I have absolutely no interest in convincing anyone to follow a particular religion. My only desire is, in these extremely troubled times, to give comfort to as many as possible, and to encourage everyone to become a better person—whether he/she believes in God or not.

History

In Genesis 12, God reveals Himself to Abraham and has him relocate to the land of Canaan. God tells him he will father a great nation that centuries later will inherit the land, currently held by various Canaanite tribes. Subsequently, his wife Sarah gives birth to Isaac, who marries his cousin Rebecca. They have twins, Esau and Jacob, and the latter returns to Abraham's birthplace, lives with his uncle Laban, and falls in love with Laban's daughter, Rachel, whom he agrees to work for seven years. But Laban substitutes his older daughter, Leah, and Jacob is forced to work an additional seven years for Rachel. Altogether, he is at Laban for twenty years, and with two other concubines, Bilah and Shifrah, sires twelve sons;[65] the most notable being Judah, Levi, and Joseph.

Back in Canaan, the brothers become insanely jealous of Joseph, who was Jacob's favorite, and sell him as a slave to Egypt. But God is with Joseph, and at the age of thirty he appears before Pharaoh and interprets some troubling dreams, which predict seven years of the most severe famine, preceded by seven years of abundance. Joseph becomes Pharaoh's minister, supervises the gathering and storage of grain during the abundant years, and its allocation during the famine. Eventually, Jacob sends his sons to get food from Egypt; Joseph reveals himself to

---

[65] The Twelve Tribes of Israel: They include: Reuven, Simon, Levi, Judah, Issacher, Zebulun, Dan, Naftali, Gad, Asher, Joseph, and Benjamin.

them; and they reconcile. He then supervises his family's relocation to Egypt.

Jacob, whose name was changed by God to *Israel*, dies sometime later, and eventually so do Joseph and his brothers. A new king arises who is antagonistic toward the Israelites, as they have greatly multiplied, and he fears they would side with Egypt's enemies during a war. Initially, Pharaoh directs that they be enslaved. Later, he decrees that all the males be killed at birth.

Through different stratagems, many males survive, including one from the house of Levi, whose mother hid him for several months, after which she placed him in an ark in the river. Pharaoh's daughter was bathing at the time and took pity on the boy, named him Moses, and raised him as her son. When he grew into adulthood, he witnessed an Egyptian taskmaster beating a Hebrew slave, so he slew him and buried him in the sand. But word got out to Pharaoh who sought to kill him, and Moses had to flee to the land of Midian, where he remained, married, and had two children.

Many years later, while Moses was tending sheep, God appears to him and informs him that He is the God of Abraham, Isaac, and Jacob, that He has heard the cries of the Hebrews in Egypt, and will deliver them through him. Accordingly, Moses returns to Egypt and requests that the Israelites be allowed to go into the desert to pray to their God. But as Pharaoh refuses, Egypt is ravaged by ten plagues—the last being the slaying of the first born—and, in a panic, the Egyptians beg the Israelites to leave, and give them their jewelry, flocks, and other valuables.

A year later, God reveals Himself to the Children of Israel on Mount Sinai and charges them with the Ten Commandments. (See Appendix I.) But as they repeatedly sin, He causes them to wander in the desert for the next 40 years. During that period, God gives Moses detailed laws that the people are to follow.

Ultimately it is Joshua who leads the Children of Israel across Jordan River into Canaan. They quickly conquer and displace the nations residing there, but turn away from God and worship idols or *Baalim*, so God subjugates them to the surrounding nations for years, until a savior or judge is sent to save them. For a time, they return to God, then rebel again. This goes on for three centuries.

Eventually, the people demand a king from the last of the judges, Samuel, and after the first one, Saul, displeases God, David is anointed.[66] In his forty-year reign, he conquers the nations surrounding Israel and leaves his son, Solomon, the most powerful nation in the world. Solomon also rules for 40 years, and builds the First Temple in Jerusalem, supervised by priests from the Tribe of Levi. But he foolishly marries foreign women and allows them to worship their idols, causing God to uproot ten tribes from Solomon's kingdom, now known as Judea. They are consolidated into a northern kingdom known as Israel.

---

[66] David wrote over half of the 150 psalms; many are used in both Christian and Jewish worship.

For centuries, both kingdoms, especially that of Israel, are ruled by kings who rebel against God and commit all sorts of abominations. Although God appoints prophets, such as Elijah, Isaiah, and Jeremiah to urge the people to return to Him and become righteous, the kings, officers, and people do not listen. Accordingly, they are plagued by wars, usurpations, assassinations, and fratricidal murders for another three centuries. Then, Assyria conquers Israel and disperses the "Ten Lost Tribes." A century and a half later, the same fate befalls Judea when, in 587 BCE, the Babylonians sack Jerusalem, burn the First Temple, and carry off the greater part of the people into captivity.

After two generations, under the Persian king, Cyrus, the Jews receive permission to return to Jerusalem and rebuild the Temple, but for the next three centuries, Judea is a vassal of Persia, Greece, Egypt, or Syria depending upon the political situation at the time. During that period, a new group of non-priests, known as Pharisees, arise to interpret the laws of the Pentateuch, which sharply conflict with those of the priestly sect known as the Sadducees. Eventually, the Roman Empire conquers the Middle East, and, after a number of rebellions by the Jews, sacks Jerusalem and destroys the Second Temple.

As the Jews were required to face a new reality, that of Judaism without a Temple and Judea without autonomy, the Pharisees, now known as rabbis and sages, take over the religion. There is a flurry of legal discourse, ultimately recorded in the writing of the Talmud, and resulting in a major transformation of the religion, so that virtually everything thing in the life of an Observant Jew, is regulated by thousands of very detailed laws, or *halachah*.

Over the centuries, two other branches of Judaism evolved, Reformed and Conservative, which liberalized many of the Rabbinic decrees; the details unnecessary to go into for the purposes of this work.

Laws

Judaism has over six hundred laws that are specified directly in the Five Books of Moses. They consist of civil and criminal statutes, sacrificial rites, laws of the priest, animal rights, laws of slavery, etc., which at the time were the most humanitarian laws one can imagine. Unfortunately, the overwhelming majority of people—Jew and non-Jew alike—have little, if any, knowledge of these laws, and do not appreciate the justice and compassion the Children of Israel were commanded to adhere to during a time in which paganism, violence, and evil were rampant. Hopefully, summarizing many of the Biblical laws by category will have an impact, and educate you about the true nature of the religion.

As we shall see, there are numerous laws God wanted the people to follow that go way beyond the scope of modern civil and criminal law, yet to Him they are equally important. For in God's eyes, a Hebrew breaking one of His statutes is considered to have sinned.

Laws Relating to Animals

We begin with the laws relating to the well-being of animals. They include:

- *If you see a mule whose burden is too heavy, you shall not pass him by, but remove enough of his load that will allow him to rise up!*[67]

An amazing humanitarian law directs us to have consideration for beasts of burden, such as horses, camels, asses, mules, and oxen, such that if their loads are too much for them, one must remove enough to allow them to rise and continue on.

- *Do not mate animals of different species!*[68]

Animals would not normally mate outside their species. Forcing them to do so would make them extremely distraught, so God forbids Jews from doing so, showing how much He cares about their feelings and well-being.

- *Do not plow with an ox and an ass together!*[69]

Differing greatly in size and strength, it would be cruel to the weaker animal to yoke them together.

- *Do not muzzle a beast of burden when it is working in the field!*[70]

It would be cruel to stimulate an animal's desire for food without allowing it to eat. As Professor C. H. Cornill wrote, "what a truly human sentiment finds expression in this law. . . . The beast of burden should not perform hard labor and at the same time have food before its eyes without the possibility of eating therewith."[71]

---

[67] Deuteronomy 23:4
[68] Leviticus 19:19
[69] Deuteronomy 22:10
[70] Deuteronomy 25:4
[71] Cornill, Carl Heinrich (1854-1920), cited in *The Pentateuch and Haftorahs*, ed. by J. H. Hertz (London: Socono Press, 1985) p. 833.

- *Rest beasts of burdens on the Sabbath!*[72]

Although God gave the Sabbath—a day of rest—to humans, His consideration for animals demonstrates that even *they* should not be overworked, and need—deserve—a day of rest.

- *Do not castrate an animal!*[73]

Although these days we routinely geld horses, cats, and dogs for our convenience, God considers it cruel, and commanded the Hebrews not do to so.

- *If you see your enemy's ass or ox go astray, you shall surely return it!*[74]

An amazing law. First, although the property is that of your enemy, one should not be vengeful by looking the other way—taking satisfaction that your enemy's loss will cause him dismay. But more importantly, a domestic animal could not survive without being taken care of. Therefore, it must be returned to its owner to ensure its well-being—even if there might be some danger to the one returning it—seeing that its owner is his enemy.

- *Do not seethe a calf in its mother's milk!*[75]

Somehow the mother will sense the fate of her calf, causing her anguish.

- *Do not take a mother and her young from a bird's nest together, but chase the dam away!*[76]

Not only are the Children of Israel commanded to have consideration for a mammal, as above, but for birds as well—removing both together would cause the mother great distress.

---

[72] Exodus 20:10
[73] Leviticus 22:24
[74] Exodus 23:4
[75] Exodus 23:19
[76] Deuteronomy 22:6

Laws of Slavery

Although slavery is allowed in Scripture, it is nothing like the slavery that took place in the 17th-19th centuries when imperialist nations would kidnap people from backward countries, bring them to their colonies, and work them harshly. Under no circumstances were Hebrews allowed to steal slaves, as Europeans and Americans did. That would be punishable by death.

Biblically, slavery was more like indentured servitude. For Hebrews, if one could not pay his debts, he would become a servant to his creditor, although there are laws that he must be redeemed by his family—or if there is no one to redeem him, after six years he must be freed. Gentile slaves arose from wars in which Israel was victorious, or alternately, could be purchased by Hebrews from other nations that had enslaved them. Also, captured women could be taken as wives. Note that Gentiles might have Hebrew slaves as well, in the case where an Israelite cannot pay his debts to them.

Finally, while there are some differences between the laws for a Hebrew and Gentile, all slaves must be well-fed, clothed, housed, and treated with dignity. Laws include:

- *If a Hebrew man or woman is sold to you as a servant, he must go free after six years and must be furnished liberally with flock, herds, and seed!*[77]

---

[77] Deuteronomy 15:12

- *You shall not sell a Hebrew bondman by public auction nor shall you work him harshly.*[78]

- *If during war, you capture a young woman, you must give her thirty days to mourn her mother and father, then if you desire her, you may take her as your wife, but if you do not desire her, you cannot sell her as a slave, but must let her go free!*[79]

To avoid excess cruelty having first subjected her to the slaying of her family, and then humbling her by taking her into your household, only to reject her.

- *A slave that has escaped from his master and comes to the Hebrew territory shall be given asylum and not returned to his master. He shall dwell in the midst of you, wherever he chooses!*[80]

Another amazing law! Escaped slaves from other nations would normally be treated very harshly, but the Hebrews are commanded to provide him/her a place of asylum.

Laws of the Judiciary

Judaism demands justice and God demands the Hebrews to be totally impartial. This contrasts sharply with our own laws, in which *winning* is the norm, and our courts are filled with procedures and technical issues that have little to do with justice. Unfortunately, in America it is the rare exception in which a case, criminal or civil, is decided solely upon its merits.

- *A Judge is not to decide in favor of poor man out of pity, nor favor a litigant who is wealthy or powerful, but in righteousness shall you judge your neighbor.*[81]

This law is fundamental, relating to God's desire for strict impartiality.

---

[78] Leviticus 25:42
[79] Deuteronomy 21:10
[80] Deuteronomy 23:15
[81] Leviticus 19:15

- *A Judge shall not accept a gift, for gifts perverts the words of the righteous.*[82]

This law is not so much against bribery—although, obviously, it is not permitted—but even a gift without strings attached is forbidden.

Other examples include:
- *Treating litigants equally before the law.*[83]
- *Condemning witnesses who testify falsely.*[84]
- *One must not suppress evidence unfavorable to a litigant.*[85]
- *A Judge may not avoid a just judgment through fear of an evil person.*[86]
- *A Judge may not pervert justice against any litigant, whether a Hebrew or an alien.*[87]
- *A Judge may not pervert justice that is due aliens.*[88]
- *A Judge must not hear one litigant in the absence of the other.*[89]

Criminal Law

Following are a number of what may be termed criminal laws in the Bible. A major theme is that whatever the crime, the accused must get a fair trial and be treated with dignity.

- *Do not put a murderer to death without a trial!*[90]
- *There is no capital punishment on the testimony of a single witness!*[91]

---

[82] Exodus 23:8
[83] Leviticus 19:15
[84] Exodus 23:16
[85] Deuteronomy 1:17
[86] Deuteronomy 1:17
[87] Deuteronomy 1:16
[88] Exodus 23:9
[89] Deuteronomy 19:17
[90] Numbers 35:12
[91] Deuteronomy 19:15

Although capital punishment was decreed for certain acts such as murder, both a trial and at least two witnesses were mandatory. These two laws demonstrate a death sentence was not made indiscriminately, but only after careful consideration. Significantly, capital punishment could not be based upon circumstantial evidence.[92] (If no one saw the act of murder, it is presumed God will execute the judgment.)

- *Do not inflict excessive corporal punishment!*[93]

This important law not only states that criminals should be treated with dignity, but also clearly *prohibits* torture!

- *After execution, there must be burial on that day. Do not leave the body of an executed criminal hanging overnight!*[94]

Even for capital crimes, the individual shall die with dignity and his body should not be subject to dismemberment by the birds.

- *Witnesses to a crime must give testimony!*[95]

Unlike these days when most people do not want to get involved, God commands the Hebrews that they *must* testify if they see criminal activity—especially a murder. Not doing so is considered a major sin, and God will punish the witness.

- *For witnesses who testify falsely, what they would have the court do to the man on trial should be done to them!*[96]

Another amazing law! Although perjury is a crime in modern law, the punishment is rarely implemented, and its severity is not remotely connected to the matter on trial. But in Hebrew law, those who testify falsely in a capital case would be put to death themselves! While some readers may have issues with this, it is a

---

[92] Interestingly, on August, 2017, the Supreme Court of India commuted a death penalty to life imprisonment for a conviction based solely on circumstantial evidence. They determined that there are authorities for the proposition that capital punishment should not be handed out under those conditions.

[93] Deuteronomy 25:3

[94] Deuteronomy 21:23

[95] Leviticus 5:1

[96] Deuteronomy 19:19

strong deterrent for testifying falsely—one of the Ten Commandments. Moreover, just as one is guilty of murder who hires someone to kill another, although he doesn't actually pull the trigger, so too, these false witnesses would be engineering the death of the man on trial.

- *You shall not fraudulently alter your neighbor's land boundary.*[97]

Doing so is considered worse than theft, since land was the basis for the economy in those times, and altering boundaries could easily provoke violence.

- *Do not keep false weights and measures.*[98]

This prohibition, such as overcharging for grain or other commodities that must be weighed, clearly indicates that even petty theft is abhorrent in God's eyes and will be punished.

Civil and Business Law

Dozens of civil laws attest to the humanitarianism of Judaism, whether they relate to debts, loans, or other themes. Most would not be considered actionable in our court system, but God demanded the Children of Israel act with justice, and protect the dignity of all concerned.

- *Do not oppress a stranger.*[99]

Aliens in the land must be treated with dignity. Contrast that to how Jews have been treated throughout the past 2000 years, even when they were citizens of the countries who persecuted them.

- *Wages must be paid on a daily basis.*[100]

This is an important humanitarian law. Unlike modern times in which wages might not be paid for weeks or even months,

---

[97] Deuteronomy 19:14
[98] Deuteronomy 25:14
[99] Exodus 22:21
[100] Deuteronomy 24:15

Judaism required payment the same day, as the worker might need it immediately for life's basics, such as food, shelter, and clothing.

I can personally attest to the wisdom of this law, as there was a time in my life during which I had literally less than a dollar to my name. Fortunately, I procured a job driving for a car-service, and at the end of the day was paid my percentage of the fares. That enabled me to continue to pay my rent and buy food.

- *Do not wrong one another in business.*[101]
- *Do not cheat a Gentile in business.*[102]
- *If you take your neighbor's garment as a pledge, return it by sunset, because the garment is the only covering your neighbor has. What else can they sleep in? When they cry out to Me, I will hear, for I am compassionate.*[103]
- *Do not take one's work implements as security for a loan. How then would he earn living?*[104]
- *You may not enter the home of a debtor to take security for a loan, but must wait outside.*[105]
- *Do not demand payment from a debtor unable to pay.*[106]
- *Do not infringe on any vow or oral obligation.*[107]

How often do we *not* keep our word. But that has profound implications, especially in business when we make decisions based on another's promise and can incur a substantial loss if he reneges. God, Who always keeps His word, considers that it a major sin.

---

[101] Leviticus 19:13
[102] Leviticus 19:33
[103] Exodus 22:26
[104] Deuteronomy 24:6
[105] Deuteronomy 24:10
[106] Exodus 22:22
[107] Deuteronomy 23:23. See also Leviticus 5:4.

Laws of Compassion

Besides the laws delineated above, there are dozens of additional laws that charge the Hebrews to have compassion. While none could be brought in U.S. civil courts, failure to follow them is considered a sin.

- *You must leave the corners of gleanings for the poor.*[108]
- *Do not take a widow's garment as a pledge against a loan.*[109]
- *You must leave fallen grape clusters and ears of corn that fall during harvesting for the poor.*[110]
- *If one is poor among you in the cities the Lord allots to you, do not remove your hand from your needy brother. But you shall surely lend him whatever he needs. Beware lest you harden your heart against the poor and give them naught so that they cry unto the Lord against you. For you will be found guilty of sin. Rather give generously to them and without a grudging heart. Thus the Lord your God will bless you in all your work and in everything you do.*[111]

These laws are further proof of God's concern for the poor. When gathering up one's produce, any that fall by the wayside are to be left for the needy, even if they are totally usable. It also teaches Hebrews not to be greedy by trying to bring every last fruit or vegetable to market.

- *Both a traveler and one working the field may eat the produce from any field that does not belong to him.*[112]
  Since traveling long distances in those days was tedious and tiring, God allows travelers to nourish themselves from produce they came upon on the way, without needing

---

[108] Leviticus 19:9
[109] Deuteronomy 24:17
[110] Leviticus 19:10
[111] Deuteronomy 15:7
[112] Deuteronomy 23:25

permission from the owner. Likewise, one performing hard labor by working the land also has the right to be nourished properly. It should be noted, a corollary of this law is that neither has the right to take produce home to eat later or to sell. That would be considered theft.

- *You shall not see your fellow's donkey or ox fallen on the road, and hide yourself from him: you shall surely help him lift them up again.*[113]

Complementary to the law about struggling animals, this law is concerned with the human whose burden is too great. God makes it clear you must not look away, but must help him. These days, that includes offering to help one who is struggling with packages or materials too heavy for him/her.

- *Do not place a stumbling block before the blind.*[114]

One might ask why the law doesn't state, "You shall remove a stumbling block from the blind," but the former shows the depth of God's wisdom. For what one considers a stumbling block may, in fact, be a "marker" to a blind person and must not be removed.

Laws of Personal Relationships

- *Do not utter a false report or gossip.*[115]
- *Do not wrong your brother by speech.*[116]
- *Do not wrong a Gentile by speech.*[117]
- *If you find property of your neighbor, you must return it.*[118]
- *Do not be the bearer of tales.*[119]
- *Do not put another to shame.*[120]
- *Do justice to orphans and strangers in your midst.*[121]

---

[113] Deuteronomy 22:4
[114] Leviticus 19:14
[115] Exodus 23:1
[116] Exodus 20:16
[117] Exodus 23:9
[118] Deuteronomy 22:1
[119] Leviticus 19:16
[120] Leviticus 19:16

- *Do not bear a grudge.*[122]
- *Do not stand idly by if your brother is endangered.*[123]
- *Do not take vengeance on another.*[124] *(i.e. Let God do so.)*
- *Love the alien in your midst.*[125]
- *Love your neighbor like yourself.*[126]

The above laws charge the Hebrews to show respect for their fellow man/woman and to treat them with dignity.

Completing this rather detailed elucidation of Judaic law, we hope it has provided you with insight into Judaism—especially how important compassion and justice is to God. Most of the above laws would hardly be considered as incumbent upon the citizens of any country in this day and age.

---

[121] Deuteronomy 24:17
[122] Leviticus 19:18
[123] Leviticus 19:16
[124] Leviticus 19:18
[125] Leviticus 19:34
[126] Leviticus 19:18

Chapter 11
Christianity

History

Arguably, more than any other religion, the beginnings of Christianity is shrouded in controversy. The four Gospels were not written when Jesus was alive, but forty to one hundred years after his death. There are also some significant differences between them, such as his birth—Matthew and Luke trace Jesus as descending from King David through his father, Joseph; John and Mark state he was miraculously conceived by Mary. As we have seen with Judaism and will see with other religions, Christianity has become much more complex than the initial founder conceived.

Born in Nazareth during the time of the Roman Empire's supremacy, and versed in Jewish law, Jesus traveled about Judea teaching the doctrine of a universal loving God and the coming of His Kingdom of Heaven. Moreover, God had no favorites, but was the loving Father of everyone. Jesus urged those he met to cease their evil and become righteous.

Jesus was thirty when he began preaching and filled his adherents with love and hope. Ailing people were heartened and healed by his presence. Within three years, he had quite a large following. Then he came to Jerusalem, got embroiled in controversy with the leaders of Judaism—both the Sadducees, who ministered to the Temple, and the Pharisees. Subsequently, he was accused by the Romans of fomenting rebellion, tried, and executed.

Within days, there were claims that his body was not in his tomb, and there were numerous reports of his sighting. Soon, his disciples became convinced that he had risen from the dead and had ascended to heaven. A faith evolved upon the stories of his resurrection, ascension, and a promised return; his followers identified Jesus with the Messiah, so long expected by the Jewish people.

However, the real founder of Christianity, as ultimately practiced, was Saul of Tarsus, or Paul. A Jew by birth, he was at first a bitter critic and antagonist of the Nazarenes, who were considered heretical by traditional Judaism. However, after an epiphany, he became convinced Jesus was the "sacrificial servant" referred to in Isaiah 53, who was afflicted by God as an atonement for the sins of the people. Although Paul never met Jesus, he built this new sect into a theological system, converting what was largely a faith into a creed.

Yet, questions abounded. Was Jesus the Messiah? Was Jesus an aspect of God? Had God created him? Centuries went by with three major Christian sects in dispute: the Arians, the Sabellians, and the Trinitarians. The Arians asserted that Jesus was the son of God who was begotten by the father at a point in time—therefore distinct from the father and subordinate to Him. The Sabellians held that God reveals Himself in three "manifestations," so that He is successively, father, son, and holy spirit—temporary manifestations in the operations of a one Divine Being. The Trinitarians taught that the three "persons" are distinct, have one essence or nature, and are co-equal and eternal.

In the interim, Christianity was regarded as a rebellious movement by Rome and there were systematic attempts to suppress it. By the fourth century, however, the Roman empire could barely manage its vast holdings, as its subjugated nations were constantly rebelling. The Emperor Constantine concluded that Christianity could be a major unifying force throughout the empire, and made it the official religion of Rome. Needing to establish an inviolate canon, he called a council of the Church at Nicaea in 325, to once and for all decide upon a theology. Known as the Nicene Creed, the Trinitarians prevailed and became authoritative—not to be questioned. Shortly thereafter, Christianity developed a centralized organization which ran parallel to the empire—although subservient to it.

Yet, like the differences between Biblical and Rabbinic Judaism, there were profound differences between this Christianity and the teaching of Jesus. His was a simple teaching. It had no temple, no priests, no rites or ceremonies, and ritual was secondary. Rather, the "sacrifice" was a contrite heart. Under Paul, Constantine, and those that followed, Christianity was transformed. Now its core centered about sacrifice—if symbolic—the altar, and the essential act of worship, the Mass, which could only be serviced by a consecrated priest. It soon had an organization of deacons, priests, and bishops.

Slowly but surely, the next thousand years saw the development of the Roman Catholic Church, led by a Pope who claimed he was God's representative on earth, and expected total adherence to the Roman Catholic creed and doctrine. Indeed, the thirteenth century saw the development of a new institution, the Papal Inquisition—discussed more fully in Part III—organized as a standing inquiry into heresies under the Pope's direction. With fire and brimstone, anyone whose views were contrary to that of the church was assailed, excommunicated, and later, arrested and tortured.

The Reformation

Despite or because of the above, by the fourteenth century voices started to be heard in opposition to the *Church*—not Christianity *per se*. One was that of England's John Wycliffe (1320-1384), a parish priest who alleged the church and clergy were corrupted by garnering wealth and living in luxury, while engaging in heavy papal taxation. Translating the Bible into English, his ideas spread throughout the British Isles. Additionally, Wycliffe criticized certain doctrines, such as the consecrated bread used in the Mass becomes in some way the actual body of Jesus. Such a doctrine mandated the consecration could only be performed by a priest, resulting in the necessity of the priestly order, when, in fact, it was merely a symbol of the personal remembrance of Jesus, without the need for a papal hierarchy. Later, in 1396, a Czech, John Huss, criticized the church for similar reasons, but was not as fortunate as Wycliffe whom the Catholic church could not get to. Huss was put on trial for heresy, and burned at the stake.

The major break with Roman Catholicism, however, came when Martin Luther, a German, published, in 1517, his Ninety-Five Theses criticizing the Church for, among other things, the selling of indulgences which purported to offer remission of sin, as well as their doctrinal policies about purgatory, and the authority of the Pope. Luther's translation of the Bible into German was critical in helping him gain a large following; now the average German could learn it—whereas before it was in Latin and only the Church could interpret it. Somewhat later, John Calvin, in England, also broke from the church for most of the same reasons. The result was *The Reformation*—doing away with the Roman Catholic hierarchy and allowing the average individual to commune directly with God. Protestantism spread in Europe during the 16th century, and itself became divided theologically and ritually, but maintained their total rejection of papal supremacy over the Church.

Creed and Beliefs

Roman Catholicism

According to Roman Catholicism, God established the Church, headed by a Pope, to guide and lead men into salvation. In general, Catholics did not need to—nor did they—understand the plan of salvation, or even God. Catholics were discouraged from studying the Bible, but only were required to believe that God has created a channel for saving mankind—the channel being the Church. Salvation was necessary because of the original sin of Eve, and Jesus through his suffering, paid the debt that allowed Christians to receive it.

Salvation includes the *Beatific Vision* which brings the greatest happiness it is possible to experience. It consists in coming face to face with God in heaven and be given full knowledge of truth. Catholics believe the Bible—for over a Millennium available only in Latin—contains no errors. There are also seven Sacraments that one must partake of during his/her life to pave the way into heaven. They are structured rituals—five occur once, the two others performed frequently—the details beyond the scope of the book. The former consists of *Baptism* (at birth), *Confirmation* (an anointing with oil when an adolescent), *Matrimony*, *Ordination* (for those becoming priests), and *Extreme Unction* (or the last rites). The latter are the *Eucharist* (a merging with the body and blood of Jesus) and *Penance* (confession and absolution).

Protestantism

For Protestants, such as Lutherans, Calvinists, Baptists, Methodists, etc., whatever their differences, there are five major principles (*solae*) they hold in contradistinction to the teaching of the Catholic Church.

Sola Scriptura ("By Scripture alone") asserts all church traditions, creeds, and teachings must be in unity with Scripture, which is the divinely inspired Word of God. The Bible alone is the ultimate authority. This principle contains four sub-doctrines: that its teaching is needed for salvation (necessity); that everything necessary for salvation comes from Scripture (sufficiency); that everything taught in the Bible is truth (inerrancy); and that, by the Holy Spirit overcoming sin, believers may read and apprehend, however difficult, truth from the Bible itself (clarity).

Sola Fide ("By Faith alone") asserts salvation occurs without the necessity for good works on the part of the individual. Faith in Jesus is sufficient. A believer is accepted without regard for merit, as no human deserves salvation.

Sola Gratia ("By Grace alone") specifically excludes the deeds of a person during his life in order to gain salvation. Rather, it is by divine grace or "unmerited favor" only, since man is too much the "sinner" to merit it. It is an unearned gift from God, for the sake of *Jesus*.

Solo Christus ("By Jesus alone") is the teaching that Jesus is the only mediator between God and man. Thus, the priestly class, including the Roman Catholic hierarchy and the Pope, are unnecessary for the sacraments. Salvation cannot be granted through another human being.

Soli Deo Gloria ("Glory to God Alone") is the teaching that all glory is to be given to God alone, since salvation is accomplished solely through His will. Human beings—saints canonized by the Roman Catholic Church, the Popes, and the ecclesiastical hierarchy—are not worthy of the glory accorded them.

In short, Protestants reject the Roman Catholic Church's doctrine that it is the one true, indivisible church.

This review of Christianity is, of course, brief and very much simplified, as this not a book about religion. Rather it is man's relationship to God that is its focus, and general religious concepts are necessary to understand Part III, which demonstrates why God's love, "is on the rocks."

Chapter 12
Islam

History

Mohammed, the founder of Islam, was born around 570 AD in Mecca. Poor and uneducated, he was for some years a shepherd's helper. Later, he became the servant of a certain Kadoka, the widow of a rich merchant, who eventually married him. He was 25 at the time. At forty, he declared that the reality of *one* God, known as *Allah*, had been revealed to him by an angel. This contrasted sharply with the religions of the desert people, who believed in and worshipped multiple gods.

Mohammed wrote down his revelations, known as the *Koran*, which asserted among other things, the unity of God, the charge to be righteous, a future life in paradise for the upright, and hell for the disbeliever and the wicked. Mohammed claimed that the prophets before him, such as Moses and Jesus, had been divine teachers, and that his revelations completed their undertaking.

At first, only his wife and a few intimates were privy to his revelations. Then Mohammed began to preach more openly. As word got around, his teaching aroused the ire of the elders in Mecca, whose polytheistic cult was critical to numerous pilgrimages to the town—the source of considerable income. They harassed Mohammed's followers, some of whom were forced to leave Mecca, but as Mohammed was well connected, they did not personally harm him.

114 God and Man: Love on the Rocks

After ten years of largely unsuccessful proselytizing, Kadoka died, as did several of his chief supporters. Medina, a nearby city, however, was intrigued by Mohammed's teaching, and arranged for him to come and rule in the Name of his God. Those that followed him were now known as *Moslems*, and the religion he preached became *Islam*.

Meccans, however, were threatened by this development as they would lose revenue if they allowed this new "religion" to take hold in a town on a major caravan route. They attempted to put an end to Mohammed and Islam by force, and for several years there were periodic battles between the two towns; neither side prevailing. The Koran records the situation:

> "Oh, you who believe! If you obey those who disbelieve, they will turn you back upon your heels, so you will turn back losers.
>
> "Nay, Allah is your Patron, and He is the best of the helpers.
>
> "We will cast terror into the hearts of those who disbelieve, because they set up with Allah that for which He has sent down no authority, and their abode is the fire; and evil is the abode of the unjust.
>
> "And certainly Allah made good to you His promise, when you slew them with His permission, until you became weakhearted and disobeyed, after He had shown you that which you loved; of you were some who desired this world, and of you were some who desired the hereafter; then He turned you away from them, that He might try you; and He has certainly pardoned you, for Allah is gracious to the believers. . . .
>
> "As for those of you who turned back on the day when the two armies met, only the devil sought to cause them to make a slip on account of some deeds they had done, and certainly

Allah has pardoned them; surely Allah is forgiving; forbearing."[127]

Finally, an agreement was made with Mecca, which became the center of the new faith—as the town's only concern was economic; whether pilgrims came in the name of one god or many was unimportant. Meanwhile, Mohammed tried to convert Jews and Christians, but was unsuccessful, so he began asserting that Allah was Islam's own special god, and less the father of all mankind.

Amazingly, Islam became widespread in a very short time—much of it through conquest—and Mohammed became master of all Arabia by the time he died in 632. Abu Bekr, his father-in-law, succeeded Mohammed as *caliph*, or leader; he prevented a split between Medina and Mecca, and carried out the first Holy War against a nation: Syria. Although Moslems encountered large and disciplined armies, they continually defeated them, and gave those they conquered three choices: join Islam by confessing the one true God is Allah, agree to pay tribute, or die. Under these threats, Christian Arabs joined the invaders very readily, as did some Jews.

When in 634 Abu Bekr died, Omar, Mohammed's brother-in-law became caliph, and under him major conquests of the Moslems continued. The Byzantine Empire was evicted from

---

[127] The Koran: Sura 3. Cited in Wells, H. G., *The Outline of History*, (The Project Gutenberg eBook, 2014), Vol. 2, Chapter XXXII, No. 3. www.gutenberg.org/files/45368/45368-h/45368-h.htm#v2-page_090

Syria, Armenia was overrun, Mesopotamia was conquered, and so was Persia. Egypt became a Moslem nation, and Jerusalem a Moslem city.

But then, family jealousies led to civil war. Abu Bekr, Omar, and Othman, the third Caliph, were all chosen by the majority of adherents, known as *Sunnis*. However, Ali, Mohammed's son-in-law who was the husband of Fatima, his youngest daughter, considered himself the rightful Caliph, claiming Mohammed told him that it was divinely ordained that he succeed him. Vying for power among the two groups, Othman was assassinated in 656, and Ali became Caliph. Those believing that Ali and his descendents were the rightful caliphs would be known as *Shiites* (who themselves splintered into several subgroups, and for centuries were a minority in all the countries Islam conquered).

But Ali was murdered in 661, and Islam was taken over by Mu'awiya, a Sunni and member of the Umayya, one of the most prominent families of Mecca. Mu'awiya decreed that the role of a caliph was to become hereditary, rather than elected. The Umayyad family became ascendant, and provided rulers to Islam for almost a century; its power base in Damascus, Syria.

But they were not unopposed, and in 750, after a three-year civil war among rival Sunnis, Marwan II, the last of the Umayyad caliphs, was captured and executed, and Abu Abbes became the first of the Abbasid caliphs; which now included non-Arabs, and whose capital was Baghdad, Persia.

There was still opposition however, of those who desired Shiites for leadership, but they remained a minority faith until about 1500, when Ismail founded the Safavid dynasty in what is now Iran, and made Shi'itism the official creed of his realm. *Shi'itism*, that claimed leadership could only come from direct descendants of Ali, continued to grow in several other regions, but still is a minority within the Islamic world, comprising approximately 15 percent of Moslems.

Creed and Beliefs

A year before he died, Mohammed made a last pilgrimage from Medina to Mecca. His sermon included:

> "Hearken to my words. . . . Your lives and property are sacred and inviolable amongst one another until the end of time. . . .
>
> "The Lord hath ordained to every man the share of his inheritance; a testament is not lawful to the prejudice of heirs.
>
> "The child belongs to the parent; and the violator of wedlock shall be stoned.
>
> "Whoever claims falsely another for his father or another for his master, the curse of God and the angels and of all mankind shall rest upon him.
>
> "You people! You have rights demandable of your wives, and they have rights demandable of you. Upon them it's incumbent not to violate their conjugal faith nor commit any act of open impropriety, which things if they do, you have authority to shut them up in separate apartments. . . . But if they refrain, clothe and feed them suitably. And treat your women well, for they are with you as captives and prisoners; they have not power over anything as regards themselves. And you have verily taken them on the security of God, and have made their persons lawful unto you by the words of God.
>
> "And your slaves, see that you feed them with such food as you eat yourselves, and clothe them with the stuff you wear.

And if they commit a fault which you are not inclined to forgive, then sell them, for they are the servants of the Lord, and are not to be tormented. . . .

"Know that every Moslem is the brother of every other Moslem. All of you are of the same equality."[128]

Note how this excerpt is remarkably similar to a number of laws of Judaism. Woman and slaves must be treated kindly and with dignity. If every Moslem is a brother and equal in the eyes of God, so also is every Hebrew, as in, "Love your neighbor as yourself." "Property is inviolable until the end of time," echoes Judaism's, "lost property must be returned to its owner and it is prohibited to change the boundaries of one's neighbor's fields."

As in Judaism and Christianity, Islam insists upon kindness, compassion, and brotherhood, although it differs ritually, as there is no priestly caste, nor is the core of Islam centered around the sacrifice. Worship is simpler, but more frequent—Moslems pray five times a day—while monotheism is more uncompromising. It is opposed to theological elaborations of the Trinity that divided Christianity at its outset.

As stated above, Islam split and has been divided to this day. One main division are Shiites, who maintain the hereditary right from Mohammed to be spokesmen for Islam, and accept only the written Koran, claiming two chapters were omitted that specifically stated the leadership was to go to his descendants. They prevail in Iran and India. The Sunnis, the bulk of Moslems today, deny this, claiming the so-called two chapters were

---

[128] Wells, *The Outline of History*, Vol. II, Chapter XXXII, No. 4.

fabricated. They rely on the *Sunna*—the verbally transmitted record of Mohammed's teachings, deeds and sayings, and prophetic oral tradition—in addition to the *Koran*, as their canon.

For Sunnis, an Imam is one who leads Islamic formal prayers, typically, but not necessarily, in a mosque. At times, he may be a member of the congregation.

For Shiites, an Imam is much more attuned to Allah and considered chosen by Him to lead the community in all aspects of their lives. Imams are thought to be free from sin, and must be followed since they are appointed by God.

In many ways, Islam is the simplest of all the religions we will review and its theology the most understandable. To convert to Islam there is no complicated procedure, as in Judaism or Christianity. One simply needs to declare his/her faith, and state in effect: "I bear witness that there is no god worthy to be worshiped but Allah, and I bear witness that Muhammad is the Messenger of Allah."[129]

Islam particularly suited the desert people, whose life was simple compared to those living in towns or cities—it appealed directly to the heart of the average man. And whether Sunni or Shiite, both agree to the six foundations of the religion.

1. *Belief in one and only one God, Allah.*
2. *Belief in the hereafter and eternal life.*
3. *Belief in spiritual beings or angels.*

---

[129] See http://Moslemconverts.com/howtoconvert/

4. Belief that revelations come from God.

5. Belief in human messengers—i.e. prophets.

6. Belief in the decree and ultimate plan of God.

Rituals include five daily prayers, fasting from sunrise to sunset during the ninth month, *Ramadan*, and donating a portion of their wealth to the poor. If possible, once in their lifetime, Moslems are expected to go to Mecca, which is in Saudi Arabia, usually during the last month of the Moslem calendar—which is based upon the lunar year.[130]

---

[130] As a result, over the course of time, the seasons associated with a given month change.

Chapter 13
Buddhism

History

Buddhism stems from the sixth century BCE, when its founder, Siddhartha Gautama, was born. He was the son of a rich Hindu Raja, and until about thirty he was pampered, protected by his family, and lived the aristocratic life. Handsome and of great intellect, at 19 he married his beautiful cousin and had a child.

Despite this, Siddhartha was not content, and his soul was troubled. He felt his existence was not the true reality, but a fantasy. The sense of suffering, disease, death, and the tenuousness of happiness descended upon Siddhartha. Then, he encountered one of the wandering ascetics who existed in great numbers in India. He perceived they were seeking some deeper meaning; living in poverty and spending their time in meditation.

A passionate desire to join them overcame Siddhartha, so he left his privileged life and entered the solitude of the forest of Bengal—the abode of hermits. There, a number of ascetics lived, going into town for their simple needs, and imparting their knowledge by word of mouth to those who sought them.

But the solutions they offered were also not satisfying. Eventually, with five disciples, Siddhartha moved to the Vindhya Mountains, and began fasting and engaging in severe penances. His fame soon spread, but this way of life also did not bring him closer to the truth. Then, one day, he collapsed. When he was revived, the preposterousness of this method in receiving enlightenment became obvious. He ceased fasting and self-mortification, understanding that whatever truth a man may reach, he could only do so by a nourished brain in a healthy body. His disciples, however, weren't pleased and left him, going off to Benares.

Alone now, Siddhartha rested under a tree by the side of a river to eat when, suddenly, all became clear. Determined to impart his vision to the world, he traveled to Benares, convinced his five disciples that he finally had arrived at enlightenment—*the reason for suffering and how it could be overcome*! They hailed him as the *Buddha*, or the "awakened" one. Soon they accumulated other followers, and traveled throughout India revealing the new teaching—all by word of mouth.

What had the Buddha discovered? That misery, torment, discontentment, and suffering could be traced to insatiable selfishness—to the craving of individuality; to greedy desire. Until one overcame living just for himself and satisfying his personal craving, his life would be one of suffering, and his end sorrow.

Buddhism began to spread, as the early teachers were noble and practiced what they preached. But it truly took off in the third century BCE because of Ashoka, an Indian emperor who invaded and conquered the east coast of Madras. Although victorious, Ashoka was horrified by the cruelties and horrors of war. He declared he would no longer seek conquest by violence, but by religion, and became a patron to the Buddhists. The rest of his life was devoted to spreading Buddhism throughout his vast empire, and it flourished.

Creed

According to Buddha, cravings take three principal forms: (1) The desire to gratify the senses, or *sensuousness,* (2) the desire for *prosperity*, and (3) the desire for *immortality*. All three must be overcome before suffering will cease and life can become serene. When desire no longer rules one's life; when the personal "I" has vanished from one's thoughts, then one has reached the higher wisdom—*Nirvana*—or the serenity of the soul. Unless one loses himself in something greater than himself, there can be no security, no happiness, and no peace.

Known as the *Four Noble Truths*, Buddha conceived the following:

(1) *Dukkha*: (*The Actuality of Suffering*) Birth is suffering. . . . Illness is suffering. . . . Not obtaining what we desire is suffering. Disharmony is suffering. . . . Death is suffering.

(2) *Samudaya*: (*The Origin/Cause of Suffering*) Suffering occurs because of our erroneous attitude towards the world and how we experience it. Giving in to our cravings and desires leads nowhere.

(3) *Nirodha*: (*Cessation of Cravings*) One doesn't have to be a slave to his cravings. One has a choice how to live. Ineffective actions and unwholesome habits must be overcome, and one needs to look at new situations with a new eye.

(4) *Magga*: (*The Path*) To end the cravings, one must restrain oneself and cultivate discipline, by practicing mindfulness and meditation. *Moderation* is a crucial key. Over-indulgence or severe asceticism never leads to anything worthwhile. Likewise, the desire for an endless continuation of this trivial individual life—and the dread of death—is unwise and an obstacle to immortality.

Instead, Buddha conceived the *Eightfold Path* that should govern one's life.

(1) *Right Viewpoint*: One must be aware that his cravings lead him astray. He must examine his attitudes, insist upon truth, take responsibility for his actions and not cling to superstition.

(2) *Right Aspirations*: Base cravings are to be denied; self-centeredness must cease. True values are love of the service of others, desire to do justice, and acting with kindness.

(3) *Right Speech*: One must no longer engage in gossip, slander, abusive or idle talk. Speech must be thoughtful, controlled, and specific. To Buddha, "the pen *was* mightier than the sword!"

(4) *Right Behavior*: Not only must a person not kill, steal, get drunk, or be impure, but he must be loving. Like Jesus, Buddha stated, "Let a man overcome anger with love; evil by doing good."[131]

---

[131] Rig Veda 79:1, cited in *The Great Religions by Which Men Live*, Floyd H. Ross & Tynette Hills (Greenwich, Fawcett Publications, 1956) p. 61.

(5) *Right Livelihood*: Certain occupations are harmful; especially those injuring any life-form. Thus, those of a butcher, a soldier, and making or selling intoxicants are eschewed.

(6) *Right Effort*: Good intentions without action are meaningless. One must keep a keenly critical eye upon his activities. He must not move too fast nor too slow on the *Eightfold* path, but in accordance with his nature and his internal time-clock.

(7) *Right Mindfulness*: One must be on constant guard against a lapse into personal feelings and not seek glory for what he does. One must not be distracted by physical desire, but keep cravings and imagination concealed, and keep calm under all stimuli; good or bad.

This idea is also expressed in the Bible:

> The Lord said to Moses, "Speak to the Children of Israel and have them make fringes on the corners of their garments, throughout their generations, so when beholding them, they will remember the commands of the Lord; that they shall not follow the promptings of their hearts or the attraction of their eyes to be misled by them."[132]

(8) *Right Contemplation*: This was aimed against the ecstasies of the devout. Instead, one must train and *silence* the mind by such disciplines as meditation and yoga.

Unlike Judaism or Christianity, Buddhism initially was not a religion of ritual, observance, and sacrifice. It had no theology, temples, or sacred order of priests. Yet like almost every other

---

[132] Numbers 15:37

religion, those that came after Buddha modified his teaching. Some early disciples lapsed into monastic seclusion—*the opposite of what Buddha had preached*—but particularly attractive in India, where the extreme simplicity of living was the norm, and exertion was more laborious than anywhere else in the world. Also, a theology evolved about Buddha and he was deemed a god—one of a series of divine beings that Indians previously had worshipped. Additionally, well-meaning souls related supposed miracles that attended Buddha's birth. And as each new assertion demanded explanation, Buddhism became filled with a theology that eclipsed the simple lessons of its founder.

Eventually, two major sects of Buddhism developed: *Hinayana* and *Mahayana*. *Hinayana* Buddhists, practicing largely in Thailand and Burma, believe a person is responsible for his own salvation. That is one's first duty, since salvation is unavailable from another. Accordingly, those following *Hinayana* tend to become isolated, their material needs minimal, and they practice self-control and moderation, if not asceticism.

M*ahayana* Buddhism, in contrast, is much more socially oriented. It posits a reciprocal relationship to gain salvation—one must give to others and accept from others. Temples and other edifices are largely the result of Mahayana Buddhists. This is the major practice in China and Japan.

In general, Buddhism came to see salvation and the hereafter as the answer to the misfortunes and sufferings of life. It thus evolved to the idea of *reincarnation*—or transmigration of the soul after death—although this was contrary to what Buddha had taught. Echoing Judaism, Christianity and Islam, the purpose of *virtue* was no longer to become serene in *this life,* but to prevent the torment of being *reborn* in a degraded or miserable condition.

Ultimately, Buddha became the savior from almost unlimited torment. And, as in Christianity, some adherents gained wealth and fame, and the simple huts of the early teachers gave way to substantial monastic temples.

Significantly, despite what later Buddhists claim, Buddha came to his realization alone, and never considered himself a prophet—in the sense of Moses, Jesus, or Mohammed. We might note that as Hinduism with its many gods, its castes, and variety of occults grew more powerful, they turned upon this caste-denying religion with persecutions, and by the eleventh century ousted Buddhism from India.

Today, the largest Buddhists populations—although far from a majority—are in China, Thailand, and Japan.

Chapter 14

Confucianism and Hinduism

Confucianism

Confucius, the founder of Confucianism, lived during the sixth century BCE in China. He was of aristocratic birth and, after occupying various official positions, founded an Academy for the imparting of wisdom.

How could man live a happy and rewarding life? His answer was largely sociological, and had to do with the concept of *harmony*. When man acts in concert with other humans, he achieves universal harmony. Thus, man's responsibility is to cooperate with others and perform the duties expected of him.

But man was not conducting himself that way, and needed structure; rules to help him achieve that goal. Confucius therefore designed a method for man to live by, consisting of very detailed rules and protocols. Centered upon the idea of a standard or ideal—the *Aristocratic* or *Superior Man*—Confucius described the devoted public servant:

> It is impossible to withdraw from the world, and associate with birds and beasts that have no affinity with us. With whom should I associate, but with suffering men. The disorder that prevails is what requires my efforts. If right principles rule through the kingdom, there would be no necessity for me to change its state.[133]

---

[133] Wells, *The Outline of History*, Vol. 1, Chapter XXVI, No. 5.

As the magistrate in the city of Chung-to, Confucius began to regulate life to that of an elaborate etiquette. Every detail was prescribed: dress, conversation, social interaction, even posture. These rules became obligatory for the people at large; even foods which different classes of people ate were regulated. Those keeping to the rules were known as *Superior Men* and considered to be noble—which anyone could aspire to.

No other people had ever approached moral order and social stability through such regulation. Only in Rabbinic Judaism, through the Talmud, are the details of everyday life so directed. But much of those regulations are rituals relating only to God, or theoretical, relating to a different time and society.

In China, however, the methods of Confucius had an enormous effect and a huge influence on the development of the Chinese national character.

Confucius identified five *Constant Virtues* which were to be practiced until they were an integral part of the *Superior Man*:

(1) *Attitude*: Man must desire to be co-operative, accommodating, and in harmony with others.

(2) *Procedure*: Man must apply the rules of conduct to all interactions he is involved in. He must understand the ceremonies and rituals: how to walk, stand, sit, and converse. He must even control his facial expressions.

(3) *Knowledge*: The *Superior Man* studies subjects such as history, literature, civics, and classics; particularly those that have to do with morality.

(4) *Moral Courage*: This virtue requires remaining loyal to oneself, while charitable towards one's neighbors.

(5) *Persistence*: Achieving the other four virtues is only part of the *Superior Man*. If they are transient, he is transient. Thus, persistence and constancy are critical to Confucius' teaching.

> The great influence of Confucius' personality on national life in China was due not only to his writings and his teachings as recorded by others, but also to his doings. His personal character, as described by his disciples and in the accounts of later writers . . . has become the pattern for millions of those who are bent on imitating the outward manners of a great man. . . . Whatever he did in public was regulated to the minutest detail by ceremony. This was no invention of his own, since ceremonial life had been cultivated many centuries before Confucius. But his authority and example did much to perpetuate what he considered desirable social practices.[134]

In general, Confucianism, like Buddhism, is a "way of life," a path without the doctrines of a church, of sacrificial rites, or of prayer. And unlike Judaism, Islam and Christianity, there is no assertion of a transcendent God.

---

[134] Wells, *The Outline of History*, Vol. 1, Chapter XXVI, No. 5.

Hinduism

Unlike the previous religions, Hinduism has no specific founder or prophet. It also has no ecclesiastical order, religious authority, or governing body. It is more a "way of life," rather than a religion. But practiced by over one billion followers in India, Nepal, and other Asian countries, we will treat it as the latter. Indeed, is not religion really a way of life?

In fact, Hinduism is by far the most complex of the religions we have reviewed. Over the centuries it has evolved into a number of different schools, with a wide range of practices—hundreds of deities in some sects—and a complex synthesis of various Indian cultures and traditions. We can only outline its major tenets.

Hinduism began to develop over 3500 years ago with the *Vedas*—poems and hymns, and rules for ritual worship. Sometime later, about 800 BCE, the *Upinshads*, the foundation of Hindu philosophy, were written. They were answers to questions about life and the universe, whose content included meditation, philosophy, and spiritual knowledge.

Basic to Hinduism is the idea that there is a fundamental unity to all existence and experience; any differences we perceive are trivial and temporary. In the *Rig Veda*, the Hindu hymn of creation, we are told that at the very beginning:

> Existence was not, nor its opposite.
> Nor earth. Not heaven, blue vault nor aught beyond.
> Death was not yet, nor deathlessness.
> The day was night, night day,

> For neither day nor night had come to birth. . . .
> Then THAT, the primal fount of light—
> Immobile—rest and action joined—
> Brooded in silent bliss.
> Itself besides, in the wide universe, there nothing was.[135]

Although the above is not meant to describe God as defined by Judaism and Islam, it very much in keeping with the Kabalistic idea of "Ein Sof"—that at the beginning there was nothing—God was alone. Rather, in Hinduism, the concept of the *Supreme One* is known as *Brahman*. It is conceived as pervasive, genderless, infinite, eternal, and unchanging. Yet it is the cause of all, including truth and bliss.

Basic to Hinduism as well, is the idea of *Maya* or illusion. Everything is constantly changing; one cannot be sure what is real, for life is like a river; flowing; always moving. Additionally, every action, every intention, every attitude has consequences. The present circumstances of an individual depend on his or her actions—which may be in a person's current life or past life. Likewise, the consequences of today's actions may affect a future life. And although one cannot know why the universe was created, by knowing *Atman*—the spirit/soul or true "self" of every person—one can apprehend its secrets. As soul is believed to be eternal, the goal of life is to realize that one's soul is identical to the Supreme Soul; that the Supreme Soul is present in everything and everyone, and that all life is interconnected.

---

[135] Ross & Hills, *The Great Religions by Which Men Live*, p. 26.

This knowledge is gained by life experience, but not all at once. *Samsara*—reincarnation or transmigration—in which one comes back in another form is crucial to Hinduism. Liberation from Samsara through *Moksha* (see below) ensures detachment from worldly desires and provides lasting happiness and peace. The ultimate goal of life is the realization of one's eternal union with the Supreme One—the realization of the unity of all existence. One returns as many times as necessary, until he incorporates the above and "regains" Atman. Then his pilgrimage, so to speak, ends and he finds happiness.

On a practical level, there are four main methods to reach this goal, which should be the aims of humans: They consist of *Dharma* (ethics/duties), *Artha* (livelihood), *Kama* (fulfillment of desires), and *Moksha* (attaining liberation).

Dharma, or the "right way of living," is considered the foremost goal of a human, and includes the moral rights and duties of each individual, as well as behaviors that nourish social order. Specifically, it includes refraining from injuring living beings, purity, goodwill, mercy, patience, forbearance, self-restraint, and generosity.

Artha is the *virtuous* pursuit of livelihood. One must honor one's obligations which will result in economic prosperity and material well-being. It is includes political involvement and diplomacy.

Kama relates to sensual pleasure: desire, passion, and longing; the aesthetic enjoyment of life, affection, and love. Kama is considered an essential and healthy goal of human life, when pursued without sacrificing *Dharma*, *Artha* and *Moksha*.

Moksha is the ultimate goal in Hinduism: liberation from the birth-rebirth cycle; the end of pain and suffering. Some sects believe this can only be attained in the after-life, while others claim it is a goal achievable in the current life—a state of bliss through self-realization.

Traditionally the life of a Hindu is divided into four stages: *Student*, *Householder*, *Retired* and *Renunciation*.

In the *Student Stage*, the individual lives with a tutor, who teaches him the ancient wisdom of Hinduism, with the aim to find the meaning of life and his place within it.

In the H*ousehold Stage*, the individual is expected to marry, have children, and make his contribution to the economic stability of the community.

In the *Retired Stage*, the individual hands over his responsibilities to the next generation, retires from public life and business, and spends time in contemplation—continuing the search for his true self and the nature of the universe.

In the *Spiritual Stage*—which very few enter—one becomes a teacher. He leaves his family, friends and village, and travels from place to place sharing his wisdom, while depending on others for his sustenance.

Hindu society has also been categorized into four classes, called *Varnas*. They are the teachers and priests; the warriors and kings; the farmers and merchants; the servants and laborers.

Finally, as a diverse system of thought, Hinduism has a wide range of gods, depending upon the individual and his tradition. Philosophically, belief in god includes monotheism, polytheism, and pantheism—the details beyond the scope of this book.

Summary

One can see that despite the complexities of each religion we have reviewed, the core values are remarkably similar. If one could summarize four major principles, they would be as follows:

- *Love your neighbor as yourself.*
- *Have compassion on those less fortunate.*
- *Be honorable in your dealings with your fellow man.*
- *Be moderate in your actions; extremism is counterproductive.*

Given the above, why then, over the centuries, has so much blood been shed by *intra/inter*-religious conflicts? Can God possibly desire this? The answer is, of course, He doesn't—and thus our relationship with Him can only be described as *Love on the Rocks*. Part III describes, in painful detail, those conflicts, both of a religious and secular nature. Part IV will suggest what we can do to repair our relationship with God—and as a result, receive His blessings and make our world a better place.

Part III

Love on the Rocks

Chapter 15
Love on the Rocks

Having discussed the nature of God and the nature of Man; having reviewed good and evil, ethical systems, and completed a survey of six religions, our task in Part III is to document how often through the Millennia, God and Man have been at odds.

Actually, the above totally understates reality. More accurately, there has been virtually no period during which God and Man have been at peace. Man is constantly provoking God by his actions—a plethora of evil—which is in direct violation of God's purpose and desire in creating our world—not to mention causing Him untold suffering.[136]

Of course, when we use the term "Man" we are not talking about a single individual, but all men everywhere—tribes, city/stares, empires, kingdoms, or nations—in both the religious and secular spheres. We will prove that you are as fortunate to be reading this, as I am for having written it; that God, in fact, hasn't *destroyed* the world He created, because of the evil of its inhabitants, not excluding myself. This does not mean there weren't or aren't good people, or even righteous nations—at least for a time—only that evil is virtually never ending.

---

[136] This would be a good time to review Chapter 7 on "evil," remembering how much of it is not necessarily obvious, but includes that which is praised by our society, such as the corporate CEO who ruins tens-of-thousands of lives because of his greed and arrogance in initiating a hostile takeover.

Our Laboratory

In science, any assertion, claim, or theory must be backed by experimental proof, which can be duplicated independently by other scientists. And so it must be with theology. If one is to make assertions about God, it must be backed up by proof as well. But in this case, our laboratory, if you will, is *religion and history*.

Specifically, if we accept that God is good, but it is man who is evil, what, if any, are the consequences? Can our laboratory prove our assertion that *evil is ultimately punished*, even if not immediately?[137]

Succeeding chapters, therefore, will take us through the conflicts *between* and *among* religions and between nations. Again and again, we will see the evil perpetuated by humans, and how through the centuries, God, because of His great compassion, has tolerated it far longer than He might.

But there *are* consequences—when God has had enough! Ultimately, while evil might flourish for a time, those engaging in it—tribes, kingdoms and/or nations—were either totally destroyed, or conquered and humbled into virtual oblivion.

And while God's retribution does not take place overnight, it *does* happen. Can anyone forget the recent destruction of Iraq by

---

[137] In fact, God's beneficence allows nations to repent from their evil, and if they do, His decrees are nullified. For one example, see the *Book of Jonah*.

the United States, especially the image of Saddam Hussein—who was arrogance and evil personified—cowardly hiding from his pursuers in little more than a hole in the ground, emerging disheveled and trembling, humbled by God, and, significantly, not executed on the spot, but given a trial before he was hung?

In poetic terms:

> The Lord controverts the conspiracies of the nations.
> He causes the intentions of the peoples to come to naught.
> The Lord peers down from heaven.
> He observes all the children of men.
> He scrutinizes all the inhabitants of the earth,
> He, Who fashioned each of their hearts individually.
> Does He not apprehend all their doings?
> A king is not saved by the multitude of his army.
> A strong man is not delivered by his might.
> Depending upon a horse is illusory;
> Its great strength and swiftness are of no avail.[138]

We also should also point out there is an important difference between religious and secular conflicts. By and large, wars among and between religions were self-cleansing! That is, when a nation kills, rapes, maims and oppresses another in God's Name, as much as it hurts Him to observe that—there is nothing He need do. The oppressor ultimately becomes the oppressed, and receives measure for measure—if not worse—for what it inflicted. As we shall see, only once did God have to intervene directly, with the *Black Plague*, which virtually destroyed over a third of the world's population—when evil in the name of religion became unbearable to Him.

---

[138] Psalm 33

In political wars, on the other hand, when one nation conquers and oppresses another, the victim is usually unable to recover to repay its conqueror. God then must intervene—sometimes directly through miracles—as He often did in Biblical times, or more subtly through the material world, by empowering other nations to destroy the nation that was oppressive and evil.

We begin our tragic odyssey detailing the incredible evil resulting from religion. Chapter 16 and 17 describe the major religious conflicts *within* and *between* religions, respectively.

Chapters 18-21 are devoted to evil in *history*, based upon greed, arrogance, and lust for power. Those chapters, separated by various periods, from Biblical times to the present, will amply demonstrate how evil has constantly flourished, and how billions of people over the Millennia have suffered, and/or been sent to a premature grave, but ultimately how the ravagers were paid back in kind.

Chapter 16
Intra-Religious Conflicts and Wars

Anyone who attempts to construe a personal view of God which conflicts with Church dogma must be burned without pity.
          Pope Innocent III

Introduction

Without doubt, religion has been the cause of greatest degree of suffering the world over; that in God's Name, people think nothing of slaughtering each other and committing the worst atrocities. Can any reasonable person possibly believe God is pleased by any religion that maims, kills, and tortures its opponents?

The author would certainly prefer not to detail the incredible violence associated with religion, but unless he does so, the reader is apt to look at religious history *abstractly*, and fail to truly realize the horror and evil that is inherent in humans—or the fact, as stated in Scripture, that "man has a tendency toward evil from his youth."[139] Unless we can *feel* this; incorporate even a modicum of the horror into our own hearts and souls, we will not only fail to see why God's love for us is, as the title states, "on the rocks"—but more importantly, fail to do anything about it.

What is especially tragic about religious wars is the fact that however different each religion appears on the surface, their foundations are remarkably similar. They include:

- *Love your neighbor as yourself (Judaism, Christianity).*

---
[139] Genesis 6:5

- *Remain loyal to yourself, while charitable towards your neighbors (Confucianism).*
- *Let a man overcome hate with love; evil, by doing good (Buddhism).*
- *Every Moslem is the brother of every other Moslem. All of you are of equality (Islam).*

Indeed, it is doubtful whether the founders would even recognize their own religion, given the changes and innovations over the centuries. Yet throughout history, the conflicts and blood curdling wars, both within and outside each faith, with those who do not believe or follow a particular creed boggles the mind. Why this should be the case is the million dollar question.

Judaism

During Biblical times, once the Hebrew kingdom was split after the reign of Solomon, there were numerous wars between Judea in the South and Israel in the North, in which millions were killed. During that period, Israel rebelled against God, set up its own Temple, removed the Tribe of Levi as priests in favor of the common man, and began worshipping a pagan Baal--ironically still following many of rituals specified in the Pentateuch. And while most of the wars between the Israel and Judea were not *religious* wars *per se*, but rather political wars, we include one particularly sad episode that took place early on, when 500,000 Jews were slain in a 24 period—by other Jews!

Abijah was the grandson of King Solomon, and during his reign, in 666 BCE, Jeroboam, king of Israel amassed 800,000 warriors and invaded Judea, whose army numbered 400,000:

Abijah stood on top of Mount Zemaraim and called out, "Hear me, Jeroboam and all Israel! Did not God give the kingship forever to David and his sons by a covenant? Yet Jeroboam, a servant of Solomon, rose up and rebelled against him. Then base men gathered about him and defied my father Rehoboam, when he was young and could do nothing. And now you defy the kingdom of the Lord in the land of the sons of David because you are a great multitude and have with you golden calves that Jeroboam made you for gods.

"Have you not driven out the priests of the Lord, the Levites, and made priests for yourselves from the common man? We keep the charge of the Lord our God, but you have forsaken Him. Behold, God is with us at our head, and His priests with their trumpets to sound the call to do battle. Sons of Israel, do not fight against the God of your fathers, for you cannot succeed."[140]

Meanwhile, Jeroboam had sent a large body of troops behind Judea, so she was surrounded. But they prayed and cried to God, the priests blew the trumpets, and the men raised a great battle shout. Abijah and his army routed Israel and 500,000 of their warriors perished.

Clearly, God was with Judea and deemed those of Israel deserved death for their rebelliousness and idolatry. Significantly, in this case God intervened *directly* when evil proliferated beyond His limits. In the examples that follow, however, we must *induce*[141] Divine retribution. But make no mistake: God ultimately will repay those who commit evil—whether an individual, tribe, city/state or nation!

---

[140] II Chronicles 13:4
[141] That is, derive the general principle from specific observations.

Our next example occurs around 140 BCE, when Judea, at the time a vassal of Syria, declared its independence under its Highpriest, Simon the Maccabee. By then, two major religious parties had been formed; the Pharisees who were composed mainly of the common man, from which the Rabbinic tradition stemmed, and the Sadducees, named after the former high priest Zadok, who were from the tribe of Levi—priestly families in charge of the Temple and the sacrificial rites, as commanded by God.

For close to a century, before Rome finally invaded and sacked Jerusalem, there was much violence between the two religious sects, each fighting for control of Judaic religious practice. The Pharisees had promulgated a great many observances which were not specifically stated in the Torah of Moses, while the Sadducees rejected them and only observed the written law.

John Hycranus, king at the time, was originally a disciple of the Pharisees, but then left the party, abolished the decrees they had imposed on the people, and punished those that observed them. He ruled for more than thirty years, and when he died in 104 BCE, his son, Alexander Janneus (103-76 BCE), took his place. Alexander continued his father's religious policy despite strong opposition, but then left Jerusalem to attack Arabia. When he returned, Jerusalem, now controlled by the Pharisees, refused to let him in; so he laid siege to the city. For over six years he was stymied, but eventually, internal divisions within Jerusalem weakened the city, and he was able to force his way in—executing over 800 Pharisees for their rebellion.

Nonetheless, on his death bed, he instructed his wife, Alexandra, to make peace with the Pharisees, since they controlled the populace at large. As Josephus tells it:

> And now the Pharisees joined themselves to [Alexandra], and artfully insinuated themselves into her favor little by little, and became the real administrators of public affairs. They banished and reduced whom they pleased; they bound and loosed [men] at their pleasure.[142]
>
> And [Alexandra] restored those practices which the Pharisees had introduced . . . which her father-in-law, Hyrcanus, had abrogated. . . . She had indeed the name of the "regent," but the Pharisees had the authority. . . . And the country was entirely at peace, except for the Pharisees; for they disturbed the queen and desired that she kill those who persuaded Alexander to slay the eight hundred men; after which they themselves cut the throat of one of them, Diogenes, and after him, they did the same to several others.[143]

Although there was constant strife between the Sadducees and Pharisees, as long as Alexandra ruled, violence was kept to a minimum. But when she died in 67 BCE, civil war broke out between the two factions, each led by one of her children, Aristobulus and Hycranus II. The Sadducees, the officers, and most of the army preferred Aristobulus, while the Pharisees and

---

[142] Josephus, Flavius: *The Wars of the Jews,* Book 1, Ch. 5, No. 2. See http://www.documentacatholicaomnia.eu/03d/0037-0103,_Flavius_Josephus,_De_Bello_Judaico,_EN.pdf

[143] Josephus, Flavius: *Jewish Antiquities*, Book 13, Chapter 16, No. 2. See http://www.ccel.org/ccel/josephus/complete.ii.xiv.xvi.html

the common people aligned themselves with Hycranus. Aided by a large Arabian army, Jerusalem was besieged by Hycranus and fell into his hands, forcing Aristobulus to retreat to the Temple Mount.

At the time, Rome was the foremost power in the world and the Roman general Pompey had conquered much of Asia Minor. Emissaries from both sides appealed for his support and Pompey began moving his forces to Jerusalem, believing he would be welcome as a mediator. But when it became clear that he, himself, had designs upon the city, the Sadducees and many of the common people resisted the Romans, so Pompey was forced into a long and costly siege. When the Romans finally breached the walls, they slaughtered a great number of Jews in retaliation:

> And now did many of the priests [Sadducees], even when they saw their enemies assailing them with swords in their hands, go on with their Divine worship, and were slain while they were offering their drink-offerings and burning their incense; preferring the duties of their worship to God, before their own preservation. [Yet] the greatest part of them were slain *by their own countrymen;* of the adverse faction [the Pharisees], while an innumerable multitude threw themselves down precipices. . . . Now of the Jews, twelve thousand were slain; but of the Romans very few were slain.[144]

The Romans eventually withdrew from the city, and Judea became its vassal. Pompey appointed Hycranus as High-priest—but not king—and for a time the Pharisees were back in control, allowing the Jews aligned with them to practice their religion.

---

[144] Josephus, *Wars of the Jews*, Book 1, Chapter 7, No. 5.

Intra-Religious Conflicts and Wars 147

Jerusalem, however, remained a powder keg, and for the next 100 years there was sporadic violence between the sects, and even an occasional rebellion against Rome.

The Sadducees still, however, were responsible for Temple worship, and held it was permissible for non-Jews to bring sacrifices to the Temple—against the opposition of the Pharisees. Additionally, and critically, the Sadducees thought it best to submit to Roman rule as long as the Jews were able to practice their religion; the Pharisees, who had the multitude their side, were much more zealous, and wanted to expel Rome once and for all from Judea and Jerusalem.

Finally, in 70 AD, a major rebellion resulted in the Romans amassing a large force, invading Judea, and beginning a siege of Jerusalem. The Sadducees wanted to submit to the Romans, whereas most of the Pharisees were violently opposed to it. At the time, the high priest was one, Ananias, whose son, Eleazar, was governor of the Temple situated in lower Jerusalem and controlled by the Pharisees. Eleazar came over to their side as religion *pitted son against father and father against son.* Josephus describes a most shameful episode in the history of the Jews:

> Eleazar, the son of Ananias the High Priest . . . was governor of the Temple, and persuaded those that officiated in the Divine service to receive no sacrifice from any foreigner. . . . [But] when many of the high priests and their leaders besought them not to omit the sacrifice, which was customary to offer for their princes, they would not be prevailed upon . . .

[relying] much upon their multitude, for the . . . [Pharisees] assisted them.

Hereupon the men in charge told the [Pharisees] that their forefathers had always received [offerings] from foreign nations. . . . [but you] "have brought up novel rules of a strange Divine worship, and are determined to run the hazard of having the city condemned [by Rome] for rebellion, by not allowing any foreigner, but only Jews, to sacrifice or worship there."

But still those innovators would not hearken to what was said . . . and prepared for war. Seeing this, the governors with the high priests, and the part of the multitude that were desirous of peace, seized the upper city [Mount Zion], as the Pharisees controlled the lower city and the Temple. Now both sects made use of stones and slings perpetually against one another . . . and thus was there perpetual slaughter on both sides for seven days; but neither side would yield.[145]

On the eighth day, the High Priest [Ananais] was caught where he had concealed himself and was slain. . . . Now his death so incensed Manahem [a Jewish leader of the peace party], that he became barbarously cruel and thinking he had no antagonist to dispute him, he adorned himself with royal garments and proceeded to the Temple—his followers with him in their armor—to worship in a pompous manner. . . . But Eleazar and [the Pharisees] . . . fell violently upon them, as did the rest of the people. . . . Manahem and his party fled and those that were caught were slain. As for Manahem himself . . . they took him alive and then tortured him with many sorts of torments, and afterwards slew him, as they did to those that were captains under him.[146]

The intra-religious wars within Judaism ended after the Second Temple was destroyed, as the Jews were dispersed throughout Asia, Europe, and Africa. Having no Temple to

---

[145] Josephus, *Wars of the Jews*, Book 1, Chapter 17, No. 4.
[146] Josephus, *Wars of the Jews*, Book 1, Chapter 17, no. 9.

administer to, the Sadducee party dissolved, while the Pharisees evolved into Rabbinic Judaism, which took over control of religious practice. While words and occasional edicts of excommunication took place between the rabbis and the heretical sects that cropped up here and there, violence ended, as the Jews no longer had a state, but were subject to the whims and political fortunes of the nations in which they resided.

Religious conflict was responsible for the death of several million Jews, but that was only a small fraction of the *hundreds of million*s affected over the next 2000 years in wars within and between Christianity, Islam, and Hinduism. We continue our tragic saga by turning next to conflicts *within* Christianity.

Christianity

It is an undeniable fact that the internecine wars *within* Christianity were the most egregious, lasted the longest, and resulted in the most atrocities and the deaths of the most people, affecting hundreds of millions of families. *Can any reasonable reader imagine that this state of affairs was acceptable to God?* Such monstrosity in His Name? And for what: in most cases, for a simple belief or two not in accordance with the Roman Catholic or established Protestant national church; or even worse, using religion as a pretext to confiscate land and possessions.

Having already described the differences and conflicts between the Arians, the Sabellians, and the Trinitarians in the early phases of Christianity, we will focus on later conflicts that led to untold suffering; the *Inquisition*, the *Crusades*, and the *Reformation*:

The late thirteenth century saw the formalization of new and insidious policies of the Church. Previously, the Pope would make occasional inquiries into the heresy of one region or another, to combat religious sectarianism—but now crusades and the Inquisition were *formalized* with fire and brimstone, unleashing unprecedented horror in the Name of God for the next five hundred years.

Early Crusades

In the mid-twelfth century, a movement known as Catharism began in Western France, but was considered heretical by the Church. By the early 13th century, their beliefs spread to other areas and attracted many followers and sympathizers. Cathars called for a return to Jesus' message of humility, poverty, and preaching—reforms that were a reaction against the often scandalous and dissolute lifestyles of the Catholic clergy. Theologically, in contrast to the Church, the Cathars had but one sacrament, the *Consolamentum*, or consolation before death. They denied the Sacrament of the Eucharist, stating that it could not possibly be the body of Jesus, and refused to be baptized.

Because they dared oppose the doctrines of the Church and orthodox interpretations of the Bible, Pope Innocent III called for a crusade against them. He offered the lands of those presumed heretics to any French nobleman, willing to take up arms. The Albigensian Crusade (1209–1229) became a 20-year military campaign to expunge Catharism. It was prosecuted largely by the French king and soon took on a political flavor, resulting in not only a significant reduction in the number of practicing Cathars, but also a realignment of various counties, bringing them into the sphere of the French crown.

In one notable horror, crusaders invaded the city of Beziers in 1209. After a short siege, the entire population of between 15,000 and 20,000 was slaughtered and the city burned to the ground. By 1225, the Cathars were virtually eliminated from their lands; after 1233, the Inquisition crushed what remained of Catharism.

The Waldens were even more offensive to the Catholic Church because they denounced the riches and luxury of the clergy. The movement originated in the late twelfth century by

Peter Waldo, a wealthy merchant who gave away his property—preaching poverty as the way to heaven. The Waldensian movement was characterized by lay preaching, voluntary poverty, and strict adherence to the Bible.

Waldens asserted that pomp and ceremonies of the Church were not meant for preachers of the Gospel; relics that were sold were nothing more than old bones; pilgrimages served no end other than to enrich the Church; holy water was not any more efficacious than rain water; and that prayer in a hut was just as effective as one offered in the most grandiose temple. In short, they rejected what they perceived as the hypocrisy of the Roman Catholic Church and considered the Papacy as the Antichrist of Rome.

Pope Innocent III denounced the Waldensians, and, in 1211, over eighty of that sect were burned at the stake in Strasbourg. This began several centuries of persecution that virtually destroyed the movement.

> We have the spectacle of Innocent III preaching a crusade against these unfortunate sectaries, and permitting the enlistment of every wandering scoundrel at loose ends to carry fire and sword, to rape and [commit] every conceivable outrage among the most peaceful subjects of the King of France. The accounts of the cruelties and abominations of this crusade are far more terrible to read than any account of Christian martyrdoms by the pagans, and they have the added horror of being indisputably true.

This black and pitiless intolerance was an evil spirit to be mixed into the project of a rule of God on earth. This was a spirit entirely counter to that of Jesus of Nazareth.[147]

As centuries passed and the Waldensians still proved problematic, Innocent VIII in 1487 began a new crusade for their extermination. An offensive was launched in the provinces of Dauphine and Piedmont, and devastated the area, forcing many Waldensians to flee to Provence and south to Italy. In 1545, the *Arrêt de Mérindol* assembled 2,000 professional soldiers returning from the Italian wars, against the Waldensians of Provence. Deaths in the Massacre of Mérindol were in thousands, and over 25 villages were razed. Those that survived were forced to serve in the French Navy.

The Inquisition

Innocent III also organized a new order known as Dominicans, as a standing inquiry under the control of a Grand Inquisitor. In 1252, Innocent IV's papal bull explicitly authorized the use of torture by the Inquisition for eliciting confessions. Penalties were usually confiscation of property and/or imprisonment. This often led to false charges to enable the Church and Crown to gain land.

As an ecclesiastical court of the Roman Catholic Church, Inquisitors wielded immense power, brutally repressed all alleged heretics of their rights, and deprived them of their estates and assets, which became subject to the Catholic treasury. Inherently corrupt, the Church was relentless to destroy anyone who spoke,

---

[147] Wells, *The Outline of History*, Vol. 2, Chapter XXXIII, No. 13.

or even thought, against established canon. And this continued throughout most of Europe for almost *six centuries*—until the mid 1800s—one of the most monstrous polices in the history of man.

As reported by H. G. Wells:

> The church set itself . . . to assail and weaken the human conscience in which its sole hope of world dominion resided. Before the thirteenth century, the penalty of death had been inflicted but rarely upon heretics and unbelievers. Now in a hundred market-places in Europe, the dignitaries of the church watched the blackened bodies of its antagonists, for the most part poor and insignificant people, burn and sink pitifully, and their own great mission to mankind, burn and sink with them into dust and ashes.[148]

Regardless, there were those who continued to speak out against the Church. We spoke earlier of England's John Wycliffe (1320-1384), who criticized the corruption of the Church—garnering wealth and living in luxury while engaging in heavy papal taxation. He also denied that the doctrine of the eating of consecrated bread and drinking of wine in the Mass ceremony becomes, in some mystical way, the actual body of Jesus. Rather, the sacrament was merely a personal remembrance of him—making it unnecessary for consecrated priests altogether. Organizing a number of followers, known as the Wycliffes, he translated the Bible in English, so people could determine for themselves whether, in fact, the Church's claims were true to the

---

[148] Wells, *The Outline of History,* Vol. 2, Chapter XXXIII, No. 13.

teachings of Scripture. The Pope raged against him and ordered him imprisoned, but was helpless as Wycliffe had supporters in high places.

We spoke, too, of John Huss, a Czech who incorporated the ideas of Wycliffe in Bohemia. In 1396, after lecturing at the University of Prague based upon Wycliffe's doctrines, the Church excommunicated him. In 1415, Huss was convinced to go to Constance to debate his ideas under promise of a safe conduct, but instead was put on trial for heresy. Refusing to recant, and despite his safe conduct guarantee, *he was burnt alive*!

This resulted in an insurrection of the Hussites, which became the first of a series of religious wars that marked the breaking-up of Christendom and ultimately led to the Reformation. In 1420, the Pope, Martin V, called for the destruction of the Wycliffes, Hussites, and all other heretics in Bohemia, and, not surprisingly, attracted the dregs of Europe who couldn't care less about ecclesiastic theory, but simply needed an excuse to rob, kill, rape and collect booty. However, they would be gravely disappointed. The Hussites were very well organized, and the country was aflame with enthusiasm. Despite infantry of over 100,000 and 40,000 cavalry, four crusades over a period of ten years were totally unsuccessful.

As H. G. Wells tells it:

> The crusaders, advancing by slow marches, penetrated further into Bohemia, till they reached the neighborhood of the town of Domazlice . . . [when] on August 14th, 1431, [they] received the news that the Hussites . . . were approaching. Though the Bohemians were still four miles off, the rattle of their war-wagons and the song, "All ye warriors of God," which their whole host was chanting, could already be heard.
>
> The enthusiasm of the crusaders evaporated with astounding rapidity . . . [and] the Papal representative and the Duke of Saxony ascended a convenient hill to inspect the battlefield. [But] they discovered . . . the German camp was in utter confusion. Horsemen were streaming off in every direction, and the clatter of empty wagons being driven off almost drowned the sound of that terrible singing. The crusaders were abandoning even their loot. Came a message from the Margrave of Brandenburg advising flight; there was no holding any of their troops. They were dangerous now only to their own side, and the papal representative spent an unpleasant night hiding from them in the forest. . . . So ended the Bohemia crusade.[149]

Another sect considered heretical by the Church was the Anabaptists. They were founded in Wittenberg in 1521 and believed that baptism is only valid when the candidate freely confesses his/her faith in Jesus and *desires* to be baptized. To them baptism of infants was irrelevant and not supported by Scripture. They adhered to a literal interpretation of the Sermon on the Mount, which precluded taking oaths, participating in the

---

[149] Wells, *The Outline of History,* Vol. 2, Chapter XXXV, No. 2. (Not, however, before the crusaders stormed the small town of Most, and committed horrible atrocities on a population that was entirely innocent of any form of heresy.)

military, or taking positions in civil government. Persecuted by the Church, in 1525 they broke out into an insurrection. Between 1532 and 1535 the insurgents held the town of Minster in Westphalia, but were besieged by the local bishop who eventually gained control. After the surrender, the bishop had the Anabaptist leaders brutally tortured and executed in the marketplace, their mutilated bodies hung in cages from a church tower, to show the entire world the fate of heretics.

Before long, the Inquisition expanded to a number of territories. Particularly atrocious were those in Spain and Portugal against *New Christians*. As a result of violent anti-Semitism and pogroms in the late 14th century, thousands of Jews were killed and their synagogues burned. That, and very oppressive laws of the 14th and 15th century, forced many Jews—known as *Conversos*—to convert to Christianity to save their lives. Those who did not fully embrace Catholicism and continued to practice Judaism secretly were referred to as *Marranos*. As Christians conquered areas of Spain and Portugal from Islam, Moslems also converted to avoid eviction or worse.

Accordingly, Ferdinand and Isabella established the Spanish Inquisition in 1478, targeting the above groups. Then, in 1492, Jews who had not converted were expelled from Spain, while in Portugal, the Inquisition targeted largely Sephardic Jews, who left Spain years earlier to avoid conversion.

The Spanish Inquisition, was, arguably, the deadliest and most notorious of all; highly organized, yet its association with Rome was deliberately hidden so punishment could be much crueler, and property could be confiscated without blaming the Pope. In one month alone in 1556, 25 Jews were burned alive, 26 were hung, and 30 more were liberated only after they had paid a substantial bribe. Rome became veiled by secrecy, and it falsified, concealed, and forged the reports of thousands of trials. In some districts, Inquisitors were ordered to round up the wealthiest heretics, so their property would be confiscated and divided between the Spanish Throne and the Church.

During the late Middle Ages the scope of the Inquisition significantly grew in response to the Protestant Reformation and expanded to most other European countries. All told, the number of the victims of the Inquisition is estimated to have been close to ten million, not including, the wives, husbands, parents, children, and other relatives of those evicted, tortured, and slaughtered by the Church.

The Inquisition - Not Very Jesus Like

Citizens accused of heresy would be awakened in the dead of night, often gagged, and removed to the Inquisition prison for closer examination. . . . [Orders were that] no husband should be spared because of his wife, nor wife because of her husband, and no parent spared because of a helpless child. Once in custody, victims waited anxiously before their judge, while he perused through the document of their accusation. During the first examination, enough of their property was confiscated to cover the expenses of the preliminary investigation. The accused would then be asked incriminating and leading questions calculated to entangle him/her.

During their trial, defendants had no right to counsel, and were even denied the right to know the names of their accusers. No favorable evidence or character witnesses were permitted. Nor would a prisoner of the Inquisition have seen the accusation against himself, or any other. All references relating to time, place, and person were carefully concealed. One who spoke up for an accused heretic would, himself, be arrested as an accomplice.

When a sentence of torture had been handed down, Inquisitors were instructed to make fresh attempts to persuade the accused to confess the truth. "The executioners, while stripping him, should affect uneasiness, haste, and sadness, endeavoring thus to instill fear into his mind; and when naked, the inquisitors should take him aside, exhorting him to confess; promising him his life upon the condition of his doing so, provided that he is not a relapse."

Most defendants confessed in order to escape the great anguish and bitter torture. If found guilty, they were handed over to the civil authorities to be "relaxed"—that is, burnt alive. Refusing to confess at the first hearing, saw heretics being remanded to the prisons for several months. The dungeons were situated underground, so that the outcries of the subject might not reach other parts of the building. In some medieval cells, the victims were bound in stocks or chains, unable to move about and forced to sleep standing up or on the ground. In some cases there was no light or ventilation, inmates were generally starved, kept in solitary confinement, and allowed no contact with the outside world, including that of their own family. In 1252, Pope Innocent IV officially authorized the creation of torture chambers, and perpetual imprisonment or death at the stake, without the bishop's consent. Acquittal of the accused was now virtually impossible. Thus, with a license granted by the Pope himself, Inquisitors were free to explore the depths of horror and cruelty. Dressed as black-robed fiends with black cowls over their heads, Inquisitors could extract confessions from just about anyone. The Inquisition invented every conceivable devise to inflict pain by slowly dismembering and dislocating the body. Many of the devices were inscribed with the motto, "Glory be only to god."

Very few who entered the doors of those halls of torment emerged whole in mind and body. If they escaped with their life, they were, with rare exceptions, maimed forever—physically and/or mentally. Those who managed to endure the dungeons generally went mad in captivity, screaming out in despair to escape their purgatories. Others committed suicide during their confinement.

Defendants were known to incriminate themselves, given any chance they could escape the horrors. Some might be let free by revealing all they knew of other heretics and apostates. Under the general terror, there was little hesitation in denouncing not only friends and acquaintances, but the nearest and dearest—parents, children, brothers and sisters, whose houses . . . were razed to the ground. Anyone who allowed a heretic to remain in his country, or who shielded him in the slightest degree, would lose his land, personal property, and official position; the local magistracy joined in the search for heretics; males from the ages of 14, and females from 12, had to swear that they would inform on heretics, renewable every two years.[150]

---

[150] Excerpted from: http://istrangehuman.blogspot.com/2013/03/the-holy-inquisitions-dark-side-of.html

Catholics vs. Protestants

By the sixteenth century, with the invention of the printing press and the beginning of the Industrial Revolution, people began to perceive that the Church was not a spiritual refuge; that the Pope and the hierarchy were not spiritual leaders, as much as wealthy, earthly princes who lived in luxury. Furthermore, as the Bible was translated into various languages, people realized that many of Church's rituals and assertions had nothing to do with Jesus' teachings, but only served as an excuse to line the church's pockets—ironically, practicing what Jesus rebelled against 1500 years earlier, when he turned over the table of money changers in Jerusalem.

Now, between the efforts of Martin Luther and John Calvin, people all over Western Europe were gaining familiarity with the newly translated Bible. And in many cases they were supported by the secular rulers—princes, who not necessarily for religious reasons, also resented the Church's claim to power in their territory. Soon, Great Britain, Sweden, Norway, Denmark, and Bohemia, among others, broke away from Roman Catholicism, while new *Protestant* churches were popping up all over Europe, protected and controlled by the nobility. Adding to the mix, a third group of "Nonconformists" declined to have their religion determined by any authority—the Pope or the State—but held that the Bible is the only divinely inspired and authoritative guide.

It did not take long before the assertions of Luther and Calvin were firmly established in Germany and England, and various monarchies took on the creed. This resulted in major conflicts between Catholics and Protestants in which blood on both sides was shed by the tens of millions. Catholic governments tried to stop the spread of Protestantism in their territory, leading to civil war in France from 1562 to 1598, including the notorious St. Bartholomew's Day Massacre.

Before dawn on the morning of August 24, 1572, church bells tolled in the Saint-Germain l'Auxerrois quarter of Paris. Just moments earlier, soldiers under the command of Henri, Duke of Guise, had overcome resistance and assassinated the Admiral of France and Huguenot leader, Gaspard de Coligny, in his bedroom. They threw the body from the window to the ground below, where angry crowds mutilated it; cutting off the head and hands, and dragging it through the streets of Paris. As Guise walked away from Coligny's lodging, he was overheard to say "it is the king's command." (See inset.)

The killing unleashed an explosion of popular hatred against Protestants throughout the city. In the days that followed, some 3,000 Huguenots were killed in Paris, and another 8,000 in other cities. This spilling of blood decisively ended Huguenot hopes to transform France into a Protestant kingdom. It remains one of the most horrifying episodes in the Reformation era.

St. Bartholomew's Day Massacre – France: 1572

Determined to exterminate all Protestants . . . the Duke of Guise who was put in command of the enterprise, summoned captains of the Catholic Swiss mercenaries and commanders of French companies, and told them that it was the will of the king that they should take vengeance on the band of rebels while they had the beasts in the toils. Victory [would be] easy; the booty great and obtained without danger. The signal to commence . . . would be given by the bell of the palace . . . [while they would] recognize each other by a bit of white linen tied around the left arm. . . .

Meanwhile, the head of the Huguenots, Gaspard de Coligny awoke, and recognized . . . that a riot was taking place. Nevertheless he remained assured of the king's good will . . . that quiet would be restored as soon as it was seen that soldiers of the guard, under command of Cosseins, had been detailed to protect him and his property.

But when he perceived that the noise increased and that some one had fired a musket into his courtyard . . . conjecturing what it might be—but too late—he arose . . . and said his prayers. Labonne [his servant] held the key of the house, and when Cosseins commanded him, in the king's name, to open the door, he obeyed at once, apprehending nothing. But scarcely had Cosseins entered, when Labonne was killed with a dagger thrust. The Swiss who were in the courtyard fled into the house and closed the door, piling against it all the furniture they could find. But finally the conspirators broke through . . . and mounted the stairway, including Cosseins [and the other captains] of the regiment of the guards—all with [armor].

Still, after his prayers, Coligny said without any appearance of alarm to those who were present, "I see clearly that which they seek, and I am ready steadfastly to suffer that death which I have never feared and which for a long time past I have pictured to myself. I consider myself happy . . . in being ready to die for God, by whose grace I hope for life everlasting. . . . Go then from this place, my friends, as quickly as you may, for fear lest you shall be involved in my misfortune, and that some day your wives shall curse me as the author of your loss. For me it is enough that God is here, to whose goodness I commend my soul, which is so soon to issue from my body." After these words, they ascended to an upper room, whence they sought safety in flight over the roofs.

Shortly thereafter, the conspirators burst through the door of the chamber, and [demanded to know whether he was Coligny.] "Yes, I am," he replied with a fearless countenance. "But you, young man, respect these white hairs. What is it you would do? You cannot shorten by many days this life of mine." As he spoke, a conspirator thrust a sword through his body, and having withdrawn his sword, thrust it again in his mouth, by which his face was disfigured. So Coligny fell, killed with many thrusts. . . .

They then threw the body through the window into the courtyard, disfigured though it was. When the Chevalier d'Angouleme, had wiped the blood away with a cloth, he said: "Cheer up, my friends! Let us do thoroughly that which we have begun. The king commands it." He instructed the bell of the palace clock to ring . . . and the people ran to the house of Coligny. After his body had been treated to all sorts of insults, they threw it into a neighboring stable, and finally cut off his head, which they sent to Rome. They also shamefully mutilated him, and dragged his body through the streets to the bank of the Seine, a thing which he had formerly almost prophesied, although he did not think of anything like this.

The body was then placed upon the gibbet of Montfaucon, where it hung by the feet in chains of iron and they built a fire beneath, by which he was burned without being consumed; so that he was, so to speak, tortured with all the elements, since he was killed upon the earth, thrown into the water, placed upon the fire, and finally put to hang. Having served for several days as a spectacle to gratify the hate of many—he also aroused the just indignation of many others, who reckoned that the fury of the people would cost the king and France many a sorrowful day.[151]

---

[151] http://www.historyguide.org/earlymod/massacre.html

Elsewhere, in 1556 Philip II sent Spanish troops into the Netherlands under the ruthless Duke of Alva, who sacked towns and massacred the populace. But that only resulted in a rebellion led by William the Silent. Religion was also the major issue in the war between Spain and England from 1585 to 1604.

The collapse of a unified Christendom had the most consequences in Germany, a patchwork of domains controlled by sovereign princes, dukes, electors, and bishops—far less centralized than France or England. As a result, some territories went Protestant while others stayed Catholic, resulting in a civil war known as the Thirty Years War. The Emperor was not strong enough, nor the Protestant princes sufficiently united for a decisive conclusion. The fact that it was not fought along a pre-determined frontier, but all over an empire consisting of multiple domains—Protestant here, Catholic there—made it one of cruelest and most destructive wars that Europe had ever known—especially coming at a time when military tactics and technology had developed to a point that rendered citizen armies virtually useless against trained professional soldiers.

Under these conditions, compensation of soldiers was as important as food or munitions. As the long struggle dragged on and the financial distress of Germany increased, both sides were forced to loot towns and villages for supplies and soldiers' pay. Increasingly, armies gathered into brigands living off the country—as looting and committing outrages became a legitimate operation in warfare and a soldier's privilege. So devastated was the land that farming ceased, what crops could be harvested were hidden away, and great crowds of starving women and children became army followers, desperate for some food. By 1648, Germany was ruined and desolate. It did not fully recover for a century.

All told, tens of millions were killed in these intra-faith wars—supposedly in the Name of God.

> **The Siege of Alkmaar – The Netherlands, 1573**
> And now . . . did the handful of people shut up within Alkmaar prepare for the worst. Their main hope lay in the friendly sea. The vast sluices called the Zyp, through which the inundation of the whole northern province could be very soon effected, were but a few miles distant. By opening these gates, and piercing a few dykes, the ocean might be made to fight for them. To obtain this result, however, the consent of the inhabitants was requisite, as the destruction of all the standing crops would be inevitable. The city was so closely invested, that it was a matter of life and death to venture forth, and it was difficult, therefore, to find an envoy for this hazardous mission. At last . . . one Peter Van der Mey by name, undertook the adventure. . . .
>
> Affairs soon approached a crisis within the beleaguered city. Daily skirmishes, without decisive results, had taken place outside the walls. Soon, two choice regiments, recently arrived from Lombardy, led a major attack, rending the air with their shouts and confident of an easy victory. They were sustained by what seemed an overwhelming force of disciplined troops. Yet never, even in the recent history of Haarlem, had an attack been received by more dauntless breasts. Every living man was on the walls. The storming parties were assailed with cannon, with musketry and pistols. Boiling water, pitch and oil, molten lead, and unslaked lime were poured upon them every moment.

> Hundreds of tarred and burning hoops were skillfully quoited around the necks of the invaders, who struggled in vain to extricate themselves from these fiery ruffs, [but] as fast as the soldiers planted foot upon the breach, they were confronted face to face with sword and dagger by the burghers, who hurled them headlong into the moat below.
>
> Thrice was the attack renewed with ever-increasing rage—thrice repulsed with unflinching fortitude. . . . Meantime, as many of the dykes hand been opened, the land in the neighborhood of the camp was becoming splashy, although as yet the threatened inundation had not taken place. The soldiers were already very uncomfortable and very refractory; [Peter Van der Mey] had not been idle."
>
> He returned with dispatches for the city. By accident or contrivance, he lost these dispatches as he made his way into the town, so that they fell into Alva's hands. They contained a definite promise from the Duke of Orange to flood the country so as to drown the whole Spanish army. . . . But Alva, when he had read these documents, did not wait for opening of any more sluices. Presently the stout men of Alkmaar, cheering and jeering, watched the Spaniards breaking camp.[152]

---

[152] Motley, John Lothrop, *The Rise of the Dutch Republic,* as cited in Wells, *The Outline of History*, Vol. 2, Chapter XXXVI, No. 3.

Islam

Sunni vs. Shiite

As we described in Chapter 12, Islam split after Mohammed's death into two major sects: Shiites, or partisans of Ali, Mohammed's nephew and adopted son, who claimed only he and his descendants were part of the Divine order, and Sunnis, who opposed political succession based on Mohammed's bloodline, but believed the Imam should be elected by the religious leaders of the community. Unlike Shiites, they also subscribed to the oral traditions passed down of the interpretation of the Koran.

While Sunnis triumphed politically, Shiites continued to look to the blood descendants of Ali as their legitimate political and religious leaders. Since then, most Shiites have vested religious authority in their senior clerical leaders, called *Ayatollahs* (Arabic for "Sign of God").

Although differences between Sunnis and Shiites has led to sporadic violence, it did not approach that previously detailed among Christians. Still, conflicts between Shiites and Sunnis have been ongoing to this very day. Until 1258, all of the caliphs of Islam were from Mohammed's tribe, the tribe of Quraysh, and Shiites were harshly persecuted in every Islamic country where they did not rule. In Persia, Sunnis dominated until the Safavid dynasty was established in 1501. Then Shiite Islam became the state religion, and over the following two centuries they fought with the Ottomans, the seat of the Sunni caliphate. As both empires faded, their battles roughly settled the political borders of modern Iran and Turkey, and by the seventeenth century their legacies resulted in the current demographic distribution of Islam's sects: Shiites comprising the majority of Moslems in Iran, Iraq, Yemen and Lebanon, while Sunnis make up the majority of more than forty countries from Morocco to Indonesia.

It is in the 20th and 21st centuries that the violence between Sunnis and Shiites has escalated exponentially, and arguably has been the cause of more suffering than the previous centuries put together. Often, the population was largely of one sect, but those in power of the other—or a secular Islamic party, such as the Ba'aths in Iraq—had the former persecuted.

In Pakistan, for example, there has been violence for decades between Sunnis, who comprise 90 percent of the Moslems, and Shiites, who comprise the remainder. But the largest intra-faith conflict occurred in the nine-year war (1980-1988) between Iran and Iraq. The former was ruled by the Shiite Ayatollah Khomeini, who called for a Moslem revolution. He desired to control Mecca and Medina, which is in Saudi Arabia, removing the Sunnis from these Islamic holy places and restoring the Shiites to power. While Saudi Arabia and Iran did not go to war, Iraq, led by Saddam Hussein, and supported by the Saudis, persecuted Shiites—for example, forbidding the celebration of their holy days or gatherings in groups of more than three. The war itself between Iraq and Iran resulted in well over a million deaths on both sides, all of whom were *Moslems killed by other Moslems*!

In the 21st century, sectarian war still plagues Iraq; Sunni jihadists blow up Shiite neighborhoods with car and truck bombs, and in revenge Shiites blow up Sunnis neighborhoods with vehicles similarly loaded. At this writing, the violence between Sunnis and Shiites is especially acute in the Syrian Civil War, which the Islamic State of Iraq and Syria have launched against the Shiites. This needless and insane fighting has cost the lives of tens of thousands of men, women, and children with no end in sight.

Chapter 17
Inter-Religious Wars and Conflicts

He who takes not his cross and follows me is not worthy of me.
Pope Urban II

Christian vs. Moslem

Continuing our saga, we now turn to inter-religious wars or conflicts *between* religions. By far, the one causing the greatest suffering and devastation have been between Christian and Moslem.

The Crusades

By the eleventh century, with the advance of the Moslem Turks into areas that had long been Byzantine, the Eastern Emperor, Alexius Comnenus, appealed to Pope Urban II for aid. Separated from Roman Catholicism for centuries, this was a unique opportunity for Rome to assert its authority over the entire Christian world. Urban wasted no time and, in 1095, called for a crusade led by one, Peter the Hermit, who, barefoot, clad in a coarse garment, and bearing a huge cross, travelled across France and Germany and riled up vast crowds about alleged atrocities the Turks had perpetuated on Christians.

Soon, a largely leaderless mob made their way east. As told by H. G. Wells:

> From the very first this flaming enthusiasm was mixed with baser elements. . . . There was something in the multitude that now turned their faces east, something deeper than love in the human composition, namely, fear-born hate, that the impassioned appeals of the propagandists and the exaggeration

of the horrors and cruelties of the infidel had fanned into flame. . . . The first forces to move eastward were great crowds of undisciplined people rather than armies. . . .

This was a "people's" crusade. Never before in the history of the world had there been such a spectacle as these masses of practically leaderless people moved by an idea. . . . [But] when they got among foreigners, they do not seem to have realized that they were *not* among the infidel. Two great mobs, the advance guard of the expedition, committed such atrocities in Hungary, where the language was incomprehensible to them, as to provoke the Hungarians to massacre them. A third host began with a great pogrom of the Jews in the Rhineland—for the Christian blood was up—and this multitude was also dispersed in Hungary. Two other hosts under Peter reached Constantinople, to the dismay of Emperor Alexius. They looted and committed outrages as they came, and at last, he shipped them across the Bosphorus, to be massacred . . . by the Turks.[153]

So much for disorganized mobs. But then, Rome got serious. In 1097, the First Crusade was authorized with a professional army led by Stephen of Blois. They crossed the Bosphorus and took Antioch after a year's siege. Then they proceeded to Jerusalem:

After a little more than a month's siege, the city was finally captured. The slaughter was terrible [Jews and Moslems alike] . . . the blood of the conquered ran down the streets, until men splashed in blood as they rode. At nightfall, "sobbing for excess of joy," the crusaders came to the Sepulcher from their treading of the wine-press, and put their blood-stained hands together in prayer. [And so ended the First Crusade.][154]

---

[153] Wells *The Outline of History*, Vol. 2, Chapter XXXIII, No. 10.
[154] Wells *The Outline of History,* Vol. 2, Chapter XXXIII, No. 10.

Accomplishing the Pope's goal, the authority of the Patriarch of Jerusalem was usurped by the Roman Catholic clergy, and Latin kingdoms were set up in Syria and Jerusalem in communion with Rome. Soon Rome's lust for Byzantine Christianity became more obvious. In 1147, a Second Crusade, in which both the Belgium Emperor Conrad III and King Louis of France participated, attacked, and subjugated the still pagan lands east of the Elbe and captured Lisbon—which became the basis of the Christian kingdom of Portugal.

During these centuries, the Church had become "a state within a state" competing with secular emperors. It had its own law courts for cases involving priests, monks, students, crusaders— even widows, orphans, and the helpless. Whenever the rules of the Church were involved, it claimed jurisdiction; so wills, marriage, oaths, and, of course, heresy, sorcery, and blasphemy were tried in their courts. Numerous clerical prisons were built in which offenders would rot until they died. The Pope was the supreme law-giver, and Rome was the final and decisive court of appeal. The Church not only held vast properties, but gained great income from fees and taxes. Nor was this voluntary; the church demanded it as its right. Yet the clergy, itself, claimed exemption from the taxation of the emperor. Rome had forgotten—better ignored—the Kingdom of a loving God in hearts of men that Jesus had preached, but rather asserted its own godliness—not one of compassion and justice, but of fire and brimstone married to wealth and splendor.

But the Moslems were not idle. In 1169, Saladin, the founder of the Ayyubid dynasty, reunited Egypt and Bagdad and led a Holy War, or a counter-crusade, against the Christians. It was now crusader against crusader, Islam against Christianity, and in 1187, Jerusalem was retaken. This provoked the Third Crusade in 1189. It failed to recapture Jerusalem, but the Christians still remained in possession of the sea-coast of Palestine. Finally, a Fourth Crusade in 1204 conquered Constantinople—after more than eight centuries of separation from the Latin Church. Now, Latin and Greek Churches were declared to be reunited, and Latin emperors ruled until 1261. Alas, Eastern Orthodox Christians found themselves in rather a worse situation under Papal rule than under the Moslems.

The Black Death

But neither was God idle. In one sense, for centuries God needed to do nothing nor intervene in the wars between and among religions in His Name. They were all were self-cleansing. *Those who lived by the sword, died by the sword. Men reaped what they sowe*d. Whatever atrocities were committed by one religious group, would be reciprocated somewhat later by their antagonists.

But by the middle of the 13th century, Christianity as just described, got completely out of hand, and cruelties and suffering knew no bounds. The Church, now dominant, with greed, power, and wealth the great motivators, subjected anyone in their territories, whatever religion, to its whims and fancies. God could no longer stand by quietly. He had had enough!

So—the author has absolutely no doubt—God unleashed a pestilence, the *Black Death* or Bubonic Plague, unprecedented in the history of man. It devastated Europe and Asia—where the Roman Catholic Church was most exploitive. The number of deaths from the plague was an estimated twenty million in Europe alone, virtually one-third of the population. Tens of millions died, as well, in Asia.

> "In men and women alike," the Italian poet Giovanni Boccaccio wrote, "at the beginning of the malady, certain swellings, either on the groin or under the armpits . . . waxed to the bigness of a common apple, others to the size of an egg; some more and some less, and these the vulgar named plague-boils. Blood and pus seeped out of these strange swellings, which were followed by a host of other symptoms—fever, chills, vomiting, diarrhea, terrible aches and pains—and then, in short order, death."[155]

Overall, these symptoms were very much alike those that were inflicted upon Job,[156] although in his case, they were neither contagious, nor as a result of any sin he committed. Still, never was there so clear a warning to mankind to cease their evil, seek wisdom, and unite against the dark powers of nature. The massacres of Hulagu[157] were as nothing compared to the plague.

---

[155] http://www.historyguide.org/ancient/lecture29b.html
[156] See Job 2:7
[157] For centuries, Baghdad was the capital of the Abbasid Caliphate, whose rulers were descendants of Abbas, an uncle of Muhammad. Although, by the middle of the 13th century, the power of the Abbasids had declined, Baghdad still retained much symbolic significance, and it

Its ravages were worst in the larger towns, where filthy and undrained streets afforded a constant threat to leprosy and fever.

In the burial ground of London . . . more than fifty thousand corpses are said to have been interred. Thousands of people perished at Norwich, while in Bristol, the living were hardly able to bury the dead. But the Black Death fell on the

---

remained a rich and cultured city. In 1257, Möngke Khan gave his brother, Hulagu, authority over a subordinate khanate and army, with instructions to compel the submission of various Moslem states.

Hulagu assembled what may have been the largest Mongol army to have existed: 150,000 strong. The Mongols established themselves on both banks of the Tigris River so as to form a pincer around the city. The Caliph, Al-Musta'sim, finally decided to do battle with them and sent out a force of 20,000 cavalry to attack the Mongols. The cavalry were decisively defeated by the Mongols, whose sappers breached dikes along the Tigris River and flooded the ground behind the Abbasid forces, trapping them.

On January 29, the Mongol army began its siege, constructing a palisade and a ditch around the city, and, by February 5, had seized a significant portion of the defenses. Around 3,000 of Baghdad's notables tried to negotiate with Hulagu, but were murdered. Five days later, on February 10, the city surrendered, beginning a week of massacre and destruction.

The Grand Library of Baghdad, containing countless precious historical documents and books on subjects ranging from medicine to astronomy, was destroyed. Survivors said that the waters of the Tigris ran black with ink from the enormous quantities of books flung into the river, and red from the blood of the scientists and philosophers killed. Citizens attempted to flee, but were intercepted by Mongol soldiers who killed in abundance, sparing neither woman nor child. 90,000 people are said to have died. Other estimates are much higher. Ian Frazier of the *New Yorker* says estimates of the death toll ranged from 200,000 to a million.

The Mongols looted and then destroyed mosques, palaces, libraries, and hospitals. Grand buildings that had been the work of generations were burned to the ground. Hulagu had to move his camp upwind of the city, due to the stench of decay. Baghdad was a depopulated, ruined city for several centuries and only gradually recovered some of its former glory. (en.wikipedia.org/wiki/Siege_of_Baghdad_(1258))

villages almost as fiercely as in the towns. More than one-half of the priests of Yorkshire are known to have perished; in the diocese of Norwich two-thirds of the parishes changed their incumbents. The whole organization of labor was thrown out of gear. The scarcity of hands made it difficult for the land tenants to perform the services due, and only a temporary abandonment of half the rent by the landowners induced the farmers to refrain from the abandonment of their farms. For a time cultivation became impossible. "Sheep and cattle strayed through the fields and corn," says a contemporary, "and there were none left who could drive them."[158]

Of course, not all inter-religious conflicts were initiated by Christians. Moslems, throughout their history, gained power and adherents less with persuasion than by the sword. One particularly egregious example occurred in 1784, when Tipu, the Sultan of the Kingdom of Mysore in southern India, attacked the Catholic population of Mangalorean. An estimated 60,000 people, or 90 percent of the Catholic community were captured by his army; only 7,000 escaped. They were forced to march through the jungles and mountains of the Western Ghat Range.

Twenty thousand prisoners died on the way, and 30,000 of them were forcibly converted to Islam. Women and girls were forcibly taken as wives of the Moslems, and men who offered resistance were disfigured by cutting off their noses, upper lips, and ears.[159]

---

[158] Wells, *The Outline of History*, Vol. 2, Chapter XXXV, No. 3.
[159] See https://en.wikipedia.org/wiki/Tipu_Sultan

Moslem vs. Hindu

Besides Christian vs. Moslem, over the centuries there has been continual violence between Moslem and Hindu, and no dearth of atrocities on either side. This was especially true in India, which at one time was Hindu until the Moslems invaded in the 11th century. Records of religious violence are extensive, and according to many estimates, between 100 and 200 million Hindus died over the course of the Moslem invasion and occupation, between 1000 and 1500 AD.[160]

As a result, over the centuries most Hindus fled India, and it is largely Moslem now. Ironically, as we have noted, it was the Hindus, who, centuries earlier, forcibly ejected the peace-loving Buddhists from India.

---

[160] According to Moslem historian Firishta Muhammad Qasim Hindu Shah, (1560-1620), over *400 million Hindus* got slaughtered during the Moslem invasion and occupation of India. Survivors got enslaved and castrated. India's population is said to have been around 600 million at the time. By the mid-1500's, the Hindu population was only 200 million.
At https://themuslimissue.wordpress.com/2015/08/31/islamic-invasion-of-india-the-greatest-genocide-in-history/

Timurlane

A particularly abominable example of Moslem atrocities was that of Timurlane, whose conquering exploits were among the most evil in all of history. He lived in the 14th century and was the founder of the Timurid dynasty that lasted until about 1500. During a military career spanning 50 years, his empire conquered much of Asia, Russia, Iran, and India. He boasted that he was the "Sword of Islam." Whether invading lands of "infidels" or other erring Moslems made no difference. His treatment of both made it necessary to define a new meaning for sadism and cruelty.

Timurlane's invasion of India was marked by systematic slaughter and other atrocities on a truly massive scale, inflicted mainly on the Hindu population. Massacres of conquered armies included throwing men off cliffs. Entire populations were wiped out and cities razed to the ground, leaving behind nothing but rubble. In Haryana, his force of 90,000 soldiers each killed 50 to 100 Hindu men, women, and children, and included such atrocities as be-headings of most of the enslaved Indian women after they were raped by Timurlane's soldiers, resulting in a massive depopulation of the region.

After a military rampage across the Middle East in Sistan, 2,000 people were laid in wet plaster and built into a living tower.

In Delhi, Timurlane slaughtered 80,000 individuals, and built grisly pyramids of their skulls to commemorate his victory.

Timurlane, himself, wrote about the Delhi massacre:

"Before my final assault on Delhi . . . it was brought to my notice that we had taken more than 100,000 Hindu prisoners. I asked my courtiers for advice about them, and they said that on the great day of battle . . . it would be entirely opposed to the rules of war to set these idolaters and foes of Islam at liberty. [Accordingly,] I gave my command to proclaim throughout the camp that every man who had infidel prisoners was to put them to death, and whoever neglected to do so should himself be executed and his property given to the informant. When this order became known to the warriors of Islam, they drew their swords and [executed] their prisoners. [Even] Maulana Umar, a counselor and man of learning, who, in all his life had never killed a sparrow, now, in execution of my order, slew with his sword fifteen idolatrous Hindus who were his captives.

"When the soldiers encountered the Hindus, many [of the latter] drew their swords. The flames of strife were thus lit and spread through the whole city from Jahanpanah to Old Delhi, burning up all it touched. The savage Turks fell to killing and plundering. The Hindus set fire to their houses, burned their wives and children in them, rushed into the fight and were killed. They showed much alacrity and boldness in fighting. On Thursday and all the night before Friday, nearly 15,000 Turks were engaged in slaying, plundering and destroying. When morning broke out on Friday, all my army, no longer under control, [invaded] the city and thought of nothing, but killing, plundering, and taking prisoners. All that day, the sack was general—because that was a holy Moslem day to celebrate, and *what could be a greater celebration than slashing the throats of infidels*!

"The following day, a Saturday, all passed in the same way and the spoil was so great that each man secured from 50 to 100 prisoners, men, women and children and all their bullion, gems, rubies, diamonds, garnets, pearls, gold, silver, and brocades and silks of great value. The booty was immense and excepting the Moslem quarter, the whole city was sacked."[161]

---

[161] At: www.ibiblio.org/britishraj/Jackson5/chapter09.html

Inter-Religious Conflicts and Wars 181

Another major Moslem/Hindu conflict occurred in the late 15th century. Baber, the Emperor of Northern India, was the founder of the Mughal dynasty. According to his own autobiographical record, his campaign in northwest India targeted Hindu and Sikh "pagans," and an immense number of "infidels" were killed, with Moslem camps building "towers of skulls of the infidels" on hillocks. There were numerous massacres of Hindu towns and villages by his army, in addition to the numerous deaths of both Hindu and Moslem soldiers on the battlefields.

> In the night, the Moslem assailants forced their way into the fortress in several places, and fell to slaughtering and plundering. At early dawn, the Emperor went in mounted on an elephant, attended by his nobles and chiefs on foot. The order was given for a general massacre of the infidels as punishment. The number exceeded 8,000. Those who escaped the sword were made prisoners and their property came into the hands of the Moslems.[162]

In the late 17th century, Aurangzeb, the last effective Mughal Emperor, ruled over most of the Indian subcontinent. After he assumed power, one of the worst campaigns of religious violence in Moslem history began, with an estimated 4.6 million people killed. He issued orders to all his provincial governors to "destroy with a willing hand the schools and temples of the infidels. . . . to put an entire stop to the teaching and practice of idolatrous forms of worship."[163] Over 60,000 temples were destroyed during this period. Idols were smashed, and the cities, towns, and provinces

---

[162] At: www.gutenberg.us/articles/eng/religious_violence_in_india
[163] At: www.gutenberg.us/articles/eng/religious_violence_in_india

became depopulated from the religious violence. Alas, too late, Aurangzeb on his death bed lamented in writing that he had "greatly sinned," and "it should not happen that Moslems be killed and the blame for their death rest upon him."[164]

We already referenced Tipu, Sultan of the Kingdom of Mysore. Allied with the French and Napoleon, he fought a number of battles in the late 18th century against the British, but saved his greatest persecution for Hindus, particularly in the Nair and Kodava regions. The Nairs were treated with extreme brutality for their Hindu faith and martial tradition. They were subjected to forcible conversions to Islam, or torture and death. Out of the 30,000 Nairs in captivity, the vast majority perished, including women and children.

Under British rule in the 18th century, Hindus and Moslems were considered as two divided groups, both culturally and for the purposes of governing. That could not prevent religious riots in their territories. Then, in 1905, after Bengal was partitioned along religious lines, waves of religious riots between Moslems and Hindus were the order of the day; beginning from about 1910 and lasting through the 1930s.

In 1947, India and Pakistan become independent, but that meant over 10 million people had to cross borders to ensure their safety in an increasingly lawless environment. Once Great Britain left the area, massive violence and slaughter occurred on both

---

[164] At: www.gutenberg.us/articles/eng/religious_violence_in_india

sides of the border along sectarian lines. The number of deaths is estimated to have been well over a million. Since then, hundreds of religious riots have been recorded in every decade of an independent India—victims included Moslems, Hindus, Sikhs, Christians, and Buddhists.

Last, but far from least, in December 1992, members of the Vishva Hindu Parishad destroyed the 430-year-old Babri Mosque in Ayodhya. It was claimed by the Hindus that the mosque was built over the birthplace of the ancient deity Rama. This action resulted in religious riots and caused at least 1200 deaths. And in 2002, in the Godhra train, Hindus were burned alive, allegedly by Moslems, who sealed the doors of the train. This led to the Gujarat riots, in which mostly Moslems were killed.

Dozens of other examples of violence between and among religions could have been cited, but the author suspects by now, you, the reader, may be cringing, just having read how monstrous humanity had become. In fact, you may wish to take a break here, as the next few chapters continue this abominable saga, except the conflicts are no longer religiously based, but secular. Yet as we have stated, and we shall see repeatedly, there *is spiritual* justice! When God has had His fill of evil, He sees to it that the oppressors become the oppressed!

Chapter 18
War and Evil: 3000 BCE–350 BCE

Because there are literally hundreds of times cities, states, regimes, and nations were humbled or completely wiped out because of the evil by their leadership and constituents, of necessity we must limit our examples. But by the end of this section, it will be hard to deny that: *"Evil never pays,"* and *"Those who live by the sword will surely die by the sword*!"

We begin with history as reported in Scripture, during which Divine Providence is more overt, detailed, and clearer than any other time. Because it *explicitly* shows God's hand, over a dozen examples testify to our thesis.

Biblical History

The Flood

No greater example of the consequences of evil can be found than the flood which nearly destroyed our world. Depravity and violence abounded; God was in anguish because of His creation and was about to destroy it—except that one man, Noah, was found who was righteous. So for his sake, we are here today, able to read about it:

> The Lord saw how great the iniquity of man had become upon the earth, and that every inclination of his thoughts was continually for evil. And the Lord regretted that He had made man, and *His heart was deeply grieved*. So He said, "I will remove from the face of the earth man that I have created, for

I deeply regret that I have made them." But Noah found favor in the eyes of the Lord![165]

In fact, despite all their evil, God still gave mankind a way out. From the time He first had enough, man had 120 years to repent. He commanded Noah to build an ark to survive the coming flood, knowing he would be observed by those around him, and that God's threat would be promulgated throughout the world. So God postponed His decree, hoping Noah would be taken seriously, and with the realization the world was about to be destroyed, man would cease his wickedness. For the Lord said, "My Spirit will not contend with humans forever, for they are mortal; their days will be a hundred and twenty years."[166]

Alas, we did not repent. Thus, the die was cast, and everyone except Noah and his family was destroyed. If God hoped that Noah's offspring would be of a different nature, He was sorely disappointed.

This episode, besides being an historical event—at least for those that accept the Bible as God's Word—has a profound message; namely: *Anyone can save the world*! That includes *you*! Of course, you are important to your family and friends, but you are also important to God! Did not David declare:

> The Lord searches from heaven
> among the children of men,
> To determine if there is one of understanding
> who seeks Him.

---

[165] Genesis 6:5
[166] Genesis 6:3

> But they have all turned aside.
> Together they have become vile.
> There is no one who does good—
> *Not even one!*[167]

Perhaps it is you, whom God is waiting for!

Imagine the world is equally balanced between good and evil on two ends of a scale. Who knows that by doing one good deed, *you* tip the scale and bring on for the entire world redemption and salvation—as believed, regardless of the specific details—by Christians, Jews, and Moslems alike.

The Tower of Babel

While evil is usually associated with violence—murder, war, terrorism, etc., in God's eyes it is much, much more. Arrogance and haughtiness, the belief that one is superior to his neighbor, while not obvious at first, eventually turns into a cancer that ends in imperialism, war, and genocide. Even here in America, the white man's claim to superiority led to the virtual destruction of Native Americans and the slavery and mistreatment of Afro-Americans.

In Biblical times, this was borne out by the attempt of the inhabitants of Shinar to build a tower to the heavens.

> Now the entire world was of one language and of a common speech. As the people migrated eastward, they settled in the plain of Shinar. They said to one another, "Come, let us build ourselves a city with a tower that reaches to the very heavens, and make a name for ourselves lest we be scattered over the face of the earth."

---

[167] Psalm 14

But the Lord descended to see the city and the tower they were building. And He said, "If one people speaking a common language will do this, then nothing they plan will be impossible for them. Let us therefore confound their language so they will not understand one another." So the Lord scattered them over the face of the earth, and they ceased from building the city. That is the reason why it was called Babel—because there the Lord confounded the language of the whole world.[168]

It is reasonable to ask, what sin did these people commit in erecting a tower in the city they lived in? In fact, it seems they were cooperating with one another, if anything. But further thought would show aside from their arrogance in attempting to build such a structure—to become like God—the tower was not being built for the view, but rather to flaunt their power; so other tribes or cities would fear them. This eventually would lead to the subjection of those not of their kindred—not immediately, perhaps—with violence and exploitation clearly on the horizon.

Sodom and Gomorrah

The destruction of two cities, Sodom and Gomorrah, is especially significant because for the first time—but not the last—an individual spoke out on behalf of others.[169] Scripture specifically states both cities were evil, as shown by their proposed treatment of two "strangers" who came to warn Lot about the city's imminent destruction, and remove him.

---

[168] Genesis 11:1
[169] See Job 23:23. "If one out of a thousand defends one who has incurred God's wrath, God will forgive him."

Now the people of Sodom were evil and sinned greatly against the Lord. . . . And two angels [in the guise of humans] arrived in the evening, and when Lot saw them, he said, "My lords, please stay overnight in your servant's house. . . . But men from every part of Sodom—both young and old—surrounded the house and called to Lot, "Where are the men you brought to your home tonight? Bring them out so that we can violate them."

Then Lot went outside to meet them and said, "No, my friends. Don't do this evil thing. See, I have two virgin daughters. . . . Let me bring them to you, and you can do what you wish with them. Only, don't violate these men, for they have come under the protection of my roof."

"Move out of our way," they replied. "This fellow came here as a foreigner, and now he wants to play the judge! We'll treat you worse than them." And they moved forward to break down the door, but the men inside pulled Lot back into the house and struck the men with blindness so that they were unable to find the door.[170]

Earlier, God revealed to Abraham what He was going to do: "Shall I hide from Abraham that which I am intending, seeing that he will surely become a great nation, and he will be the standard in which the entire earth will be blessed?"[171] And Abraham, in one of most poignant parts of Scripture, pleads for the cities.

Then Abraham approached the Lord and said, "Will You sweep away the righteous with the wicked? What if there are fifty righteous people in the city? Will You not spare the place for the sake of the fifty righteous? Far be it for You to do such a thing—to kill the righteous with the wicked; not distinguishing those who are evil from those who are good. Should not the Judge of all the earth do what is just?"

---

[170] Genesis 19:1
[171] Genesis 18:17

So the Lord answered, "If I find fifty righteous people in Sodom, I will spare the city for their sake."

Then Abraham spoke up again: "Now that I have been so bold as to speak to the Lord, though I am but dust and ashes, what if the number of the righteous is five less than fifty? Will you destroy the city for lack of five people?"

"If I find forty-five there, I will not destroy it."[172]

Abraham continues "negotiations," prevailing to get God to agree to spare the cities if there were ten righteous, but apparently there were not, and so both cities were destroyed. Yet it is clear that God is open to changing His mind; that one can *reason* with Him. For as we shall see in Part IV, *God desires a relationship with humans*!

> **What if there was One Righteous**
> We have no way of knowing how God would have responded had Abraham asked Him to spare the city for the sake of five, or even one righteous, but it is likely there weren't any righteous in either city. While Lot, his wife, and his two virgin daughters were saved, it doesn't appear from the rest of Scripture that he was particularly righteous; rather only because he was the nephew of Abraham did God grant him mercy.

---

[172] Genesis 18:23. Note the righteousness, and especially *compassion,* of Abraham during times in which virtually everyone in power was evil. This had to mean a lot to God—which is why He loved him and blessed him exceedingly.

Egypt

The history of Egypt—which still exists today although it is nothing like the Egypt of Biblical times—provides additional insights of God's Providence and nature. In the days of the Hebrew patriarch Jacob, it was the most powerful nation in the world. For Joseph, after being sold as a slave because of his brothers' jealousy, eventually became Pharaoh's second in command and enabled the king's wealth and power to increase exponentially. Joseph prepared Egypt and the nations in the entire Middle East for seven years of the most severe famine in antiquity. Having stored grain throughout the kingdom during the prior seven years of abundance, people from other nations came to purchase food, while in Egypt itself, all its citizens assigned over their land to Pharaoh, when they ran out of money.

> [The Egyptians] came to Joseph and said, "Since our money is gone and our cattle are already yours, we have nothing left for our lord except our bodies and our land. Why should we die before your eyes—we and our land? Purchase us and our land in exchange for food, and we will be servants to Pharaoh."
>
> So the Egyptians sold their fields, because the famine was very grave, and their land became Pharaoh's. And Joseph said to the people, "I have bought you and your land this day for Pharaoh. Here is seed so you can plant the ground. And when you reap the crops, give a fifth to Pharaoh, while four-fifths you may keep as seed, and as food for yourselves, your households and your children."
>
> And the people said, "You have saved our lives."[173]

---

[173] Genesis 47:8

Meanwhile, Jacob, his eleven sons, and their entire family consisting of 67 males, relocated to Egypt under Joseph's protection, and Pharaoh, seemingly righteous and generous, gave them the choicest land. But within several decades, the original generation died out, and a new king came to the throne who was antagonistic towards and enslaved the Children of Israel.

> Now the Children of Israel were exceedingly fruitful; they greatly multiplied and the land was filled with them. Then a new king arose and said to his people, "The Children of Israel have become too many for us. . . . Should war break out, they will join our enemies and fight against us."
>
> So the Egyptians enslaved them and oppressed them with forced labor. . . . They worked them ruthlessly and made their lives exceedingly bitter. But the Children of Israel continued to multiply. . . . So Pharaoh commanded his people, "Every Hebrew male that is born, you must throw into the Nile, but let every girl live."[174]

With the ten plagues, the freeing of the Israelites, and the destruction of the Egyptian army in the Red Sea, God humbled Egypt greatly, but did not *completely* destroy it—as He did to earlier kingdoms, and would do to later nations. That was because of Egypt's initial kindness to the children of Jacob by taking them in during the famine.

God, thus, balances good and evil on a scale of *Justice*. Indeed, between 1200 BCE to 300 BCE, Egypt regained much of its power, fought against other nations—sometimes even with Israel as an ally—and, at times, was the foremost power in the Middle East. Eventually, however, it was conquered by

---

[174] Exodus 1:9

Alexander the Great and transformed into a Greek state. Centuries later, it was re-conquered by the Roman Empire, and became Christian—only to be overrun by Moslems in the tenth century. Finally, it was overrun by Napoleon, reconquered by the Turks, and became part of the Ottoman Empire, only gaining its independence after World War II.

Canaanite Nations

Our next example relates to Canaan, the land west of the Jordan River that God promised the Children of Israel through Abraham. Seven nations lived there in antiquity, such as the Amorites, Jebusites, and Hittites, who were continually committing abominations:

> The Lord appeared to Abraham and said, "To your offspring I will give this land. . . . Look about; to the north and south, east and west. All that you see I will give to you and your offspring forever. I will make them like the dust of the earth, so that if one could count the dust, then your offspring could be counted. Now go, walk through the length and breadth of the land, for I am giving it to you."
> Then the Lord said to him, "In the fourth generation your descendants will return here, for the iniquity of the Amorites has not yet reached its threshold." On that day the Lord made a covenant with Abraham.[175]

Again, we see God's beneficence. Despite the evil of the inhabitants, God gave them *centuries* to repent and turn away from evil. And indeed, one nation, the *Kenites,* did eschew their evil ways and attached themselves to the Children of Israel. As related in Jeremiah, they evolved into the Rechabites, who,

---

[175] Genesis 13:14

because of their righteousness, would always have a place in God's heart.

So God was with the Children of Israel, who conquered the Canaanite nations, deservedly so, because of their evil—not only idolatry and sexual depravity, but violence and murder were par for the course. Rulers even sacrificed their own children to their gods.

The Kingdom of Israel

As described in Chapter 10, about 500 years after the Exodus, Israel under, King Solomon, was the foremost power in the East. Solomon built the First Temple, had great wisdom, and the surrounding nations paid him tribute. But as he aged, he turned away from God. He allowed his many wives and concubines, most of them foreign, to worship their own gods. This displeased God greatly and He split up the kingdom.

Thus, after Solomon died and his son Rehoboam became king, the other tribes rebelled, killed his tax collector, and recalled Jeroboam from Egypt to rule over them. This began more than 300 years of dual kingdoms; those comprising the ten tribes were called Israel, while the remaining tribes of Judah and Benjamin were known as Judea. Wars between the two were frequent, and other nations rose against both kingdoms, as well.

In Israel, just about every king rebelled against God, worshipped idols, and acted immorally. In Judea, on the other hand, there were long periods during which the kings were righteous and followed God, followed by equally long periods during which they would turn away from Him and act abominably.

And although the prophets Elijah and Elisha, among others, pleaded repeatedly with the kings of Israel to cease their abominations and return to God, they were unheeded. Finally, God had enough. Assyria, a nation northeast of Israel, began a century of conquest, until they were the foremost power in the region. Then, in 745 BCE, they invaded and conquered Samaria, the capital of Israel, and deported the population—known today as the "Ten Lost Tribes"—across its vast empire. In this case, the destruction and dispersion of Israel resulted because of the evil they committed over the centuries, as prophesized in Deuteronomy 11:26.

Assyria

But Assyria overdid it, having a policy that caused untold suffering to the nations it conquered. Considered the most ruthless nation in antiquity, "her warfare abounded in atrocities; cutting off the heads of conquered peoples was a common procedure. The kings of Assyria boasted of the towns destroyed, dismantled, or burned; leveled as if by a hurricane and reduced to heap of rubble."[176]

Thus, while God desired Assyria to be His instrument to punish Israel for their centuries of abominations, Assyria also invoked His wrath by being exceptionally cruel.

---

[176] Heschel, A. J. *The Prophets*, (NY, Harper Collins, 1962) p. 207.

Woe to the Assyria, in whose hand is the rod of My anger! I sent him against a godless nation. I dispatched him against a people who angered me, to loot and plunder, and to trample them like mud in the streets. But this is not what he intends, this is not what he has in mind; his purpose is to totally destroy, to put an end to many nations.

But he [Assyria] says, "As my hand has seized the kingdoms of the idols—shall I not deal with Jerusalem and her images as I dealt with Samaria? For by the might of my hand and by my wisdom, have I done this. I removed the boundaries of nations. I plundered their treasures. Like a great warrior I subdued their kings. As one reaches into a nest, so my hand reached for the wealth of the nations; not one flapped a wing or opened its mouth to chirp."

"Does the ax raise itself above the woodcutter or the saw boast against the carpenter," says the Lord? Therefore, He will send a terminal disease upon [Assyria's] warriors; for their arrogance, a blazing flame will be kindled among them. The Light of Israel will become the fire, their Holy One the flame. In a single day it will burn and consume his thorns and his briers, destroying the splendor of his forests and its fertile fields.[177]

Accordingly, during the following century, God arranged that Babylon (the Chaldeans) conquer Assyria, and do to them what they had done to Israel and other nations.

The Kingdom of Judea

Now, only the kingdom of Judea remained of the original Children of Israel. It would struggle on for another century and a half, but never again approach the glory it had during the time of David and Solomon. Some kings, such as Hezekiah, were righteous and brought the people back to God, but others, such as

---

[177] Isaiah 10:5

the notorious Manasseh, did more evil than the Canaanites and Amorites, whom God had evicted from Canaan in the first place. Manasseh made altars for Baalim, worshipped the stars of heaven, and desecrated the Temple of God. He passed his son through fire, read omens, performed necromancy, conjured up spirits, and led the people of Judea astray. Besides that, he shed so much innocent blood, and his evil was so profuse, that God could no longer forbear His inheritance. Through His prophets, He said He would remove His Presence from His Temple and from Jerusalem, and bring evil upon the nation and the city—that Jerusalem would be sacked and the Temple burned.

Thus, the evil of the Children of Israel proved their undoing, as prophesied. The die was cast and in 587 BCE, Nebuchadnezzar—the king of Babylon and "a servant of the Lord"—besieged and conquered Jerusalem, burned the Temple, and dispersed most of the survivors all over his vast empire.

Babylon

But like Assyria, the Chaldeans—God's instrument—were much crueler than God desired.

> Babylon will be humiliated. A nation from the north will attack her and devastate her land. It will become empty; both man and beast will flee.
>
> "Flee out of Babylon, like the goats that lead the sheep. For I will raise a banner against Babylon; an alliance of nations from the north. Their arrows will not return empty-handed. Babylon will be plundered; all who spoil her will have their fill," says the Lord. "Because you rejoiced; you who ravished My inheritance; who jumped about like a yearling, and neighed like a stallion; you will be disgraced."

No longer will Babylon be inhabited but will become completely desolate. All who pass by will be astonished; they will whistle because of her afflictions.

Israel is a flock that lions have scattered about. The first to devour them was Assyria; the last was Nebuchadnezzar king of Babylon. Therefore the Lord declares, "I will do to the king of Babylon and his land as I did to the king of Assyria."[178]

Accordingly, their reign as the most powerful nation in the East barely lasted a century before they themselves were invaded and conquered by a combined force of Medes and Persians. The latter treated the Jews far better, and eventually allowed them to return to Jerusalem and build the Second Temple. Thus, it is important to note that God not only punishes evil, but *rewards* righteousness! And because of their kindness to the Jews, Persia remained for centuries the most powerful nation in the East.

---

[178] Jeremiah 50:2

Nebuchadnezzar Learns His Lesson

Nebuchadnezzar was the king of Babylon who sacked Jerusalem and destroyed the First Temple. As his success, wealth, and prestige grew, so did his arrogance and haughtiness. He directed that a golden statue of himself, ninety feet high and nine feet wide, be constructed in the plain of Dura, and commanded that "when you hear the sound of the horn, or any musical instrument, you are to fall down and worship the golden image of King Nebuchadnezzar. Whoever does not do so shall immediately be cast into a fiery furnace."

Therefore, as soon as anyone heard the sound of the horn, regardless of their culture, language, or "religion," they fell down and worshiped the golden image of the king.

At that time, there were some Chaldeans who hated the Jews. So they informed Nebuchadnezzar that there were certain men—Shadrach, Meshach and Abednego, companions of Daniel—who ignored the king's decree, did not serve his gods, or prostrate themselves to his statue at the sound of the horn.

This enraged Nebuchadnezzar, who had the three youths brought before him. "Is it true, that you do not serve my gods or worship my golden image? For if not, you shall immediately be cast into the fiery furnace. And who is the god who will deliver you out of my hands?"

Shadrach, Meshach and Abednego replied to the king, "We have no need to answer you in this matter. If this be so, our God Whom we serve will deliver us from the fiery furnace, and He will deliver us out of your hand. But even if not, we will not serve your gods or worship your golden statue."

This filled Nebuchadnezzar with so much fury his face grew to double its size, and he ordered the furnace be heated seven times more than usual. The three were then bound and thrown inside. But the flames of the overheated furnace only served to kill the men carrying them.

Then Nebuchadnezzar rose up perplexed and summoned his wise men. "I commanded three men be bound and cast into the furnace, but I see four men unbound, walking in the midst of the fire, and they are not hurt. And the appearance of the fourth is like a son of the gods." Approaching near the door of the furnace,

> Nebuchadnezzar called out, "Shadrach, Meshach and Abednego, servants of the God Most High, come out." And the prefects, the governors, and the king's counselors gathered together and saw that the fire did no harm to the men. The hair of their heads was not singed, their cloaks were not harmed, and no smell of fire was upon them.
> Nebuchadnezzar then declared, "Praised the God of Shadrach, Meshach and Abednego Who has sent His angel and delivered His servants who trusted in Him, and set aside the king's command, and yielded up their bodies, rather than serve and worship any god except Him."[179]

Nebuchadnezzar then decreed that any people or nation, whatever their language, that speaks against the God of Shadrach, Meshach, and Abednego shall be torn limb from limb, and their houses burnt to the ground.[180]

Other Mid-Eastern Nations

Last, but not least, we note that a number of nations of antiquity that surrounded Israel are no longer extant. They were destroyed, not only for *their* evil and abominations, but because they had no pity for Israel and Judea, and exulted when God punished those two nations. In fact, like vultures they swooped down to pick at the remains. But that only increased God's wrath. Among others, those nations include Moab, Ammon, Edom, and the Philistines—all of whom were greatly humbled or destroyed completely.

Regarding **Moab**: Moab will be praised no longer; in Heshbon, they will plot her downfall. "Come, let us eliminate

---

[179] See Daniel, Chapter 3.
[180] Daniel 3:29

Moab from the family of nations." You, the people of dunghills, will become mute; the sword will follow you. Cries of anguish will arise, because of the destruction. Moab will be shattered; her children will cry out, weeping as they run to and fro.

"Flee! Run for your lives. Become like thorns in the desert." Since you relied upon your might and wealth, you too will be conquered. The destroyer will go up against every town—not one will remain. Your valleys will be trampled and your plains laid to waste, for the Lord has spoken. Put salt on Moab, for she will be crushed, her towns desolate, empty of people.[181]

Regarding **Ammon**: Thus says the Lord: "Because you said 'Hurrah' over My Temple when it became profaned, over the land of Israel when it was trampled upon, over the people of Judea when they were dispersed, I am going to give you to the people of the East as an inheritance. They will set up their tents among you, eat your fruit, and drink your milk."

Put on sackcloth and cry out. Wander about here and there, for Molech [Ammon's god] will go into exile, together with his priests and officers. Why do you bluster of your valleys so fruitful—you, unfaithful daughter? You trusted in your wealth and said, "Who can conquer me?" But I will bring terror upon you from all sides," declares the Lord. "Every one of you will be scattered and no one will give refuge to your fugitives."[182]

Regarding **Edom**: "Because Edom wreaked havoc on Judea, I will stretch out My hand against it and slay both man and beast. I will lay it to waste from the South to Dedan, and there the people will fall by the sword.

"I will make you inferior among the nations, despised by all. The fear you inspired and your haughtiness have led you astray. You, who dwell in the clefts of the rocks and who occupy the heights; though you build your houses as high as the eagle, from there I will bring you down."

---

[181] Jeremiah 48:1
[182] Jeremiah 49:1

Edom will become an object of astonishment; she will evoke scorn from all those that pass by. At the sound of her fall, the earth will stagger. In that day, the hearts of her warriors will be like those of a woman in labor.[183]

Thus said the Lord: "Because the **Philistines** acted in vengeance and with great hatred sought to totally destroy Judea, I am about to extend My hand against them with great wrath."[184]

"Behold the waters are rising from the north. They will become a torrent and overflow the land, the towns, and all who live in them. The population will cry out; they will wail at the sound of the horses and at the thunder of the enemy chariots. Parents will ignore their children's cries; their hands paralyzed. For the day has arrived to destroy the Philistines."[185]

Summary:

In a fairly extensive survey, we have seen God's Providence during Biblical times, and provided many examples of evil nations that lasted for a while, and then were permanently destroyed or subject to abject humility. Here, God's hand could be seen directly, as He sent prophets to state what He intended to do. Retribution was explicit and specific. In the next three chapters, however, while Providence is present, it is no longer obvious. No longer are there prophets to inform the world of God's word. Indeed, it appears God is hiding from us.

"Days are coming," declares the Lord, "when I will send a famine throughout the land—not a famine of food or of water, but one of hearing the words of God. People will wander from

---

[183] Jeremiah 49:7
[184] Ezekiel 25:15
[185] Jeremiah 47:2

north to south and east to west seeking the word of the Lord, but they will find none."[186]

However, even those skeptical of Scripture and its assertions, will be unable to deny God's hand in the secular world—from the disintegration of the Roman Empire to the devastation of Nazi Germany. Again and again, we shall see that evil is ultimately punished, though not necessarily immediately. All have paid the price, and by the end of Part III, it should become manifest that "evil just does not pay!"

---

[186] Amos 8:11

Chapter 19
War and Evil: 350 BCE-1900 AD

The Roman Republic/Empire (350 BCE–575 AD)

The Roman Empire (formerly the Republic) at its height was the greatest power on the face of the earth. In fact, by 285 AD, the empire had grown too large to be ruled from one central location at Rome, and the Emperor, Diocletian, divided it into a Western and Eastern half (known as the Byzantine Empire), with the latter's capital at Constantinople. But the division resulted in a number of civil wars, as various military leaders fought for control of both. Yet today, you can only read about the Roman Empire in history books and/or tour the extensive ruins testifying to how great it once had been.

Because Rome was not always and not entirely evil, and gave civilization some positive benefits, it lasted for as long as it did. Ultimately, however, its evil finally caught up with it, and it became another example of Divine retribution. Two monstrosities, especially noteworthy, are the Punic Wars when Rome was a Republic, and the Gladiator games, later in its history.

The Punic Wars

By 275 BCE, Rome had unified Italy and had become more than a city/state. At that time, Carthage, who controlled Sicily and its surroundings, was a great power with an especially formidable navy. Rome and Carthage fought three wars between

264 and 146 BCE known as the Punic Wars, and after the second in 218 BCE, Carthage was defeated, forced to concede territory, and pay tribute to Rome.

It is the Third Punic War that interests us, and we could do no better than quote H. G. Wells:

> For twenty-two years there was peace between Rome and Carthage. . . . The territories of Carthage seethed with violent disorder; the returning soldiers could not get their pay, and mutinied and looted; the land went uncultivated. We read of horrible cruelties in the suppression of these troubles by Hamilcar, the Carthaginian general; of men being crucified by the thousands. . . . The peace of [Rome] was scarcely happier. The Gauls rose and marched south; they were defeated, and 40,000 of them killed at Telamon. . . . But it shows the moral and intellectual degradation of this post-war period that when the Gauls were threatening Rome, human sacrifices were proposed and carried out. . . .
>
> The evil side of life was uppermost. The history of the Second and Third Punic Wars (219 to 201 and 149 to 146 BCE), it is plain, is not the history of a perfectly sane people.
>
> It was a time when reasonable men were shouted down or murdered. . . . The western world was indeed black with homicidal monomania. Two great peoples . . . fell foul of one another, and at last Rome succeeded in murdering Carthage.[187]
>
> The spirit of [Rome] had become harsh and base. . . . [Romans] regarded alien populations abroad merely as slaves. Sicily was handed over to the greedy enterprise of tax-farmers.
>
> The sole offence of the Carthaginians, which brought about the third and last Punic War, was that they continued to trade and prosper . . .[which] aroused that passion of envy which was evidently more powerful even than avarice in the "old Roman" type.

---

[187] Wells, *The Outline of History*, Vol. 1, Chapter XXVII, No. 5.

Rome [thus] provoked a war [by the pretext of a broken treaty]. . . . The Carthaginians surrendered their arms; they prepared to surrender territory. But submission only increased the arrogance of Rome and their pitiless greed. . . . She now demanded that Carthage should be abandoned, and the population removed at least ten miles from [their lifeblood]—the sea.

This preposterous order roused the Carthaginians to despair. They recalled their exiles and prepared for resistance. There followed the most obstinate and dreadful of sieges. . . . [Rome] cut off all supplies by land or sea. The Carthaginians suffered horribly from famine; but they held out until the town was stormed. The street fighting lasted for six days, and when at last the citadel capitulated, there were fifty thousand Carthaginians left alive out of an estimated population of half a million. These survivors went into slavery, the whole city was burnt, the ruins were ploughed to express final destruction, and a curse was invoked with great solemnities upon anyone who might attempt to rebuild it.[188]

To blame Rome entirely, is, of course, not totally fair. Carthage was exceptionally cruel as well, and so was destroyed—with Rome being God's agent, if you will.

Gladiator Games.

The Punic Wars—as almost all wars—demonstrated the evil of the leaders of both Rome and Carthage, as well as that of individual soldiers. But on some level, the policy of the Rome relating to Gladiator combat was far, far worse. It degraded anyone who was not of their class. Here, there was no pretense, as there is in war, when citizens are deluded into thinking that there is a legitimate reason for. *Here, murder was legalized for*

---

[188] Wells, *The Outline of History*, Vol. 1, Chapter XXVII, No. 7.

pure sport! In God's eyes, this had to be nefarious. *This* was evil personified! Again H. G. Wells records:

> In 264 BCE . . . the first recorded gladiatorial combat took place in the forum at Rome, to celebrate the funeral of an old Roman family . . . a modest display of six combatants. But soon gladiators were fighting by the hundreds. The taste for these combats grew rapidly and the wars supplied an abundance of captives. The old Roman moralists, who were so severe upon kissing and women's ornaments . . . had nothing but good to say about this new development. So long as pain was inflicted, Roman morality, it would seem, was satisfied.
>
> [Within] two centuries, the gladiatorial shows of Rome grew to immense proportions. . . . To begin with, the gladiators were prisoners of war. . . . Then criminals condemned to death were also used. The ancient world did not understand that a criminal condemned to death still has rights, and at any rate the use of a criminal as a gladiator was not so bad as his use as "material" for the vivisectors of the Museum at Alexandria. But as the profits of this sort of show business grew and the demand for victims increased, ordinary slaves were sold to the trainers of gladiators, and any slave who had aroused his owner's spite might find himself in an establishment for letting out gladiators. And dissipated young men who had squandered their property, and lads of spirit, would go voluntarily into the trade for a stated time, trusting to their prowess to survive. . . .
>
> Gladiators who objected to fight for any reason were driven on by whips and hot irons. A wounded man would sometimes call for pity by holding up his forefinger. The spectators would then either wave their handkerchiefs in a token of mercy, or condemn him to death by holding out their clenched fists with thumbs down. The slain and nearly dead were dragged out to a particular place, the *spoliarium*, where they were stripped of their arms and possessions, and those who had not already expired were killed.[189]

---

[189] Wells, *The Outline of History*, Vol. 1, Chapter XXVII, No. 9.

Organizational murder as a sport—and cheering while men tore each other apart—could only engage God's wrath, hastening the Empire's ultimate destruction!

The Mongols: (1200-1400)

The Mongols were a group of independent tribal nomads led by warlords, originally from the region around Manchuria. Then around 1206, Genghis Khan came to the scene, conquered some tribes, made treaties with others, and unified them into a federation. For over a century, their empire was virtually invincible as they conquered extensive regions of Asia and Northeastern Europe. Ultimately, however, their empire self-destructed. They merged into the peoples they had conquered and were lost to history as a separate entity.

The son of a Mongolian chieftain, Genghis initiated the reign of terror and conquest, invading North Western China settled by the Tanguts, and forcing the emperor to submit to vassal status. Shortly thereafter, Genghis invaded the Jin empire, massacring hundreds of thousands of their troops. He then besieged, captured, and sacked the Jin capital of Zhongdu (modern-day Beijing). This forced the emperor, Xuanzong, to abandon the northern half of his empire.

As his empire expanded, Genghis imposed restrictions on Moslems and Jews therein. He considered both as "slaves"; circumcision was prohibited, as was Moslem and Jewish rituals in slaughtering animals, forcing them to comply with Mongolian methods. Genghis stated, "If you slaughter sheep, you will be considered guilty of a crime. . . . Moslems say: 'if someone else slaughters [the animal] we cannot eat.' But people are upset by this, so from now on, no matter who kills [the animal], [Moslems] and [Jews] will eat it, and you must cease slaughtering sheep yourself."[190]

By the time Genghis died in 1227, the Mongol Empire already extended from the Pacific Ocean to the Caspian Sea—twice the size of the Roman Empire at its peak. He divided his empire among his sons and immediate family, who, along with the Mongolian aristocracy, constituted the ruling class. But those that followed Genghis were far worse than he, as the Mongols evoked terror wherever their forces invaded.

The empire continued expanding under Ogedei, Ghengis' grandson, who established his capital at Karakorum in northwestern Mongolia. Before long, nations of the southern Russian Steppes, such as the Bulgars, and the Alans were conquered. When the Mongols captured the city of Kiev, they massacred its inhabitants, as Giovanni de Plano, the Pope's envoy to the empire, related first-hand:

> Mongols attacked Russia, where they made great havoc, destroying cities and fortresses and slaughtering men; they laid siege to Kiev, the capital of Russia; after they had besieged the city, they took it and put the inhabitants to death.
> We came across countless skulls and bones of dead men lying about on the ground. Kiev had been a very large and thickly populated town, but now it has been reduced almost to nothing; there are at the present time scarce two hundred

---

[190] See https://en.wikipedia.org/wiki/Mongol_Empire [29].

houses there, and the inhabitants are kept in complete slavery.[191]

The Mongols now advanced into Europe, invading Poland and Hungary. Soon, Mongol armies advanced across Bohemia, Serbia, Austria, and even into the Holy Roman Empire itself, saved only by Ogedei's sudden death in 1241. His widow, Töregene, took over, removing and persecuting Moslem officials, and the Mongols turned southward invading Hungary, where they massacred or assimilated the Maygar—just as they (the Maygars) had massacred and assimilated the Scythians, Avars, and Huns before them—recalling the days of Assyria and Babylon, and God's promise that a nation shall reap what it sows!

By 1250, some Moslem provinces began to rebel, precipitating the ruling Khan, Guyuk's, invasion of the Islamic Abbasids in what is now Iran and Iraq. When its caliph, al-Mustasim, refused to submit, Bagdad was besieged and captured, an event considered one of the most catastrophic in the history of Islam. After the destruction of the Abbasid caliphate, the Mongols invaded Syria capturing local states en route. Antioch and Tripoli quickly submitted and joined the Mongols in their assault against the Moslems. Some cities surrendered without resisting, but those that did not—their populations were massacred and the cities were sacked.

---

[191] From: Carpini, Fr. Giovanni, *The Story of the Mongols: Whom We Call the Tartar*, Circa 1240.

In 1271, Kublai Khan, another grandson of Genghis, conquered the Song dynasty in South China, renamed the new regime the Yuan dynasty, and initiated the assimilation and cultural imperialism of neighboring regions to gain control of the Chinese people.

In the first half of the 14th century there was relative stability, but soon the power of the Mongols declined and chaos erupted throughout the empire. By 1370, the Ukraine, Poland, and Lithuania were free of Mongolian administration, while in Asia, territory was lost as well.

Overall, the Mongol Empire was governed by a code of law which was quite severe. Any resistance to Mongol rule was met with massive collective punishment. "Terror and mass extermination of anyone opposing them was a well tested Mongol tactic."[192] Cities were destroyed and their inhabitants slaughtered if they defied Mongol decrees. In one egregious example, during the Black Plague, Caffa, a great trade emporium in the Crimea, came under a protracted siege during which the Mongol army was reportedly withering from the plague. So they catapulted infected corpses over the city walls, infecting the inhabitants.

The number of people killed during the reign of the Mongol Empire is estimated at between 30 and 60 million,[193] with the

---

[192] Nicole, D., *The Mongol Warlord*s, cited at: www.wikipedia.org/wiki/Destruction_under_the_Mongol_Empire [6]..
[193] en.wikipedia.org/wiki/Mongol_Empire#legacy

largest population decrease within China and Indo-China. During the Mongol invasion of Russia, almost all major cities were destroyed, and it is estimated that half of the Russian population may have died; up to half of Hungary's two million people were victims as well.[194]

According to one "eyewitness," the Mongols killed everybody regardless of gender or age. . . . They especially found pleasure in humiliating women.[195] The city of Hamadan, in modern-day Iran, was destroyed, and every man, woman, and child was executed by the Mongol general Subadai—even after surrendering, because they failed to provide enough provisions for his Mongol scouting force. Several days after the initial razing of the city, Subadai sent a force back to the burning ruins and the site of the massacre to kill all inhabitants of the city who had been away at the time of the initial slaughter.

By the time Kublai died, in 1294, the main Mongol empire was situated in China with Peking as its capital. But Mongolian conquests had reached its zenith, and the long decline began. Thereafter, the Mongol story is one of division and decay. *God had had enough!*

---

[194] https://en.wikipedia.org/wiki/Mongol_Empire [14].
[195] https://en.wikipedia.org/wiki/Mongol_Empire [142].

The Spanish Empire (1525—1825)

For close to three centuries, the Spanish Empire was one of the largest in the world, reaching its military peak in the 17th/18th century, when it was the first to be called the empire "in which the sun never sets." And although to most historians both its rise *and* fall was unexpected, to us, its fall was par for the course, because of the great cruelty and evil associated with its conquests.

By 1492, Castile and Aragon, two major regions of what is now Spain became united, and Granada was conquered under Ferdinand and Isabella. Significantly, that year all Jews were expelled from Spain—unless they converted. Many did, and were called *Conversos*, and later *Marranos,* if they practiced Judaism secretly.

Although Christopher Columbus[196] set out under Spain's auspices for what he believed to be the West Indies, he instead chanced upon the Caribbean. By 1515, Cuba was conquered and Havana founded—and the Caribbean became the base for further conquests.

Soon, various South American territories fell like dominos to Spanish arms and might, despite an overwhelming disadvantage in manpower—as the natives had no knowledge of firearms or horses. By 1521, the Aztecs in Mexico were subdued; by 1530, the Maya in Yucata, and Central America from Guatemala to

---

[196] Some historians believe he was a Marrano.

Nicaragua was under Spanish control. By 1540, the Inca kingdom of Peru, as well as Ecuador, Colombia, and most of Chile were in Spanish hands. Next, Argentina was overrun while Brazil fell to Portugal.

Amazingly, in less than half a century, a territory 50 times larger than Spain itself—on the other side of a vast ocean—was conquered and overrun. The empire included most of South America, Central America, Mexico, Florida, the Southwestern and the Pacific Coastal regions of the United States, as well as Pacific Ocean islands such as the Philippines, and significant regions in North Africa. And when in 1580 Spain and Portugal were unified, Brazil and other Portugal holdings were added to the Spanish kingdom.

But these were not conquests of liberation or to enlighten a backward population, but rather to exploit them! And exploit they did! Spanish governors, known as *conquistadors*, plundered the vast resources of gold, silver, and other precious metals in their territory. So with incredible greed—and speed—cruelty and wantonness, they entered into decades of destruction. Entire native villages were commanded by an individual conquistador, who, having a status similar to that of a feudal lord, ruthlessly treated the natives as slaves.

Meanwhile, the Catholic Church was not idle, but forged a close bond with Spain. Protestantism was all but wiped out—and for two centuries Spain enforced a policy of strict religious adherence to the Catholic Church, via, as we have seen, the

Spanish Inquisition—arguably the cruelest of all—while their European territories, such as the Netherlands, used Spanish troops under the command of the cruel, evil, and merciless Duke of Alva (See Chapter 16) to suppress heresy by any means necessary, including massacres of entire populations.

Overseas, the tragedy of the destruction of two ancient and long-time empires, the *Aztecs* and the *Incas* was horrifying and needs re-telling.

The Aztecs in Mexico were conquered by Hernan Cortes, who invaded their territory in 1519. Opposed by a much larger force of natives, Spain's cavalry and guns were quickly decisive. And although the emperor, Montezuma II, promised great wealth to Spain if they would turn back and allow them independence, Spain coveted it all. Cunningly, Cortes pretended to be a friend of Montezuma, indicating he only wanted to trade with the empire. So he was welcomed into Tenochtitlán, the capital, but kidnapped Montezuma from his palace and placed him under house arrest in the Spanish quarters, making it appear as if Montezuma was still in control—allowing him to maintain his full court under Spanish protection, while buying time. Shortly thereafter, the Spaniards assassinated Montezuma, prior to sneaking out of the city at night, and making alliances with subject tribes who were under Aztec rule. Before long, Spain built up enough strength to take control of the Aztec empire, and enslave the population to mine the huge gold and silver reserves.

Not to be outdone, Francisco Pizarro came upon the city of Tumbes in Peru the same year, discovering the fabulously rich civilized society of the Incas. Returning to Spain for arms and instructions, he was granted permission to conquer the region, and returned with cavalry and artillery.

When arriving at the Inca capital, the invaders concealed their forces in the arcades around the main square. Soon, terrifying artillery and the onslaught of unfamiliar cavalry combined to throw the Incas into a panic. Trapped by the square's narrow entrance, they were butchered. In less than two hours, thousands were killed, and the emperor, Atahualpa, was taken prisoner. His subjects tried to ransom him by offering to fill a 12 x 10 room from top to bottom with gold and silver, and the Spanish agreed. But when the room was filled with a fabulous fortune, the soldiers removed it all, and instead of returning Atahualpa, they executed him.

But God's justice prevailed. On an individual level, Pizarro's former colleague, Diego de Almagro, rebelled against him and was executed. In 1541, however, supporters of Almagro's son assassinated Pizarro, himself. A year later, Almagro's son was assassinated by Pizarro's brother, Gonzalo, who had just arrived from Spain, but he lasted only seven years before he was killed.

Finally, in the early 1800s, regions under Spanish control for two centuries began to break away. Ironically, the catalyst for the above was Napoleon—whom we shall discuss next—when in 1808 he forced the abdication of the Spanish king, Ferdinand VII, and placed his brother Joseph Bonaparte upon the throne. This was the signal for revolutions all over the empire against Spanish rule. But even before, in 1805, the Spanish fleet was destroyed by Lord Nelson at Trafalgar.

Then, in 1810, Venezuelan officers expelled the Spanish governor from Caracas and formed a junta to run the province. Later that year, a regional government took over in Argentina. In Bogota, the capital of New Granada (now Columbia), the Spanish royal officials were ejected and a local regime was established. In Santiago, the capital of Chile, locals forced the resignation of the Spanish governor and a local junta ran the province. The following year, the Spanish Governor of Paraguay was removed, and it declared its independence. Soon after, Uruguay began its struggle to throw off Spanish rule.

Some nations, such as Peru and Mexico, took longer to regain their sovereignty, but regain it they did. In Mexico, in fact, the first rebels were poor Catholic priests leading armies of Mestizos and Indians. Not surprisingly, by the mid-1820s, the great Spanish empire—in which the sun never sets—was kaput!

For again, as He did with Egypt, God initially allowed Spain to prosper, before humbling it several centuries later.

Napoleon (1790-1815)

Our last example is about the arrogance, egoism, and craze for power of an *individual,* as opposed to a nation; how one man could be responsible for the death and maiming of millions. Napoleon was not overtly evil, as say a Hitler or Stalin, but evil takes many forms. Arrogance, haughtiness, and lust for power are often worse than actual violence, since they lead to it as well, but on a much greater scale. But God, sooner or later, will destroy or humble that individual, just as He does to nations.

Napoleon was born in 1769 in Corsica, at the time controlled by France. Through patronage, he received his education at military schools and specialized in artillery. Later, in the midst of the French Revolution, he was given command at Toulon, an important French naval port, and forced the British to abandon the town. As a result, he was made a brigadier general by the new Republic of France, at only 24 years of age.

Then, in 1795, when royalists in Paris declared a rebellion against the Republican National Convention meeting in the Tuileries Palace, Napoleon was given command of improvised forces for their defense. He realized only artillery could stem the invaders, so he procured large cannons and turned them on the Royalists, killing 1,400 and causing the rest to flee. As a result, Bonaparte gained instant fame, wealth, and the patronage of the new government—all of which went to his head. Next, he was given command of the army of Italy, and his successes were brilliant—taking large regions for France, and returning incredible booty.

Back in Paris, he was a hero. He then left for Egypt with the newly developed French navy to secure the Mediterranean and make in-roads in India. First, he captured Malta, and at Alexandria in the battle of the Pyramids, destroyed the Mamuluks and took over Egypt. However, Admiral Nelson of England caught up with the French fleet and, in the battle of the Nile, destroyed most and captured the rest. Napoleon was effectively marooned, with the Turks amassing against his army, already infected with the plague. Still, he invaded the Middle East and gained victories at Gaza, Jaffa, and Haifa. However, short of provisions, *he executed 1,400 prisoners of war by the bayonet or drowning to save bullets*, and for three days he allowed the massacre of men, women, and children by the French army. When Napoleon tried to take Acre, however, his own artillery recently captured by the British was used against him. To ensure he could retreat to Egypt, Bonaparte ordered his plague-stricken men *to be poisoned with opium*. In short order, he deserted his army—allowing it to eventually be captured by the British—and surreptitiously made his way back to Paris.

Despite the major failure of this campaign, Napoleon disguised his defeats as victories, and returned to a hero's welcome. He then led a Coup to replace the National Directory by three Consuls, and had a new constitution imposed in which he became First Consul for ten years.

But that was not sufficient for the great egomaniac. So in 1802, he made himself First Consul for life, and in 1804, engineered his election as the *crowned emperor* of France!

During that period, aggression against Germany and Switzerland precipitated another war with England, who was joined by Austria and Russia into a coalition. When, in 1805, Admiral Nelson destroyed the joint fleets of France and Spain at the battle of Trafalgar, Napoleon was forced to cancel the invasion of Britain. Instead, he led his army across Europe and defeated the Austrian and Russian armies. Austria agreed to an armistice, and conceded territory. When Prussia entered the war, she was utterly defeated at the battle of Jena in 1806.

Then, in the Battle of Friedland, Napoleon destroyed most of the Russian army, and the Czar, Alexander, thought it best to seek peace—at least temporarily. The two emperors met on a raft in the middle of the Neman River at Tilst, an occasion for toasts and boasts, as children playing with toy soldiers, heedless of the fact that tens of thousands had just died because of their grandiose schemes.

> "What is Europe?" asked Alexander. "We are Europe." They discussed the affairs of Prussia and Austria in that spirit; they divided Turkey in anticipation; they arranged for the conquest of India, and, indeed, most of Asia. Russia would take Finland from the Swedes, disregarding the fact that the greater part of the world's surface is sea, and that on the seas the British fleets sailed unopposed.[197]

---

[197] Wells, *The Outline of History*, Vol. 2, Chapter XXXVIII, No. 4.

But Alexander's pretensions of friendship, led Napoleon to seriously misjudge his true intentions.

1808 was the beginning of the end. Although Spain was a loyal ally, Napoleon foolishly saw fit to depose King Ferdinand in order give his brother Joseph the crown. Not understanding the passion of the Spanish, they rebelled in fury, allied themselves with England, and began a brutal guerrilla warfare that engulfed much of the Spain. This resulted in even more atrocities, until England surrounded the French army at Baylen, and compelled it to surrender. One by one, French colonies fell to the British, aided by Spanish auxiliaries.

By 1810, Prussia had recovered from its earlier defeats and an emboldened Alexander broke off his alliance with France. Russia then made plans to invade the French Empire and retake Poland.

But Napoleon struck first, and in 1812 invaded Russia with an army of 600,000. He fought his way across Poland and Russia to Moscow—although for the most part the Russian armies declined battle. He took Moscow, expecting that this would oblige Alexander to make peace. But Alexander refused, and instead raided his communications and wasted the French army—already plagued by disease. Owing to the Russian army's scorched earth tactics, the French found it increasingly difficult to feed themselves. Finally, outside Moscow in September, the Battle of Borodino resulted in approximately 44,000 Russian and 35,000 French dead, wounded, or captured. But Russia had ample reserves and withdrew from the city, leaving it for the French troops. Napoleon, however, wrongly assumed its fall would end the war. So he refused to retreat until it was too late. Winter came with a vengeance; discipline dissolved, and the hungry army broke up into bands of marauders. The peasants, if only in self-defense, waylaid and murdered them, and Scythians cavalry hunted them down. The rest of the details need not concern us.

When Napoleon re-appeared in Germany, only his staff and a handful of royal guards were with him. The Grand Army, had only thousands remaining of the original 600,000. Everywhere scattered fugitives, ragged, lean, and frost-bitten men, spread the news of the disaster.

Napoleon fled to Paris and attempted to conscript a new army. But his previous conquests turned against him. Prussia rose, and the German War of Liberation began. Sweden joined his enemies, and Holland revolted. Napoleon became increasingly unstable, and by the end of 1813, France was invaded from the east and the south. Paris capitulated in March of 1814, and Napoleon abdicated.

He was exiled to Elba and the infamous 100 days during which he escaped, gathered an army, and returned to France makes a good story, but is not particularly important here. Suffice to say that in 1815 at Waterloo, the Duke of Wellington once and for all defeated France, and Napoleon was relegated to a small island in which he lived for 10 years, until he died of cancer.

It is estimated that over 10 million people died or were wounded because of this mis-adventurer's enormous ego.[198]

> **Whether an Individual or a Nation**
> "God repays each one for what he has done. He brings upon them what their conduct deserves. It is unthinkable that the Almighty would pervert justice. If He withdrew His spirit and breath, all humanity would perish altogether and mankind would return to the dust. Is He not the One who says to kings, 'You are worthless,' and to nobles, 'You are wicked!' He shows no partiality to princes, and does not favor the rich over the poor, for they are all the work of His hands. His eyes are on the ways of mortals; He sees their every step. There is no shadow, no darkness where evildoers can hide. He shatters the mighty and sets up others in their place. He overthrows them in the night and they are crushed. He pays them back for their wickedness, where everyone can see them, because they turned from following Him and had no regard for any of His ways; because they caused the cry of the poor to come before Him; because He heard the cry of the oppressed. *He is over individual and nation alike*, to keep the godless from ruling, from laying snares for the people!"[199]

---

[198] https://en.wikipedia.org/wiki/Napoleonic_Wars_casualties
[199] Job 34:11

Chapter 20
War and Evil: 1900-1950

World War I

Man obviously did not learn his lesson from the devastation of the Napoleonic wars. Now it was Wilhelm II, emperor of Germany and the grandson of Queen Victoria, whose arrogance and lust for territory was the catalyst of—up till then—the most devastating war of all time.

For over four centuries, most of the European powers—England, France, Spain, and Holland—were nations with vast holdings overseas, in the east, and in Africa. But Germany missed out, as it consisted of a series of independent kingdoms, duchies, principalities, and city-states. Then, in the 1870s, the Prussian Prime Minister, Otto Bismarck, unified the German states into a powerful German Empire, while somehow managing to keep Europe from war.

With the succession, in 1888, of Wilhelm II, however, Bismarck was fired. Full of the new imperialism, and always wearing a military uniform to hide his withered left arm, Wilhelm was determined to make Germany into a world power.

He began the construction of a navy, and made an alliance with Austria against Russia, supporting them when they annexed the Slav provinces of Bosnia from the Ottoman Empire.

His savagery was already evident by 1900. Addressing German troops on their way to suppress the Boxer rebellion in China, Wilhelm proclaimed:

> Should you encounter the enemy, he will be defeated! No quarter will be given! *Prisoners will not be taken! Whoever falls into your hands is forfeited.* Just as a thousand years ago the Huns under their King Attila made a name for themselves, one that even today makes them seem mighty in history and legend, may the name German be affirmed by you in such a way . . . that *no Chinese will ever again dare to look cross-eyed at a German!*[200]

When it became clear Germany was intent upon war, European nations fell into mutual alliances. Serbia and Russia were joined by France and England, while Germany and Austria were joined by Turkey. Soon the Balkans would be inundated by Germany and Russia, whose ambitions were similar but mutually exclusive.

By 1914, only a spark was necessary to set the world on fire, and was provided by the assassination of the Archduke Francis Ferdinand—the heir to the Austrian Empire—in Sarajevo, the capital of Bosnia. Although Serbia did not instigate the murder, it mattered little to the Germans/Austrians. In July of 1914, Austria declared war against Serbia.

Soon, all of Europe was at war. Germany invaded Belgium beginning over four years of horror that affected virtually every nation in one way or another. By its conclusion, besides the ten million plus soldiers who were killed through fighting, upwards

---

[200] germanhistorydocs.ghi-dc.org/sub_document.cfm?document_id=755

of close to twenty-five million civilians died through "sword, pestilence, and famine."

There were atrocities on both sides, including bombing of civilians, sinking of neutral shipping without warning—in May 1915, Germany sank the great passenger liner, the Lusitania, drowning a number of American citizens—and germ and chemical warfare. The airplane made its debut as well; their bombing, increasingly devastating.

As we shall see below, in 1917 Russia collapsed, the tsar was imprisoned and eventually executed, and after a brief interim, the elected Republican government was overthrown and power was seized by the Bolsheviks under Lenin.

Finally, the entry of the United States in 1917 proved decisive. By 1918, Germany was exhausted and Wilhelm II abdicated, fleeing into Holland *without a shred of regret or remorse for all the horror he had unleashed*!

Was he evil? Most historians do not see him that way, as they do Hitler or Stalin, but his arrogance, lust for power, and haughtiness was responsible for the death of tens of millions. And to God, that is and was evil!

The Russian Civil War

The brutality of World War I caused untold havoc with civilian life. And Russia suffered the most. People were oppressed by the tsar and his Russian aristocracy who were brutal, corrupt, and incompetent, and committed all sorts of atrocities.

> The Russian common soldiers were sent into battle without guns to support them, without even rifle ammunition; they were wasted by their officers and generals in a delirium of militarist enthusiasm. For a time they seemed to be suffering mutely as the beasts suffer; but there is a limit to the endurance even of the most ignorant. A profound disgust for the tsar was creeping through these armies of betrayed and wasted men.[201]

Finally, in early 1917, the tsar abdicated, and a Russian provisional government was formed. But a last desperate offensive effort failed amidst another great slaughter of its armies.

Food riots in Petrograd developed into a revolutionary insurrection; power was seized by the Bolsheviks under Lenin and Trotsky, who pledged to make peace regardless of Allied pressure for Russia to continue fighting. On November 7, 1917, Red Guards stormed the Winter Palace, ending the rule of the Provisional Government, and leaving all political power in the capital to the Bolsheviks. Similar parties sprang up across the country, representing workers and common soldiers.

Mutinies broke out in the Russian armies, and by March 1918, Russia officially ended its involvement in World War I. But evil did not diminish—it was only transformed from one venue to another. A Civil War ensued, between Lenin's revolutionary "Reds" and the counter-revolutionary "Whites," that lasted five

---

[201] Wells, *The Outline of History*, Vol. 2, Chapter XL, No. 9.

years and ultimately devastated Russia even more than World War I.

By mid-1918, when it became apparent that the Bolshevik army would be far too small, Trotsky, the Soviet war minister, instituted mandatory conscription of the rural peasantry. Opposition to Red Army recruitment was overcome by taking individuals who refused to serve and shooting them to set an example. Former Tsarist officers often had their families taken as hostages to ensure their loyalty. Soon, Trotsky took even more extreme measures to prevent withdrawals, desertions, and mutinies. A special military force followed the Red Army, conducting field trials and summary executions of soldiers and officers who deserted, retreated from their positions, or failed to display sufficient zeal. Later, he even authorized the formation of "barrier troops," stationed behind unreliable Red Army units and given orders to shoot anyone withdrawing from the battle without authorization.[202] In what was known as the "Red Terror," Bolsheviks executed more than 250,000 "enemies of the people," with estimates as high as a million, not including 500,000 Cossacks, who were killed or deported out of a population of around three million.

Opposed to the Soviets was the "White Army," also relying upon forced conscriptions and terror. Initially, they controlled significant parts of the former Russian Empire, and won many of

---

[202] See https://en.wikipedia.org/wiki/Russian_Civil_War

the early battles. Not to be outdone, the "White Terror" murdered an estimated 100,000 Jews in the Ukraine, and shot 25,000 people in the Ekaterinburg province alone. In total, "White Terror" killed an estimated 500,000 people.[203]

The results of the Civil War can only be described as monstrous. The worst atrocities were committed on both sides. By its end, Russia was in ruin. Droughts of 1920 and 1921 brought on a severe famine that added to the disaster. Disease had reached epidemic proportions; in 1920, typhus fever alone took three million lives. Millions more died of starvation and wholesale massacres by both sides. There were pogroms against Jews in Ukraine and southern Russia. The Russian economy was devastated; factories and bridges destroyed; cattle and raw materials pillaged; machinery unusable, and mines flooded.[204]

Finally, by 1922, the Communists were victorious, forming the Soviet Union and the unification of Russia. But by then, there were at least 7,000,000 homeless orphans as a result of nearly ten years of devastation from both wars. All told, an estimated 10–12 million died during the Civil War, mostly civilians.

---

[203] See https://en.wikipedia.org/wiki/Russian_Civil_War
[204] See https://en.wikipedia.org/wiki/Russian_Civil_War

Communism and the Soviet Union

Following Lenin's death in 1924, Joseph Stalin came to power. Communism, under Stalin, would prove to be even more abominable and deadly than Russia under the tsar. From the outset, Lenin had used repression against perceived enemies of the Bolsheviks as a systematic method of instilling fear and facilitating social control. This greatly intensified under Stalin, as he suppressed all political opposition to his rule through the mass arrests of military leaders, Communist Party members, and ordinary citizens, who were sent to correctional labor camps (Gulags) or executed. Large numbers of Jews were sent to Siberia, and intellectuals persecuted. Both Christian and non-Christian places of worship were shut down by the thousands. By 1940, as many as 90 percent of churches, synagogues, and mosques that had been operating in 1917 were closed or razed.

From 1936 to 1938, Stalin's instituted the "Great Purge"; a campaign of terror and political repression of unprecedented dimensions. It involved a large-scale dismemberment of the Communist Party and government officials; both the leadership and bureaucrats, and included the Red Army hierarchy—most of whom were party members. The Russian Orthodox clergy was virtually annihilated: 85 percent of their 35,000 members were arrested.[205]

---

[205] See https://en.wikipedia.org/wiki/Great_Purge

There was repression of peasants and widespread police surveillance, imprisonment, and arbitrary executions. The Soviet secret police (NKVD) persecuted various minorities, accusing them of being "fifth column" communities. Hundreds of thousands of victims were accused of various political crimes; from espionage and sabotage to anti-Soviet agitation, and were quickly executed by shooting, or sent to the labor camps. Many died of starvation, disease, exposure, and overwork. Purges were officially explained as elimination of saboteurs and foreign agents. There were show trials in which due-process was denied, while accusations were based on forced confessions—usually obtained through torture.[206]

A distinctive feature of the Great Purge was that, for the first time, members of the ruling party were included on a massive scale. As the purges began, the NKVD shot Bolshevik heroes, as well as the majority of Lenin's Politburo, for alleged disagreements with Stalin. The NKVD persecuted the supporters, friends, and families of these "heretical" Marxists, whether they lived in Russia or not. According to declassified Soviet archives, during 1937 and 1938 alone, the NKVD detained 1,548,366 persons, of whom 681,692 were shot—a*n average of 1,000 executions a day*.

Most estimates were that close to 3 million people died at the hands of the Soviet government during the Great Purge, although

---

[206] See https://en.wikipedia.org/wiki/Great_Purge

one source estimated that the number of people arrested by authorities in that period to be about 5.5 percent of the total population—virtually 8 million![207]

But that was not sufficient for Stalin, so he entered into a secret treaty with Nazi Germany allowing the latter to invade Poland; the spoils of which were split. But every once in a while—in God's eyes—two wrongs *do* make a right. Accordingly, He saw to it that Hitler invaded Russia in 1941, and for the first few years virtually wiped out the Communists; ravishing their land, raping their women, and torturing and killing millions of Soviet citizens. Later, Russia returned the favor by devastating Germany and committing equal atrocities, as they rampaged through the Reich to Berlin.

After the war, Stalin was up to his old tricks, executing tens of thousands of citizens, but ultimately the executioners themselves were executed. Stalin died in 1953 and Nikita Khrushchev eventually won the power struggle. It is unnecessary to continue with the history of the Soviet Union after World War II, or the fact that Communism imploded in 1990. That was simply the end of a dying nation and decaying regime. Alas, it is now our task to briefly review the ultimate evil; the largest affront to God since He created the world—the rise and fall of Nazi Germany.

---

[207] See https://en.wikipedia.org/wiki/Great_Purge

World War II, the Nazis, and the Holocaust

As evil as Stalin and the communists were, it was surpassed by Hitler and the German people who perpetrated the greatest crime in world history by the calculated extermination of a people that had been around for 4000 years, simply because they were Jews. Of course, they were not the only group targeted by the Nazis, which included gypsies, the disabled, intellectuals, and certain Christian sects, among others. No one really knows how many people were executed for committing no crime, for doing nothing remotely harmful to the state, but simply because they were, according to the Nazis and Germans, racially inferior to those that gloried in their power and whose arrogance and cruelty knew no bounds. Yet it must be clear it was not just Hitler and his henchmen, but a nation of tens of millions of people who relished their country's monstrosity. One needs only to see films of the ranting Hitler and the millions of Germans marching and preparing for war to confirm the above. Then there are the films of concentration camp survivors, the bombing of Britain, and other horrors, all testifying to the *absolute evil* of the German people. Not to mention that besides the individuals subject to the Nazi terror, Germany invaded and raped country after country, forcing millions of those citizens into slave labor.

Truthfully, the author cannot conceive of what historically occurred. It seems like a nightmare or science fiction. This could not really have happened.

But it did, and God saw to it that the Germans would pay the price. In less than three years, the two evil nations, Russia and Germany, virtually destroyed one another. We already reported the non-aggression pact Russia made with Germany, after which the two countries invaded Poland, and the Soviet Union occupied Lithuania, Latvia, Estonia, and the east. Later the same year, Russia invaded Finland.

But as we noted above, in June 1941 Germany broke its treaty and invaded Russia. For a time they were successful, taking vast portions of land, and killing and torturing its population, both soldiers and civilians. Soon they were at the outskirts of Stalingrad and Moscow. But they failed to capture either city, and an unusually harsh winter played havoc with German troops and supplies. The Red Army turned the tide at the Battle of Moscow; and now it was the Soviet forces that drove through Eastern Europe reoccupying its land, and reaching the German borders. Paying back the Germans for their atrocities, the Russians were unusually vicious with the German civilians, who only two years earlier were slapping each other on the back because of their presumed superiority. All the while, Great Britain and the United States were bombing German cities to smithereens.

Thus, the thousand-year Reich lasted barely twelve years, and by its end, all their major cities were in ruins; their women raped or forced into prostitution to survive, and millions of their children in rags searching the rubble for scraps of food.

In truth, there was little *qualitative* difference between the events of Biblical times and the above. It was just a matter of scale. For 3000 years ago, God, through His prophets, *explicitly* declared what would happen to those nations that were evil, while in the 20th century, we can only presume the above indirectly, as there were no longer prophets to relate God's word. As we stated earlier but worth repeating:

> "Days are coming," declares the Lord, "when I will send a famine throughout the land—not a famine of food or of water, but one of hearing the words of God. People will wander from north to south and east to west seeking the word of the Lord, but they will find none."[208]

But if there was no universal announcement of what would happen to Germany, its fate was, nonetheless, sealed and easy enough to predict! Let us look at a prophesy of Jeremiah, updated for the 20th century:

> Summon archers against Babylon (**Germany**). Surround her; let no one escape. Repay her for her deeds; do to her as she has done. For she has defied the Lord. . . . Therefore, her youths will fall in the streets; all her soldiers will be silenced in that day."
>
> "See, I am against you, (**Hitler**)," declares the Lord. "You the arrogant one; for your day has come, the time has arrived for you to be smitten." The arrogant one (**Hitler**) will stumble and no one will help him up; I will kindle a fire in her (**Germany's**) towns that will consume everyone within."
>
> The people of Israel (**Jews**) are oppressed. Their captors hold them fast, refusing to let them go. Yet their Redeemer is strong; the Lord Almighty is His Name. He will vigorously

---

[208] Amos 8:11

defend their cause, but provoke unrest to those (**Nazis and their allies**) who live in Babylon (**Germany**).

"A sword against the Babylonians (**Germans**)!" declares the Lord; "against her officials (**ministers**) and wise men (**propagandists**)! A sword against her false prophets (**the German media**)! They will become fools. A sword against her warriors (**the SS**)! They will be filled with terror. A sword against her horses and chariots and all the foreigners (**Axis Powers**) in her ranks! They will become feeble. A sword against her treasures! They will be plundered. A drought on her waters!"[209]

Times may have changed, but God has not!

---

[209] Jeremiah 50:29

Chapter 21
War and Evil: 1950-Present

Alas, as dozens of examples since 1950 attest to, evil has not vanished with the destruction of the Nazis. We begin with India's independence and the partition of that vast country into the new state of Pakistan.

India and Pakistan

For several centuries a British colony, nationalism found its way into India in the late 1800s, causing dissent and riots which Britain put down forcefully—especially in April of 1919 in Punjab. There, the British military commander, General Dyer, ordered his soldiers to fire into an unarmed crowd of 15,000 men, women, and children who had assembled peacefully. Before the massacre was over, thousands of defenseless Indians had been killed or wounded.

This only intensified India's desire for independence, led by Mahatma Gandhi. The British finally gave in, and after the Second World War, India was partitioned into India and Pakistan. But as Hindu and Moslem populations were scattered unevenly in both countries, the partition immediately led to major violence between Hindus, Sikhs and Moslems for control of the various regions of the sub-continent.

Initially, there were between 500,000 and one million casualties. Unfortunately, peace is still a long way off, and since that time, there have been four wars between Pakistan and India.

Genocide

Between the Korean and Viet Nam Wars, in which the United States was involved, an estimated 2 million soldiers on both sides were killed, not to mention up to 20 million civilians (many of whom died of starvation, the plague, and other social causes), not including an untold number of wounded and homeless.

Yet we will skip over the details of those conflicts, but rather conclude Part III by tracing three instances of particularly monstrous *genocide*.

Cambodia

As a result of the Viet Nam war, the North Vietnamese allied themselves with the Khmer Rouge—Communist Cambodians, led by Pol Pot. During that time, U.S. bombings killed 150,000 Cambodian peasants, who fled the countryside by the hundreds of thousands to Cambodia's capital city, Phnom Penh. The resulting economic and military destabilization in Cambodia allowed Pol Pot to gain popular support. And when, in 1975, the U.S. withdrew from Viet Nam, Pol Pot's Khmer Rouge seized control of Cambodia.

Once in power, Pol Pot expelled all foreigners, closed embassies, shut down newspapers and television stations, and censored mail and telephone usage. Money was forbidden, businesses were forcibly closed, religion banned, education halted, health care eliminated, and parental authority revoked. In short, Cambodia was sealed off from the outside world, ruled by a one-man dictatorship.

Next, all of Cambodia's cities were forcibly evacuated. In Phnom Penh, two million inhabitants were forced at gunpoint to leave on foot into the countryside. Up to 20,000 died along the way, while millions were now forced into slave labor in Pol Pot's "killing fields," where they soon began dying from overwork, malnutrition, and disease.

Workdays in the fields began at 4 a.m. until 10 p.m., with only two rest periods—under the armed supervision of young Khmer Rouge soldiers eager to kill for the slightest provocation. Starving people were forbidden to eat the fruits and rice they were harvesting,[210] while Khmer Rouge trucks would arrive and confiscate the entire crop.

Throughout Cambodia, deadly purges continued to eliminate remnants of the "old society"—the educated, the wealthy, Buddhist monks, doctors, lawyers, teachers, and former government officials. Ex-soldiers were killed along with their wives and children. Anyone suspected of disloyalty to Pol Pot, including other Khmer Rouge leaders, was shot or bludgeoned with an ax.

In the villages, unsupervised gatherings of more than two persons were forbidden. Young people were taken from their parents and placed in communes—forced to marry in collective ceremonies involving hundreds of couples. Up to 20,000 persons

---

[210] Contrast this to Judaic law, which allows field workers to eat the produce they are harvesting. (See page 107.)

were tortured into giving false confessions, and suspects were executed on the spot without any trial or hearing.

Ethnic groups were attacked as well, including the three largest minorities: Vietnamese, Chinese, and Moslems. Fifty percent of the estimated 425,000 Chinese living in Cambodia in 1975 died. Khmer Rouge also forced Moslems to eat pork, and shot those who refused.

Finally, in late 1978, Vietnam launched a full-scale invasion of Cambodia, Phnom Penh fell, and Pol Pot was deposed, retreating into Thailand with the remnants of his Khmer Rouge army. There, he began a guerrilla war against a succession of Cambodian governments lasting over the next seventeen years. Only after a series of internal power struggles in the 1990s, did he finally lose control of the Khmer Rouge.

All told, Pol Pot's reign resulted in the deaths of twenty-five percent of the country's population from starvation, overwork, and executions.[211]

---

[211] See: en.wikipedia.org/wiki/Cambodian_genocide.
Also: http://www.ppu.org.uk/genocide/g_cambodia3.html

Bosnia

Yugoslavia, "legislated" by the victors of World War I, was a multicultural country composed of religious groups that had historically been rivals for power, if not bitter enemies. They included Serbs (Orthodox Christians), Croats (Catholics), and ethnic Albanians (Moslems). In the late 1980s, a Serbian, one Slobodan Milosevic, a power hungry former Communist, took over and started to inflame the long-standing tensions between the Christian Serbs and Moslems in the independent province of Kosovo. The Serbs, who were in the minority, claimed they were persecuted by the Moslem majority, which gave Milosevic the excuse he needed to take over the province and begin his own persecution of Islamists. He then used the same formula in Croatia—largely Catholic—where Orthodox Serbs made up only 12 percent of the population.

Allied with Serbian guerrillas, Milosevic invaded Croatia in July, 1991 to allegedly "protect" the Serbian minority. In the city of Vukovar, Serbians shelled the Croatians for 86 consecutive days, turning the city into rubble—after which the Serbs began no-trial executions of hundreds of Croatians, burying them in mass graves.

As evil as this was, we cannot but help to report that during World War II, Croatia had been a pro-Nazi stronghold, and both Serbs and Jews living there were the victims of widespread massacres—in one concentration camp alone, at Jasenovac, they were slaughtered by the tens of thousands. Now, however, it was the Croatian Catholics who were massacred by the Serbs, until a cease-fire put a temporary halt to the conflict.

But Milosevic had just gotten started. When, in 1992, the U.S. and most of Europe chose to recognize the independence of Bosnia—a mostly Moslem country where Serbs made up only a third of the population—Milosevic invaded Sarajevo, Bosnia's capital. Over the next several years, Serb snipers killed tens of thousands of innocent civilians in the streets, including over 3,500 children. With Yugoslavia's army behind the Serbs, the Bosnian Moslems were helpless. Soon, the Serbs began to systematically round them up—not unlike the horror of the Nazis in WWII—with mass executions, forced repopulations of entire towns and villages, and confinement in concentration camps. They also terrorized Moslems families into fleeing their villages by raping women and girls.

Only when, in 1994, a market in Sarajevo was struck by a Serb mortar and the bloody carnage broadcast globally, did other countries act to stop the genocide. NATO forces launched air strikes against Serb ground positions, but the Bosnians retaliated by attacking the United Nations peacekeepers, taking hundreds of them as hostages and using them as human shields, chained to military targets. Even "safe haven" agreements were violated, as in Srebrenica, where U.N. peacekeepers stood by helplessly, as the Serbs systematically selected and slaughtered 8,000 men and boys between the ages of twelve and sixty—the worst mass murder in Europe since World War II.

Finally, by late 1995, military intervention, led by the U.S., and coupled with Bosnian Moslem ground forces that received massive arm shipments from the Islamic world, forced hostilities to end. But by then, over 200,000 Moslem civilians had been systematically murdered, more than 20,000 were missing, and over 2,000,000 had become refugees.[212]

Milosevic was eventually tried as a war criminal, but five years passed during appeals, without a final decision, when he died in prison.

Rwanda

Rwanda, a country Central Africa with a population of seven million, was comprised of two main ethnic groups, the Hutu and the Tutsi. Hutus accounted for 90 percent of the population, but the Tutsi minority was considered the aristocracy and dominated Hutu peasants, especially under Belgian colonial rule.

Following independence in 1962, the Hutu majority seized power and reversed the roles, oppressing the Tutsis through systematic persecution and acts of violence. As a result, over 200,000 Tutsis formed a rebel guerrilla army, the Rwandan Patriotic Front, and forced Hutu President Habyalimana into an agreement mandating joint rule between the two ethnic groups.

But in April 1994, Habyalimana and Burundi's new President, Ntaryamira, while returning from Tanzania by jet, were shot

---

[212] See: en.wikipedia.org/wiki/Cambodian_genocide
Also: www.history.com/topics/bosnian-genocide

down by ground-fired missiles. Rwanda plunged into a civil war, as Hutu extremists began targeting prominent opposition figures.

Soon the killings spread throughout Rwanda. Hutu militia, armed with machetes, clubs, guns, and grenades, began the indiscriminate killing of Tutsi civilians, overwhelming the small U.N. peacekeeping force. Even Hutu moderates were targeted, while, significantly, the U.N. and the U.S. refused to label the killings as *genocide*, which would have necessitated some kind of international intervention.

Instead, the U.N. pulled out and the Hutu were free to engage in what only could be called "genocidal mania," clubbing and hacking to death defenseless Tutsi families with machetes. The Rwandan state radio, controlled by the extremists, further encouraged the killings by broadcasting non-stop hate propaganda—even pinpointing the locations of Tutsis in hiding. The killers were also aided by the Hutu professional class, including journalists, doctors, and educators, while unemployed Hutu youths and peasants killed Tutsis just to steal their property.

Even churches and missions were no longer places of refuge, but became the scenes of some of the worst massacres. In one case, at Musha, 1,200 Tutsis who had sought refuge in a church were systematically murdered from morning until evening. Hospitals also became prime targets, as wounded survivors were sought out then killed. In some local villages, militiamen forced Hutus to kill their Tutsi neighbors or face a death sentence for themselves and their entire families. They also forced Tutsis to kill members of their own families. By mid-May, an estimated 500,000 Tutsis had been slaughtered. Bodies were now commonly seen floating down the Kigara River into Lake Victoria.

The genocide ended only after armed Tutsi rebels, invading from neighboring countries, managed to defeat the Hutus in July. By then, over one-tenth of the population, an estimated 800,000 people had been slain—*virtually 10,000 murders every single day!*[213]

Summary

Over the previous six chapters we have seen in far greater detail than one would like, the evil in both the religious and political spheres. The author deems it important that the reader truly understand how prevalent evil has been—in all ages; past and present. Perhaps it will make a difference; perhaps not. But to ignore man's history is very short-sighted. We believe our laboratory provided ample proof that God is righteous; that evil is ultimately repaid; that Divine Providence, subtle as it may be, is as active today as it was 3000 years ago, both for nations and individuals!

> You have rebuked the nations.
> You have destroyed the wicked.
> You have blotted out their names forever and ever.
> Oh, Your enemies are astonished.
> They have been eradicated for all time.

---

[213] www: en.wikipedia.org/wiki/Rwandan_genocide
Also: www.history.com/topics/rwandan-genocide

Their cities lie in ruins—their names are extinct.
But the Lord is a refuge for the oppressed;
A fortress in times of distress.
For He pursues those who shed blood—He pays them back.
But He does not forget the exploited.
The nations descend into the pit that they have made.
In the very same net they concealed is their own foot caught.
The Lord is known by the judgment which He executes;
For the wicked is snared in the work of his own hands.
The wicked shall be cast into the depths of the abyss.
Likewise all the nations that disdain God.
But the destitute will not be forgotten,
Nor the hope of the afflicted be forever lost.[214]

---

[214] Psalm 9

Part IV

The Road Back

Chapter 22
Engaging God

But before . . . I pass on to the consideration of other truths, it seems to me proper to pause . . . in order to contemplate God Himself, to ponder at leisure His marvelous attributes, to consider, and admire, and adore, the beauty of this light so unspeakably great, at least as far as the strength of my mind, which is in some measure dazzled by the sight, will permit. For just as faith teaches us that the supreme joy of the other life [that is, the world to come], consists in the contemplation of the Divine Majesty alone, so even now we learn from experience that a similar meditation, though incomparably less perfect, is the source of the greatest satisfaction of which we are capable in this life

Rene Descartes: Meditations on a First Philosophy. No. III.

Introduction

Having just reviewed a representative sample of religious and political world history, again and again we are struck by the evil of our species. Throughout, we see that those in power continually exploit the common man. Whether their motives are for wealth or power, because of pride, for vengeance, or simply out of pure sadism, leaders of men have deliberately and calculatedly caused the death, maiming, and enslaving of hundreds of millions of humans. Of course, as often as not, the leaders only reflect the evil of those they lead.

We have also seen that evil is repaid in kind via Divine Providence. Yet one might think that only applies macrocosmically—i.e., when world events might have an impact on a large population. But what of Providence in the mundane, individual lives of the billions of people in the world—in your own life and in mine?

Accordingly, we need to look a bit deeper into this question—one that has perplexed man throughout the ages—whether God is involved in His creation on a daily basis, or, simply having created the world, He silently watches and does not intervene.

Divine Providence

Albert Einstein, no less, believed that God does not "condescend" to get involved in the everyday affairs of mankind. His point of view, however, is not supported by Scripture, logic, common sense, history, or experience. In my own life, I can cite dozens, if not hundreds, of times God has helped me out. And books such as the series of "Chicken Soup for the Soul," and "Small Miracles"[215] attest to Divine Providence by documenting hundreds of cases in which individuals have reported amazing events in their lives—that one would be hard pressed to say occurred by chance.

Nor would George Washington agree with Einstein. Amazingly, in his Inaugural Address to Congress, Washington deemed Providence so important, *it was the very first thing he invoked*!

> It would be peculiarly improper to omit in this first official Act, my fervent supplications to that Almighty Being who

---

[215] See Yitta Halberstam and Judith Leventhal, *Small Miracles II* (Holbrook, Adams Media Corporation, 1998), and Jack Canfield & Mark V. Hansen, *Chicken Soup for the Soul No. 2*, (Deerfield Beach, Health Comm. Inc., 1993).

rules over the Universe, who presides in the Councils of Nations, and Whose Providential aids can supply every human defect, that His benediction may consecrate to the liberties and happiness of the People of the United States, a Government instituted by themselves for these essential purposes; and may it enable every instrument employed in its administration to execute with success, the functions allotted to His charge. In tendering this homage to the Great Author of every public and private good, I assure myself that it expresses your sentiments not less than my own; nor those of my fellow-citizens at large, less than either. No People can be bound to acknowledge and adore the invisible hand, which conducts the Affairs of men more than the People of the United States. Every step, by which they have advanced to the character of an independent nation, seems to have been distinguished by some token of Providential agency...

I shall take my present leave; but not without resorting once more to the benign parent of the human race, in humble supplication that since He has been pleased to favor the American people, with opportunities for deliberating in perfect tranquility, and dispositions for deciding with unparalleled unanimity on a form of Government, for the security of their Union and the advancement of their happiness; so His Divine blessing may be equally conspicuous in the enlarged views, the temperate consultations, and the wise measures on which the success of this Government must depend.[216]

The response of the Senate several weeks later, likewise echoed *their* belief in Divine Providence:

When we contemplate the coincidence of circumstances, and wonderful combination of causes, which gradually prepared the People of this country for independence; when we contemplate the rise, progress, and termination of the late war, which gave them a name among the nations of the earth;

---

[216] Washington, George, *The First Inaugural Speech*: April 30, 1789, in *George Washington: A Collection,* edited by W. B. Allen (Indianapolis, Liberty Fund, 1988) p. 460.

we are like you [i.e. Washington], unavoidably led to acknowledge and adore the *Great Arbiter of the universe, by Whom empires rise and fall.* A review of the many signal instances of divine interposition in favor of this country claims our most pious gratitude.[217]

Certainly, any number of psalms testify to the above:

> He who dwells within the abode of the Most High
> Shall rest securely under the shadow of the Almighty.
> He shall deliver you from the bird hunter's trap
> And from the ravaging pestilence.
> You will not fear the terror by night,
> Nor the arrows launched by day;
> A thousand may fall at your side
> And ten thousand by your right hand,
> But it shall not approach you.
> Because you stated, "The Lord is my Refuge."
> Therefore no evil shall befall you,
> Nor shall the plague approach your dwelling.
> "Because he yearns for Me, I will deliver him.
> I will elevate him, because he knows My Name."[218]

A second question yet exists. Is God's Providence purely an act initiated by Him because of His grace and goodness, or can we affect Him to act in our behalf? We have absolutely no doubt the answer is both, but while we neither can control nor begin to fathom His reasons for the former, we can very much learn the "how" of the latter. Most obvious, of course, is prayer. Billions of people pray every day for God's blessings, and many people testify that He listens and answers their petitions. And while prayer is very powerful under certain circumstances, especially

---

[217] U.S. Senate's response to Washington's Inaugural Address, May 18, 1789, in *George Washington: A Collection,* p. 452.
[218] Psalm 91

when others pray in our behalf or we pray in others' behalf, it is only part of the story. How, then, do we engage God so that He is with us most, if not all, of the time?

We address that next as we explore the question: What does God want from humans?

Righteousness

First and foremost, God wants us to be *righteous*. Repeatedly, God has stated that is all He really *requires* of *us*. He would be so pleased that He would shower His blessings upon us. What, you ask, is righteousness? It is spelled out numerous times in various venues. Thus:

> Lord, who may dwell in Your holy mountain?
> He who walks uprightly, who acts with righteousness,
> *Whose words are heartfelt.*
> *Who does not slander with his tongue,*
> *Who has not done evil to his neighbor,*
> *Who has not cast aspersions against his colleagues.*
> *In whose eyes a contemptible person is repugnant,*
> But who honors those that fear the Lord.
> *He who keeps his vows even to his detriment.*
> *Who does not take a bribe against the innocent.*
> He who does all these things shall never come to ruin.[219]

> Who may ascend unto mountain of the Lord?
> *He who has clean hands and a pure heart.*
> *Who has not taken My Name in vain,*
> *Nor has sworn deceitfully.*
> He will receive blessing from the Lord
> And mercy from the God of his salvation.[220]

---

[219] Psalm 15
[220] Psalm 24

"Suppose there is a righteous man who does what is just and right. He does not defile his neighbor's wife. He does not oppress anyone, but returns what he took in pledge for a loan. He does not commit robbery, but gives his food to the hungry and provides clothing for the naked. He does not lend to them at interest or take a profit from them. He withholds his hand from doing wrong and judges fairly between two parties. He follows My decrees and faithfully keeps My laws. That man is righteous; he will surely live," declares the Lord.[221]

"Blessed are the meek, for they will inherit the earth. Blessed are those who hunger and thirst for righteousness, for they will be filled. Blessed are the merciful, for they will be shown mercy. Blessed are the pure in heart, for they will see God. Blessed are the peacemakers, for they will be called children of God."[222]

The above can be reduced even further.

Don't glory in your wealth. Don't glory in your strength. Don't glory in your knowledge. Rather, if you need to glory, Glory in God, Who is a God of Justice and Compassion.[223]

Again: *Those who accept God; who faithfully observe His covenants; who are men of truth; who humble themselves; who avoid vain talk; who are active in deeds of charity; these will be the heirs who will inherit Paradise.*[224]

Again: *One must remain loyal to oneself and charitable towards his neighbors.*[225]

Again: *Humans. What does God require of you? Do justice, love compassion, and walk humbly with the Lord your God.*[226]

---

[221] Ezekiel 18:5
[222] Matthew 5:5
[223] Jeremiah 9:23
[224] The Koran: Sura 33:16
[225] Confucius: Constant Virtue No. 4.
[226] Micah 6:8

Finally: *All You Need is Love.*[227]

Begin with your own *sphere of influence*! It doesn't matter whether you are a CEO or a bus driver; a professional athlete or a factory worker; a housewife and mother, or a news anchorwoman. Act righteously, so that you inspire those around you: your family, friends, neighbors, and co-workers.

If you manage others, set an example for those who report to you, for your peers, and those above you. If you hold office, act *righteously* toward your constituents. Whatever place you are in currently, *practice righteousness and inspire others*!

Every reader—and that means *you*—can change the world—even if just one person at a time! Consider:

> God repays us in equal measure for how we treat each other. When you show compassion for another, God shows compassion for you. When you are generous to those that are less fortunate, God will repay you double. When you deliberately hurt another, God will ignore your prayers when someone sets out to hurt you. But when you go out of your way for another, God goes out of His way for you![228]

These days, virtually any website you go to has a sidebar labeled: *Trending Now*. It consists of the stories, images or videos that are currently the most viewed and popular, relating to politics, sports, entertainment, business, etc.

Yet if man does indeed have a *tendency toward evil*[229]—which brought about the flood—we are not fated to always remain so.

---

[227] The Beatles: *All You Need is Love* (1967).
[228] See *God is Good* by the author: p. iii.
[229] Genesis 6:5

Each of us has the power within us to reverse that tendency! We can incline toward good—not for what *we* gain, but for its own sake!

*Let us make **Trending Now**, stories that are morally uplifting*!

A Relationship with Man

Righteousness is clearly what God desires from *Man*. But is that all? Does God not desire something for *Himself*? After all, why did He create us? It should, therefore, be clear that God desires a relationship with His creatures. At the most basic level, "God is in search of Man!"[230]

> And in the evening [Adam and Eve] heard the voice of God walking in the garden.[231]

> Now the Lord said unto Abraham, "Leave your birthplace and your family and go to a land that I will show you. And I will make of you a great nation, and make your name great. I will bless those that bless you, and curse those that curse you; and in you shall all families of the earth be blessed."[232]

> "I will be your God and you will be My people."[233]

Of course, God's desire for a relationship is not limited to the Children of Israel. In fact, He would have destroyed them seven separate times for their rebelliousness, if not for Moses—for example, when God told Moses, "Let Me be and I will destroy

---

[230] Heschel, Abraham Joshua, *God in Search of Man: A Philosophy of Judaism* (New York: Farrar, Straus and Giroux, 1955).
[231] Genesis 3:8
[232] Genesis 12:1
[233] Leviticus 26:12

them in an instant and make you a greater nation."[234] Rather, anyone who behaves morally can *seek* and *find* God.

> The Lord is near unto all that call upon Him,
> To all that call upon Him sincerely.
> He will fulfill the desire of those that fear Him;
> He will hear their cry, and will save them.[235]

Now you might think, even if true, it only relates to VIPs like Noah, Abraham, Moses, David, Jesus, or Job. Who am I, that God would want a relationship with?

The answer lies in Samuel I. Having rejected Saul as king, God instructed the prophet to go to the house of Jesse in Bethlehem, "for I have discerned for Myself a king among his sons."[236]

> When Samuel arrived, he arranged a great feast, and upon seeing Eliab, Jesse's eldest, a youth of great stature and charm, he thought he was God's choice. But God said to Samuel, "Do not look at his physical prowess, for I do not desire him. The Lord does not see as man sees. Man looks at the outward appearance, but the Lord looks *inside* the heart."[237]

God sees inside *your* heart as well, and if He likes what He sees, there is absolutely no reason in the world why *you* could not have a relationship with Him, and He with you. And I will even show you how, which you can try out. You have nothing to lose and so much to gain.

---

[234] Exodus 32:10
[235] Psalm 145
[236] I Samuel 16:1
[237] I Samuel 16:6

Engaging God

Whatever your faith; whether you pray daily, follow a specific liturgy, go to a church, synagogue, or mosque once a week, or seldom if ever go to a Temple, there are always times when you have a need for something that you cannot get just by snapping your fingers. Now I do not mean winning the lottery, or having a football team win a game so you can collect on a bet. Rather, something reasonable, perhaps even trivial, like finding a parking spot in Manhattan.

Whatever it is, entreat God for help *out-loud*—with your lips. Ask Him to help you find that parking spot or your misplaced keys; or if you need something more profound, ask Him to help you find the right doctor who can help put an end to the debilitating migraines you have suffered for years.

Now you might ask, if God knows our every thought—which He does—is it not sufficient to just think about what you need? Why do you need to articulate the words?

The answer lies in the fact that a relationship must be a two-way street. But we neither see, hear, nor, for the most part, are aware of God's presence. Accordingly, we can only gain an awareness of God by degrees: step by step; little by little; a bit here, a bit there. Thus, if you only *think* about finding a parking spot in Manhattan and actually find one without much trouble, you would conclude you were very lucky or it was a coincidence. On the other hand, if you specifically asked God to help you; if you *verbalized* your request and, lo and behold, a parking spot suddenly appeared, however unlikely you would assume that it came about because of your request—and this is key—a small part of you would argue, or at least be open to the fact that it did indeed stem from God; that He not only heard your prayer, *but effected it expeditiously and intervened on your behalf real-time.*

After all, God can do whatever He wishes. One does not need to be a priest, rabbi, pastor, or imam to get God to listen, nor should one assume God has no interest in helping anyone with something trivial—that only major diseases or potentially life changing issues are worthy of His intervention.

Au contraire! It is the little things in life that define a relationship! Even helping you find a parking spot is important to God, simply *because it is important to you*! He is more than happy to help you.

Accordingly, each time you can use some help—say to catch a bus—call on God, and if it works out, the idea that God *is* actually responding to *you real-time* begins to have greater probability. Slowly you build up your confidence in the budding relationship, and over time, as more and more requests/prayers are answered (of course, sometimes God says "no"), you get to where you have virtual certainty—however hard it might be to believe intellectually—that God is indeed with you and takes into account your daily needs.

How do you repay God? By stating simply, "Thank you God for Your help. I really appreciate it." That will give Him great pleasure, and is, at first, all you need to do in return. Soon, however, you begin to talk to Him at night, tell Him about your day, think of Him when out in the work-world, and desire to please Him by doing what is good in His eyes.

That is when your relationship truly flowers, and you begin to feel *love* for Him—I dare say, as unique for God, as it would be for the fortunate human!

Faith

If God *demands* righteousness and God *desires* a relationship with man, what descriptor should we use relating to the third item on God's "wish list"—*faith*—all of which we contend is instrumental in repairing our relationship with Him? I believe the term *dreams* is a good fit—in the sense of the boy who *dreams* of playing centerfield for the Los Angeles Dodgers, or the girl who *dreams* of winning an Academy Award for best actress.

I suggest it is God's dream that we have faith in Him. As we do not see, hear, or experience God directly, the monotheistic religions, led by rabbis, priests, pastors, and imams make faith the cornerstone of their preaching. But how many of their flock truly have faith? I suspect a large percentage of religious adherents follow their religion and culture solely out of practicality, without true faith or understanding of God. Despite their doubts, they act as if they believe because they have no choice—they would be ostracized by their community if otherwise. Alternately, being dominated from an early age until their teens by parents and/or religious leaders who demand they must conform, the guilt they would feel if they took a detour

Engaging God 259

would overwhelm them. Of course, many religious people do have faith, but so do people who ascribe to no religion, but are spiritual.

What is *faith*? Let us distinguish between two types. The faith of a *people* and the faith of an *individual*. The former is intimately bound up with religion as the following example demonstrates.

God has indicated He will help the Children of Israel conquer Canaan, but—crucially—it will not happen overnight.

> "I will send My destroyer ahead of you and throw into confusion every nation you engage. I will make all your enemies turn their backs and flee. I will send the hornet ahead of you to drive out the Canaanites and Hittites. But I will not remove them in a single year, because the land would become desolate and the wild animals would become too numerous for you. Rather, little by little I will dislodge them until you are strong enough to take possession of the land."[238]

Clearly, God, if He chooses, could drive out the nations quickly, even in a day, without the land becoming desolate or wild beasts ravaging it. Why, then, does He explicitly state the process will not happen overnight? One reason is that God, having created a material world with laws of nature, desires that man should rely upon those laws, working for the goals he wishes to achieve. In short, He wants His creatures not to depend upon miracles, but to understand: "God does help those who help themselves."

But there is even a more profound reason for the above

---
[238] Exodus 23:27

passage. If God with His infinite power, did everything for the Children of Israel; if He evicted those in the land without them lifting a finger, the people would believe in Him through *experience*—not by *faith*. By having the conquest take years, however, with the uncertainty of warfare, the Children of Israel would be risking, and in some cases sacrificing, their lives, and a true test of their *faith* in Him would have been demonstrated. And His creatures having faith means a great deal to God.

But there is another type of faith, dear reader, in the here and now; a faith *qualitatively* different, which may take a while to get used to, because it is not taught by our religious leaders.

Accordingly, take a deep breath, while visualizing the following:

> *The rest of the world goes by—but in an obscure cloud. The camera focuses on you, while God, although unseen, hovers above you, anxiously waiting to see what you will do. Gather your resources and all the power God gave you—especially that of Free Will; clear your mind and consider for a moment that you belong to no particular race, creed, culture, or religion. You are simply a human being!*

Now read the next three sentences, then close your eyes, visualizing whatever meaning comes to mind.

God is here only and solely for you!

God is here only and solely for you!

God is here only and solely for you!

STOP!

Close your eyes for 60 seconds before reading the next page.

CONTINUE

Now since God knows you cannot see, hear, touch, or tangibly experience Him, He cannot possibly *demand* or *expect* that you have faith in Him. At best, He can only *hope* you do.

But let us be clear. It is not the faith of a religion; it is not the faith that God is good; it is not the faith that there is a world to come when the righteous will be resurrected. It is a faith *in the here and now*; a faith that exists solely between you and God! There are no rabbis, priests, imams, or gurus claiming they are intermediaries between God and you—that you do not rate high enough on some arbitrary scale to interact with Him yourself! That is pure hogwash! I say, Hogwash!

This is *your* life! And God is in your life! He is protecting you, watching over you, and desires to make your life as easy as possible—*if you let Him*!

Of course, you must not take this to an extreme. *Do not test God,*[239] which among other meanings, is to do nothing in which you expect a miracle to bail you out. You may be a good, righteous, and compassionate individual. But if you place a blindfold over your eyes and walk across First Avenue in New York City, thinking nothing will happen to you because of your merit, your error will be painful at best, and fatal at worst.

Before suggesting modern day examples of this *new faith*, let us turn to Scripture to get our bearings.

---

[239] Deuteronomy 6:16

Now Ahaziah [the King of Israel] had fallen through the trellis of his upper room and injured himself. So he instructed his officials, "Go and consult Baal-Zebub, the god of Ekron, to see if I will recover from this injury."

But the angel of the Lord said to Elijah, "Go and meet the officials of the king and ask them, 'Is it because there is no God in Israel that you are going to consult the god of Ekron?' Therefore this is what the Lord says: 'You will not leave your bed. You will certainly die!'"

So Elijah met the messengers, and they returned to the Ahaziah. "Why have you come back?" asked the king.

"A man came to us and he said 'Return to the king and tell him, "This is what the Lord says: Is it because there is no God in Israel that you are sending officials to the god of Ekron? Therefore you will not leave the bed you are lying on. You will certainly die!"'"[240]

Now you may ask, why did God get angry with *Ahaziah*, if having faith in Him is like a bonus—desired by God, but nothing He can count on. Had Ahaziah simply done nothing, would he have died? Probably not. But as the king of Israel, Ahaziah is setting a terrible example for his people by declaring he has faith in a non-god of a pagan nation. That could not be tolerated, so God had no choice but to take his life.

Now for some modern day examples:

(1) You live in a big city and can barely make ends meet. You virtually never eat out, and if you go to Dunkin Donuts every morning on your way to work to buy coffee, you pass on the Boston Crème pie as much as you love it, because saving 99 cents every workday amounts to twenty dollars a month—money

---

[240] II Kings 1:2

you can put to good use. Nevertheless, you always have 10 or so one-dollar bills in your wallet, and when you pass a street beggar, you give him a full dollar even though he would be more than happy with a quarter. As financially strapped as you may be, he, of course, needs it much more. So by being generous, you are making a statement that you have faith that God will see you through this difficult period.

But let those who place their trust in You rejoice.
Forever they shout with joy, because You watch over them.[241]

(2) You have been shopping at a New Jersey mall, and have bought a 32" TV. You return to your apartment in Brooklyn, but there is so much traffic, you don't get home until after 10 p.m., exhausted. Parking is difficult, but you finally find a spot three blocks from your apartment. Unfortunately, you forgot your dolly, so you would need to go back and forth to bring the TV home. But despite the fact the TV is in the back seat because it does not fit in the trunk, and although there have been several car break-ins in the neighborhood recently, you decide to just leave it there—having faith that God will watch over it and it will not be stolen. Your friends think you are nuts for taking such a chance—which is why God is so pleased that you, one of very few, *have* faith in Him. . . . And indeed, you go to bed, have a good night's sleep, and retrieve your TV in the morning.

---

[241] Psalm 5

> Place your hope in the Lord!
> Let your heart be stalwart!
> Yea, hope unto the Lord![242]

(3) Your wife has a good friend in her thirties who is single, and very much would like to get married and have a child. At a party, you meet a man who is single, the right age, and desirous of getting married and starting a family. He is happy to meet your wife's friend, and you think it might be a good match, but your wife doesn't agree and prefers not to hook them up. However, you both have faith in God, so you agree to leave it in His hands.

During the week, your wife's friend goes out after work about half the time. So you decide to call her at 7 p.m. the following Wednesday, trusting God to do what is best for all parties concerned. If she is home, then you will tell her about the man you met, while if there is no answer, you will assume it is not a good match.

> Some trust in chariots, and some depend on horses.
> But we call upon the Name of the Lord.
> They stagger and fall,
> But we rise and stand stalwartly.[243]

(4) Our last example takes faith to another level. Once or twice a year, you get the urge for excitement by going to the race track and spending a few pleasurable hours doping out the races. But your wife has the flu and you feel guilty about leaving her. She says she will be fine, and you should go ahead. In fact, your

---

[242] Psalm 27
[243] Psalm 20

urge to go is strong, but you are still not sure if it is the right thing to do.

So you ask God to help you. Living within four blocks of two hospitals, between ambulances, fire trucks, and the police, it is rare that an hour goes by without one siren or another. As your car is a five minute walk from your apartment, you tell your wife, "As soon as I leave the building, if I hear or see any emergency vehicle before I get to my car, I will assume it is a sign God recommends I do not go. But if I get to my car before any alarm, then I will assume it is okay with Him."

What happens is secondary. Rather, having stated the rules, God knows you will be faithful to them.

> The Lord is near to all who call upon Him;
> To all who call upon Him sincerely.[244]

Very few humans would think of the above examples, and even if they did, they would not implement them, believing they are too far out. But your faith in doing so is very precious to God; it makes Him feel great, and you will be blessed because of it. For God, it is a *dream* come true!

---

[244] Psalm 145

Loss of Faith

Of course, God also understands that having faith is a tremendous challenge for us ordinary people, as He cannot be seen directly. Indeed, even extraordinary people, such as Moses, Mohammed and Jesus have had, from time to time, lapses of faith. Thus, when God told Moses the people will be getting meat for thirty days, he said, "I am one of 600,000 men on foot, yet You say, 'they will have flesh for a whole month.' If flocks or herds be slain for them, or if all the fish of the sea be gathered together, will that suffice?"[245]

God didn't get angry, but, in a masterpiece of understatement, perhaps the greatest in the Old Testament, He replied, "Does the Lord's arm wax too short? Soon you will see whether My word will come to pass, or not."[246]

And did not Jesus cry out, "Oh Lord, why have You forsaken me?"[247]

For a third example, we quote H. G. Wells:

> After all his [Mohammed's] insistence upon the oneness of God, he wavered. He came into the courtyard of the Kaaba, and declared that the gods and goddesses of Mecca might, after all, be real, might be a species of saints with a power of intercession. . . .
>
> But he had no sooner declared it than he repented, and his repentance shows that he had indeed the fear of God in him.

---

[245] Numbers 11:21
[246] Numbers 11:23
[247] Mathew 27:46

He did all he could to repair the evil he had done . . . and denounced idolatry again with renewed vigor.[248]

Finally, three days after the Exodus, when the Children of Israel were at the Red Sea with the Egyptian army hard upon their heels, they cried out to Moses.

> And the Children of Israel looked up, and saw the Egyptians, marching towards them. And they were terrified and cried out to the Lord and to Moses, "Was it because there were no graves in Egypt that you brought us to the desert to die? What have you done to us? Didn't we tell you in Egypt, 'Leave us be; let us serve the Egyptians?' It would have been better for us to serve the Egyptians than to die in the desert!"
> Moses responded, "Do not fear. Stand firm and you will see the deliverance the Lord will bring you this day. The Lord will take up your cause; only be still."
> Then the Lord said to Moses, "Why do you cry out to me? *Move forward!*"[249]

These examples should encourage us all, since God surely understands—and is not particularly perturbed—when we struggle with our own faith.

---

[248] Wells, *The Outline of History*, Vol. 2, Chapter XXXII, No. 2.
[249] Exodus 14:10

Summary

To conclude this chapter, we can thus assert without any hesitation:

- God is involved in the daily affairs of the individual, as well as mankind in general.
- One person cannot destroy the world, but one person *can* save it. *You* can save the world!
- What is important to God is one's intention. . . . Whether one succeeds or not is secondary, and in any case, is up to Him!
- Humans praise victory, success, and power. For humans it is all about winning. Some football coach was even quoted as stating, "winning is everything." Well, he may have been a good coach, but he surely lacked knowledge of God.
- God couldn't care less about winning!

Engage God, do what is right, and you will succeed!

How God Communicates with *You* Real-time

* You are planning something, when you hear a loud siren from an emergency vehicle. Consider that God is advising you, *your plan is not in your best interest and will be a waste of your time—or worse.*
* Your computer screen goes blue, or some other glitch causes you to lose power. *God may not want you to continue what you were doing or go to a particular website.*
* When printing, the printer jams at a certain line or page in your document for no obvious reason (such as when it runs out of paper). Check the page or line. *God could be giving you notice that there is some error or a typo in your document.* If you are asserting something of import, double check your proof. You might be mistaken.
* While driving to a destination for an important meeting, you see, hear or pass fire trucks, ambulances, or police vehicles with their sirens blaring. *God is letting you know to be on your toes. Something is liable to go wrong that you didn't expect.*
* You find a penny, dime, or quarter in the street. *This could indicate God is pleased with something you did recently.* It may be an act of kindness, or one in which you demonstrated integrity; i.e. insisting on paying sales tax for a large auto bill, even when told that if you pay in cash, it won't be charged.
* Something unusual in your house or apartment occurs multiple times within a short-period. For example, every few days a light blows out or an electric device goes on the blink. God *may be advising you that something needs attention in your life*—often it might be a medical test or procedure to catch a potentially severe illness in its early stages.

For a personal example, my toilet leaked for weeks despite the fact the plumber came multiple times, but was stymied in fixing it. Then the toilet seat split, and a new one split as well. God was telling me I was procrastinating and had put off my colonoscopy too long. I needed to schedule one. And in fact I had five polyps, but fortunately they were removed before developing into something serious.

* You are thinking about something profound and you hear:
(1) A phone ringing, but no one is there.
(2) Jiggling of a bell, or wind chimes echoing.
(3) A beep or two of a car outside.
Consider God is affirming your thoughts; indicating you are correct. On the other hand, an alarm could indicate your assumption is in error.
* When you try to accomplish something three different ways, and yet you still fail, consider the "three strikes and you are out" rule. That is, God is indicating *it is not in your best interest to follow that path.*

Chapter 23
Suffering

Introduction

By now, it should be manifest that since Creation, man has consistently let God down—under all religions, banners, and philosophies—whether as an individual, tribe, city/state, or nation. Throughout the Millennia, God has been ignored, abused, disparaged, and forsaken.

To be fair however, we must also ask, "Has God let down man?" Albert Einstein is alleged to have stated, "God does not play dice with the universe"—that nothing in the world happens randomly. Although his assertion is based on his understanding of science, it very much agrees with our point of view, based upon Scripture. That brings us to this very difficult, but necessary, chapter on suffering. Two questions immediately occur to us: They are not new, but have been asked by theologians and philosophers over the Millennia: (1) Does God induce suffering and (2) if not, why does God allow it? How can a just, omnipotent, and compassionate God cause or tolerate human suffering?

To date, the answers have not been satisfactory—at least to most people. Some have even stated that suffering, which they equate with *evil*, is not real; that it is the absence of "good." But tell that to someone experiencing intense pain. No, we must reject that point of view, but rather agree with Jesus, who stated, "You *will* have suffering in *this* world."[250]

This chapter will explore suffering in depth, review its causes and underlying reasons, and attempt to answer the questions posed above. We will suggest several additional reasons for suffering, not usually considered, which, while they cannot conclusively answer these two questions, should, at the very least, narrow down the playing field as to what *may* be attributed to God; that is, distinguish cases of suffering in which a legitimate question arises whether God *could* be blamed, from those that should not be part of the mix. Hopefully, it will provide you with some clarity, so you can address and understand the suffering in your own life.

To start, we assert that God does not desire—nor did He ever—that His creatures suffer. As shown in Chapter 10, God *does not* even want animals to suffer, and has instituted a dozen laws for their well- being. As far as humans, let us examine the major causes of *presumed* suffering to determine if, in fact, "suffering" is the appropriate descriptor, and, if it is, whether it is fair to blame God.

---

[250] John 16:33

Causes of Suffering

Death

"Death," *per se*, is not suffering. Rather, death is in the nature of things. We cannot claim God has let us down by taking someone away from cancer in his eighties; we all die of one thing or another. Accordingly, if one reads in an obituary, "John Doe died at 83 of a heart attack," we should not consider that an impropriety on God's part.

Looking deeper into the above, imagine you and your husband lived next door to John and Jane Doe for thirty years, and are good friends. As stated, John died at 83—a ripe old age, and did not suffer. Although he was a friend of yours and your husband for much of that time, one cannot say either of you suffer because of his death. But what about his wife, Jane? Surely she suffers emotionally. By herself after so many years of marriage, life has totally changed for her, and could easily become very lonely and scary.

But is that God's fault? Should both of them have died at the same time? Or what if Jane simply shrugged her shoulders, moved on, and never again gave a passing thought to John? Wouldn't something be wrong with her? Jane's grief is natural and understandable; the result of the love she felt for John and the fifty or so years they had together. When they married, each knew one of them would die first and the other would be bereft, but they accepted that. *It would be more than worth it*!

Would anyone say Jane and John should never have married so as to have no attachments? I don't think so.

Admittedly, more difficult to answer is when someone suddenly finds he has a terminal disease at 35—in the prime of his life; or worse, a teenager barely in high-school, who is struck by a car and killed. We will explore that further on.

Accidents

We have repeatedly stated a mainstay of Scripture is "Do not test God"—the point being not to put yourself in a situation where you expect a miracle to rescue you. God created a material world and designed laws which we can rely on. If you put on a blindfold and cross First Avenue in New York City, you will, no doubt, get hit by a car and be injured badly, if not killed. That being said, can we posit an explanation for the thousands of *accidents* that happen every day? Should we—can we—blame God for most if not all? Indeed, since we claim that there is no such thing as an "accident," the more appropriate question is: Why does God allow accidents to happen?

While each case is different, and in rare cases an accident *is* punishment for an individual's sins, the *overwhelming majority* of "accidents" *could* and *should have* been prevented! Statistically, 95 percent of auto accidents occur because of "human error or recklessness."[251] They include at least a dozen different causes—for example, when drivers have too much to

---

[251] See for example: http://cyberlaw.stanford.edu/blog/2013/12/human-error-cause-vehicle-crashes

drink. Add talking on a cell phone, and especially, texting while driving. Our attention is diverted, and even a split second, at the high speeds of automobiles, is the difference between dealing with a potential dangerous situation and a crash. In a particularly tragic, if poignant, example, a woman on her way to pick up her son, was expecting a call, but her phone, which was on the center console, fell off onto the floor of the passenger side. Instead of stopping to retrieve it, she began feeling for it on the floor; but taking her eyes off the road for no more than two seconds, she hit and killed a man walking in the crosswalk.[252]

Then there are accidents caused by speeding, tailgating, running stop signs, and improper U-turns to save time. What about *accelerating* to get through a light that is changing, when you have more than enough time to slow down and stop?

Driving when exhausted, instead of stopping at a rest area, is another cause of accidents. A friend of mine was returning from Canada to New York, over 400 miles, and by the time he was within 20 miles of the city, he was exhausted. Numerous times, his wife begged him to pull over and take a short nap, but typical of many men, he said he was fine and continued driving. So falling asleep for just 2-3 seconds was enough to hit the car in front of him—fortunately, traffic was stop and go, and at ten miles an hour, they avoided serious injury. But is that God's

---

[252] Levy, Naomi *Einstein and the Rabbi*, (New York: Flatiron Books, 2017) p. 140.

fault? My friend had a number of warnings! His behavior is no different than crossing First Avenue wearing a blindfold.

In another example, early one Sunday morning I saw a neighborhood rabbi make an illegal right turn on a red light, within New York City. I followed him, and he did it again at the next intersection. So I took the trouble to confront him, relating he should know better than to test God; that if he continued doing so, one day he *could* easily get into an accident. But that will not be God's fault. Alas, in our arrogance, we think nothing will happen to us by driving foolishly and not following the laws instituted for our safety; that *we* are the exception. But that attitude is a big mistake, and, at times, may be fatal!

Aside from the above, virtually all accidents caused by a defective vehicle could have been avoided, because God warns the victim multiple times. Ask yourself the following: If your brakes fail, or your accelerator gets stuck, or you get a blowout, does that happen out of the blue? Is it not true that you had multiple warnings by the way the car handled? Perhaps you continually had to get air for a leaky tire, or your car skidded on a rainy day when starting out. Perhaps your brakes began to squeak, or your windshield wipers became defective. Did you have your car checked out immediately, or were you too lazy and/or didn't want to spend the money, thinking you would deal with the problem when it got really bad? Not very smart!

Then, there are accidents as a result of ignoring our intuition—which we assert comes directly from God and is a short-cut for guiding us. (See Appendix V.) As an example in my own life, I was responsible for the care of my elderly father who needed a home health-aide 24/7. He lived on the fifth floor of an apartment building in New York City, and needing an air-conditioner for the summer, I placed it in his bedroom window above the main entrance. Although by law it should have been secured, I did not do so, but rather relied on the heavy window to hold it in place, believing that no aide would be foolish enough to open it. This, despite a strong sense that I wasn't doing the right thing.

You can imagine my shock when I visited my father shortly thereafter, and saw the window wide open; a new aide without thinking assumed the air conditioner was secure and opened it so my father could get fresh air. Only a flimsy screen prevented the air conditioner from falling (God really held it up), and perhaps killing someone entering the building. I was very lucky; God was good to me, and made up for my stupidity.

What about the numerous fires that, for one reason or another, start in the middle of the night in an apartment or house, and cause the loss of life or serious injury. In many, if not most, cases, there was no smoke-detector, which would have awakened the occupants in time to put out the fire or, at the very least, to escape.

To conclude, think of all the accidents you or someone you know had—large or small. Was it a complete surprise, or is it not true you/they had some sort of warning, some sixth sense.

Dear reader, please do not keep on ignoring God's signs!

Illness

Serious illness is another area that we tend to blame God for. But how many of us ignore the signs of cancer at an early stage, when it could have been "cured?" What about drinking heavily, which results in liver and kidney damage. We all know smoking results in emphysema and other lung diseases. And over indulging causes weight gain and stresses the body. Why should God have liability for what we do to ourselves? In fact, the five major killer diseases can largely be prevented. (See inset.)

How often do we ignore the signals of a potentially dangerous situation until it is too late? Because of diabetes, my friend had to be hospitalized for a major infection to his leg. Afterwards, he spent months in rehab, until it was safe to go home. Checked weekly, his doctor told him on a Wednesday that his leg looked infected and he needed to get a blood test. Understandably, perhaps, my friend procrastinated and did not do so. By Sunday, his leg was so swollen and his vital signs so off the charts that he needed to be rushed to the hospital. He was fortunate that he was stabilized, and the infection caught in time. He easily could have died. But is it God's fault that he ignored his doctor's warning?

Again, we see that suffering is too often self-inflicted.

The Most Serious Life-Threatening Diseases

Coronary Artery Disease—Coronary artery disease is the number one killer in the United States, and stroke is number three. Both can largely be prevented through good nutrition, exercise and not smoking. Controlling blood pressure, significantly decreases the chance of CAD and/or a stroke. Keeping weight down, also decreases risk of heart disease. An annual physical could detect these killers when they are treatable.

Respiratory Diseases—Diseases such bronchitis, emphysema, asthma and pulmonary disease are largely preventable. Those who smoke are at the highest risk. Unsafe working and living conditions also contribute to these diseases, such as mold, pollen, dust, and mites. Asthma symptoms can arise from food allergies, such as nuts, additives, and dairy products. In most cases, they are preventable.

Obesity—Two-thirds of Americans are overweight, according to the Center for Disease Control/Prevention, and one-third of children are obese. Eating habits are out of control—promoted by a high-speed lifestyle with fast food available at every corner. Diseases that result from being overweight include diabetes, atherosclerosis, heart disease, and even some cancers.

Diabetes—24 million people in the U.S. have diabetes according to the American Diabetes Association; one in four people are pre-diabetic and will develop it in ten years if left untreated. Diabetes can result in cardiovascular disease, stroke, blindness, and kidney disease. Yet Type II diabetes can be prevented. Those with elevated glucose can reverse the trend by exercising and a weight-loss program.

Sexually Transmitted Diseases—All sexually transmitted diseases, including HIV/AIDS, are preventable. All of them! Proper protection can eliminate every one. Yet people continue to practice unsafe sex and get diseases that are difficult to treat, and, in the extreme, fatal.[253]

---

[253] Excerpted from: www.mdvip.com/press/view/preventing-the-5-most-serious-life-threatening-diseases

Man Inflicted suffering

We now examine suffering that is caused by others, to see if we can exculpate God.

War

God cannot be blamed for death or injury to soldiers caused by war. Other than the last 100 years or so, wars, for the most part, were fought man to man. If one is maimed or killed during a battle, we must keep in mind that he would, if possible, have maimed or killed his opponent. Although in some cases men have been drafted, most soldiers were mercenaries or volunteers, believing the myths of the romantic notions of war and of becoming a hero, or more practically, being paid huge sums and promised the spoils of the enemy. Moreover, as we have seen in Part III, war has been started by humans for the wrong reasons—*not sometimes, not most of the time, but all of the time*: because of religious fervor, lust for power, greed, vengeance, pride, the arrogance of racial or religious superiority, or pure sadism.

Given we have *Free Will*, God cannot be blamed for deaths or injuries as a result of war. This applies to modern day warfare as well, in which the combatants are usually not in close contact, and many more civilians than soldiers suffer from death, injury, famine, and disease.

Exploitation

While wars, natural disasters, and terrorism get the headlines, it is likely that more suffering is caused than all the above put together by individuals who, for one reason or another, are *abusive*. This includes criminal behavior, from murder, rape, robbery, extortion, and drug abuse, but especially physical or emotional abuse by spouses, bosses, co-workers, parents, children, and even friends. The abusive relationship causes untold suffering to the victim—often lasting for years.

But God cannot and should not be blamed for these relationships; the victim usually allows himself/herself to suffer, and the bully or perpetuator chooses to act that way. Psychologists can conjure up all sorts of rationales for these behaviors, but that only shows how little they know. All explanations of abusive behavior that psychologists attribute to perpetrators have been useless. Abuse is more prevalent than ever, while their theories *never* help the *victim*, but rather give the abuser an excuse to act that way.

In truth, humans still have *free choice*—the abuser does not have to abuse, and the victim does not have to tolerate it!

Death of Children

The thesis that "God is good" arguably runs into its greatest difficulty by the death of children—for our purposes, defined as those who have not reached puberty. Presumed to be *innocent*, why should they suffer from illness, be abused, or die? Religious answers, such as there is a world to come and their souls are still alive, may in fact, be true, but are not quite satisfactory—especially when we consider a large portion of mankind does not believe in an afterlife.

Also unsatisfactory is the idea that God knows these innocent children will grow up to be evil: thieves, rapists, murderers, serial killers or terrorists, and so arranges for their early death. While this explanation may be valid for a small minority of cases, it is implausible to account for the number of children who are taken ill, or die through other means.

Another idea, is that as God is the author of life, He can take it whenever He chooses—just as an artist can despoil her painting, or a writer destroy his manuscript. But this, also, is problematic, as it is not consistent with the laws and statutes in Scripture that God has asked us to follow.

To partially answer this question—and we can only do so partially—we need to ask ourselves who *is* actually responsible for our children? Is it God, or is it their parents? Surely it must be the latter. Thus, unwed mothers who abandon a child, or parents neglecting their children who fall into harm's way, are subject to *criminal* charges!

Now God has not only given us the responsibility to take care of the physical needs of our children, but to assume moral and spiritual responsibility for them as well, until they reach the age where they can make their own decisions. Significantly, *the parents' own behavior will affect what happens to their children.* In other words, *it is the parents' righteousness or wickedness that will determine their children's fate*!

While this may sound quite radical, it is stated explicitly in the Old Testament:

So at dawn, Moses ascended Mount Sinai. Then the Lord came down in a cloud, stood there with him and proclaimed His Name. "The Lord, the Lord, a God of compassion; gracious, slow to anger, abounding in kindness and truth; maintaining His favor for thousands of generations, and forgiving wickedness, rebellion and sin, but Who cleanses, but not completely; *visiting the iniquity of the parents upon their children and grandchildren unto the third and fourth generations.*"[254]

God, in effect, is making it clear to parents that if they want their children to thrive, they best refrain from evil!

To better understand the above, let us emulate Albert Einstein who came up with his theory of relativity through a *thought experiment*. Our thought experiment, however, relates to the *moral* universe. Let us visualize a medium-sized town in Germany in early 1943. There is a roundup of Jews by the Gestapo, while a young German woman, with a three-year old—her husband away at war—looks on. She sees whole families being removed forcibly from their homes, beaten, and herded into trucks to take them to the railway station—their final destination, a concentration camp and death. She knows several families by sight, and one in particular, with whom she was superficially friendly with, lives in her building. We certainly do not expect her to interfere with the Gestapo and try to rescue that family, but indeed, she is joyful at the scene, secretly hating Jews even before Hitler. She witnesses her neighbor's child of five being torn from his parents and placed in a separate truck for who

---

[254] Exodus 34:4

knows what experiments, and thinks it serves them right. If that is not enough, as soon as the dust clears and the trucks are gone, she hurriedly makes her way to neighbor's apartment and loots whatever valuables she can carry—particularly, expensive toys to give to her own child.

Is that not evil? Should God let that pass? Now visualize it is early 1945, and the woman is outside with her child—by then five-years-old. Sirens go off as enemy aircraft from England pass over and start bombing and strafing the town. Everyone runs for cover and, somehow, she and her child get separated. Afterwards, she discovers her five-year old is dead. The shoe is on the other foot, is it not? What incredible suffering *she* must feel. But her son is innocent, you say—much too young to understand the Nazi propaganda, or what happened to the family who lived in his building two years earlier. Is that just?

I believe it is! Just as a marine is responsible for his buddy, until children are of an age to take responsibility for their own actions—at a minimum, when they reach puberty—*it is the parents that are responsible for their well-being*! If the parents are wicked, that child very likely will be in harm's way. As the German had no compassion and gloated over the suffering of her neighbors, God repaid her in kind by taking her child.

Did God not say to Moses:

"Just as they killed the first born of the Children of Israel, I will kill their first born." So say to Pharaoh, "This is what the Lord says: Israel is My firstborn son, and I told you, 'Let My son go, so he may worship Me. But you refused to let him go; so I will kill your first born son.'"[255]

We must teach each other that righteousness is not only necessary for our survival, but for the survival of our children!

Acts of God

Admittedly, when earthquakes, hurricanes, tornados, floods, etc., devastate an area, we wonder why, and we question God. However, we must also acknowledge that we are at least partially responsible. What man does to his environment—the stripping of the ozone layer, changing the course of rivers, nuclear testing in the atmosphere or below ground, deforestation, polluting air and water—results in global warming and climate change, as well as a myriad of local effects. Without question, hurricanes, flooding, earthquakes, etc., are much more devastating than they would have been otherwise.

We also need to recognize that with modern technology, most natural disasters can be predicted ahead of time. Therefore, we cannot blame God for those who are killed or injured because they did not heed warnings to get out of harm's way—whether to leave an area or seek shelter. Once again, we admonish: *Do not test God*!

Pestilence or pandemics might seem harder to justify, but it is only in the last 100 years or so that the spiritual demise of man results in questioning and indicting God for them. We already alluded to the idea that the Black Plague in the Middle Ages,

---

[255] Exodus 4:23

which killed one-third of the European and Asian population, was due to the incredible and intolerable evil at that time. But other plagues over the centuries, devastating large regions were also seen as the result of man's evil. For example, between the second and sixth century, three devastating pandemics were major factors in the fall of the Roman Empire.

> The centuries of later Roman history might be considered the age of pandemic disease. Three times the empire was rocked by mortality events with stunning geographical reach. In AD 165, an event known as the Antonine Plague, probably caused by smallpox, erupted. In AD 249, an uncertain pathogen swept the territories under Roman rule. And in AD 541, the first great pandemic of *Yersinia pestis* [known as the Justinian plague], the agent that causes bubonic plague, arrived and lingered for over two hundred years. The magnitude of these biological catastrophes is almost incomprehensible.[256]

> The Justinianic plague, apart from its devastating immediate impact, is generally viewed as undermining the late Roman Empire, politically and economically, creating conditions ripe for disaster. Coupled with the other disasters during the reign of Justinian, the plague may have reduced the population of the Mediterranean world by the year 600, [up to] 60 percent of its count a century earlier. Such a massive mortality rate would naturally lead to social and economic ruin.[257]

And while the actual cause was biological, that was only "the means to an end"—God's retribution for the evil in the world.

---

[256] Harper, Kyle, *The Fate of Rome*, (Princeton, Princeton University Press, 2017), p. 18.
[257] See http://www.loyno.edu/~history/journal/1996-7/Smith.html

John of Ephesus was a Christian writer. To him, the plague was a manifestation of divine wrath, and a call for repentance. His account vividly detailed scenes of havoc in which men collapsed in agony within the public quarters. . .

Christian writers . . . clearly felt that the plague was a justifiable punishment . . . sent by God in response to human sinfulness.

"It was known," wrote Zachariah of Mytilene, "that it was a scourge from Satan, who was ordered by God to destroy men." Near Antioch, St. Symeon the Younger tearfully prayed to Jesus, and received the reply, "The sins of this people are manifold, and why do you bother yourself about their diseases? For you love them no more than I." . . . and paralleled a common fourteenth-century interpretation of the Black Death; that is, it was caused by the wrath of God.[258]

Summary

Despite the above, admittedly we cannot explain away *all* suffering, whether from illness, "Acts of God," death of young children, etc. We can only have faith that God has His reasons—which we are not privy to—and refer you to the *Book of Job*, which discusses this idea in great detail.

---

[258] See http://www.loyno.edu/~history/journal/1996-7/Smith.html

Reasons for Suffering

Having seen that most of the *causes* of physical and emotional suffering cannot be attributed to God, we now examine the reasons we suffer—whether acutely and short term, or chronically and longer term. It may surprise you that there are not just two or three reasons for suffering, but closer to a dozen.

- *Punishment for Sins*

This is the most obvious reason, although not necessarily the most common. Whether in the Five Books of Moses, the Gospels, the Koran, the Psalms, or the Prophets, there are literally hundreds of examples in which God states directly or through His prophets, that those who sin will be punished; *that evil will not be tolerated*—as when Sodom and Gomorrah were destroyed for their wickedness!

> Praiseworthy is the one who disdains the counsel of the wicked,
> Nor follows in the way of the sinful,
> Nor sits in the chambers of the scornful. . . .
> He shall be like a tree rooted by rivers of water
> That bring forth its fruit in its season,
> And whose leaf shall never wither.
> All he undertakes will succeed.
> But not so for the wicked.
> They are like the chaff which the wind disperses.
> Accordingly, the iniquitous will not prevail when judged,
> Nor will the sinful enter into the congregation of the righteous.
> For the Lord appreciates the way of the upright,
> While the path of the wicked lies in ruins.[259]

---

[259] Psalm: 1

This holds for individuals as well as for a nation!

"[God] takes note of their actions. He overthrows them in the night and they are vanquished. He punishes them for their evil because they rebelled against Him and had no regard for His ways. They caused the poor to cry before Him, so that He heard the cry of the indigent. But if He remains silent, who can condemn Him? He rules over the *individual* and the nations alike—to keep the godless from oppressing the people!"[260]

- ***As a Preventive before one will Sin***

There are times one suffers and is afflicted, although he/she may be sin free. This happens because God knows what is in the hearts and thoughts of man, and sees, that in desperation, a normally good individual contemplates an action which would have tragic consequences. For example, a homeless person is desperate for money and plans to rob a liquor store. He procures a gun which is not loaded, as he has no intention of using it. He doesn't know, however, that the proprietor also has one, having been held up several times. God knows that in the attempt, the proprietor will make a play for his gun, the robber will panic, and in the struggle, the gun will go off and kill the owner.

As the robber will either be executed or spend the rest of his life in prison, God, in His mercy, sees to it that he breaks his leg the day before the planned robbery. Although the pain is excruciating, while the robber is immobile, he comes to his senses and figures out how to get his life back on track.

---

[260] Job 34:25

"Now, Job, hear me out. Why do you complain to [God] that He responds to no man's words? For God does not speak directly. Rather through a dream, or in a vision of the night, when deep sleep falls upon people, He will speak in their ears and give them ample warning, to turn them from evil and keep them from haughtiness; to preserve them from the pit—from their lives from perishing by the sword.

God does all these things to a person twice, even three times—to turn them back from sin, that the light of life may shine upon them."[261]

- *Self-Inflicted.*

There should be no question that much suffering is *self-inflicted*—accounting perhaps for the *major cause of suffering* in the world—brought on by our own foolishness or evil, when we do things that we know could have nasty consequences. It could be as simple as over indulging in alcohol and having a vicious hangover the next morning, eating foods we're allergic to and getting a severe rash or intractable migraine, or going off our diabetic diet—which can be life-threatening.

Also, as stated earlier, we are too often reckless, which can result in a major accident; we physically or emotionally abuse others, or abuse ourselves by becoming an alcoholic or drug addict. What about visiting a prostitute and getting beat up and robbed, or worse, coming down with a severe venereal disease?

Could anyone claim God is responsible for our own stupidity or moral weakness?

---

[261] Job 33:1

- *As a Sacrifice/Substitute for Another's Sins.*

It should not surprise some readers that an additional reason for suffering is to atone for others. For God explicitly stated that was His intention—for one to suffer for the sins of many.

> Who would believe what we have heard! For whom has the arm of the Lord been revealed! He grew up like a tender shoot, and like a root in arid ground. He had neither beauty nor majesty—nothing in his appearance that would make us desire him. He was despised and rejected by men, a man of sorrows and acquainted with grief.
> Yet in truth, he took up our pain and he bore our suffering, although *we* considered him stricken by God. But he was afflicted for our transgressions and suffered for our iniquities. What he bore was for our benefit; and through his pain we are healed. For like sheep each of us has gone astray, engaging in our own evil. So the Lord has placed upon him the iniquity of us all . . . though he had committed no evil, nor was there deceit in his mouth.
> Therefore, he will be given a portion among the nobility and he will divide the spoils with the mighty, because he gave up his life and was considered as one with the iniquitous. For though he bore the sins of many, he prayed for the people![262]

Christians, of course, believe that Jesus was the "suffering servant," others believe it was Job, while traditional Judaism holds it is the nation of Israel that God is referring to. While it is beyond the scope of this work to speculate exactly whom God had in mind, there is no reason to think *it was a one-time only prophesy*. It is more reasonable to believe that throughout the Millennia, others—maybe thousands or more—chosen by God, *have and continue to suffer for the iniquities of mankind*!

---

[262] Isaiah: 53:1

Granted, it is difficult to understand why God would cause one individual to suffer for the sins of others, yet we will not second-guess Him—why He deems it necessary or desirable. We can only point out, whether rare or not, it needs to be included as a reason of suffering.

- ***To Test our Character***

There are times God wishes to test us, whether as a nation or individual, and so He might cause us to suffer to see how we will respond. Whether physical or emotional, the suffering is usually not life-threatening, but painful enough to tempt us to do or act in ways opposed to God. This relates to what we cited in Section I.

> And it came to pass, that Cain brought the fruit of the earth for an offering to the Lord. And Abel, as well, brought of the first of his flock and of the fat thereof. And the Lord accepted Abel's offering, but as for Cain and his offering, He desired not.
> So Cain became exceedingly wroth and his countenance fell. And the Lord said to Cain, "Why are you so wroth? And why has your countenance fallen? When you do well, shall it not be lifted up? Although, be advised should you not do well, sin crouches at your door and you shall be tempted by its desire. *But you may rule over it!*"[263]

When we transcend temptation and do what is good in God's eyes, the rewards are great.

- ***As a Prophylactic/Preventive Measure***

Recently a friend told me about her six-month old granddaughter, usually an easygoing and happy infant, who was in great pain and crying during a whole weekend. Why? She had

---

[263] Genesis 4:2

just been inoculated. Her reaction, although far worse than that of most babies, was clearly "suffering," yet no one would think of blaming God for the above. Rather, she suffered somewhat now, to protect her from more devastating illnesses in the future, such as smallpox, polio, whooping cough, or pneumonia.

- ***To Teach Us Wisdom***

Knowledge can be learned, but wisdom must be *experienced.* Accordingly, there are times we suffer because God wishes us to gain wisdom in one area or another—for example, when we lack empathy, ignore, or in the worst case, treat with disrespect others, such as the poor, the physically and mentally disabled, or the elderly. Thus, if we disdain and make fun of the homeless, don't be surprised if God takes away our assets or causes us to lose our job, so we ourselves are in danger of losing our shelter. Knowing how that feels is likely to make us a better person.

In the *moral* sphere, making fun of anyone, for any reason, is very unwise. For a day will come when we will be made twice as much fun of for the same reasons.

Also in this category we can add the love affairs of our youth that go sour. While not a moral issue, there is little that causes us as much pain than the suffering of a rejected suitor. But that is for our own good; to give us experience with various partners and teach us what qualities to look for in someone we will be spending our life with.

Then there are those among us who are ambitious, and want to accomplish a lot more than the average person. To do so, one must work hard and perhaps suffer—one disappointment after another—to gain the insight and experience necessary to succeed. Like becoming a world-class marathon runner, one must suffer for his goal. Included are "paying one's dues"; for example, working in corporate "Siberia" before becoming an executive at headquarters, or killing oneself by exercising 6 days a week to lose 30 pounds.

- **As God's Emissary**

I believe that much more often than we would imagine, God needs to test the integrity of one or more individuals by creating a situation which provides them a venue for choosing between good and evil; right and wrong. But as God works in the material world, He needs someone to interact with those individuals—sort of a sacrificial lamb—whether he/she is aware of it or not. Typically, God's "emissary" suffers as the result of the interaction.

As an example in my own life, several years ago I sued Amazon for defamation, related to a review someone placed about my book, *A Guide to the Psalms of David*. The review had nothing to do with the book's content, but castigated me for marketing it by sending one-time unsolicited emails to selected individuals. Although the review was clearly a violation of Amazon's policy, and I twice asked Amazon to remove it, they refused. I had little choice but to sue them *pro se*, as I could not afford a lawyer.

I was quite content to let a jury of my peers decide if, in fact, the review *was* defamation. But Amazon's attorneys filed a dismissal motion prior to even answering my complaint, on what I assert was shaky legal grounds.[264] The lower court of one judge dismissed it for one of the reasons Amazon brought, the Appellate Court of four judges upheld the dismissal with a most superficial explanation, while the New York State Court of Appeals—the highest state court—denied my application for an appeal, despite the fact that the issue involved constitutional issues that, by law, should have given me the right to be heard.

As much stress and emotional suffering the suit cost me over three years, I was aware that God was testing at least a dozen individuals: Amazon executives who refused to remove the review, the law firm that defended them, and most importantly, the eleven judges who had to decide whether to do the right thing based upon the merits of the case.

I believe many of us are put into situations that become contentious and cause us suffering, because God needs us to interact with others to determine their character. Our consolation

---

[264] Amazon's motion for dismissal was based on the grounds that the review was an *opinion* (as opposed to a *false* statement of fact) which they claimed was not actionable. I argued that the review was a factual assertion that could be evaluated as to its truth or falsity. But more significant, even considering it an opinion, because it was obvious the reviewer deliberately and callously desired to harm me—in legal terms, known as *actual malice*—the supposed protection given to opinions is negated in New York law, and the case should have gone to trial.

is that God will take up our cause at some point, and those individuals who failed to act justly will be punished. But even more importantly, God appreciates that we had to suffer in His behalf, and we can be sure He will make it up to us in one way or another.

- ***To Identify with God***

Last, but not least, we suggest one further reason some of us suffer, although it may be questioned by many readers. But considering that a major postulate of this book is that God wants a relationship with man, we cannot rule it out.

What could be more important in a relationship than when each party has empathy for one another? Could anything bring the two closer? If God has empathy for man, should not man have empathy for God? Thus some of us may suffer for no other reason than to help us understand how God feels, and how much He suffers because of the evil in the world.

Who initiates the suffering is hard to answer; but what is important is our *perception* that the only reason we are suffering is to get closer to God. This should motivate us try to be a better person, have more integrity, and do acts of kindness that will ease God's pain.

A Final Word

Did not King David state long ago:

> The evil ones say to themselves,
> "There is no God."
> They are corrupt and have acted abominably.
> There is not even one who does good.
> The Lord searches from heaven
> among the children of men,
> To determine if there is anyone of understanding
> who seeks Him.
> But they have all turned aside.
> Together they have become vile.
> There is no one who does good—
> *Not even one!*[265]

Imagine how much of a difference it would make to God, if *you* were the one!

This very difficult, but important, chapter has not given us all the answers for why we suffer, but hopefully we will have gained greater insight into its causes and reasons—and help us see that God is usually not to blame. Clearly, suffering is very real, and all of us suffer at one time or another. There are probably other reasons for suffering, we have not thought of. Perhaps you can think of additional ones.

Finally, we hope this chapter will help *you* avoid suffering, by acting proactively, so that accidents, illnesses, and the like can be prevented or made minimal.

---

[265] Psalm 14

Chapter 24
The Meaning of Life

We are now are prepared to examine perhaps the most profound question of all: What are we here for? Are we here to do God's Will? Or is it remotely possible God wishes to do *our* Will? While virtually all religions assert the former, in reviewing all we have discovered, there is substantial evidence for the latter! While there were some individuals over the course of history; prophets such as Moses, Jonah, and Jeremiah that God specifically stated He had a mission for, which they resisted at first—but which, critically, they were *not* forced to do—that was the exception to the rule. Let us explain why the idea God desires to do *our Will* is more tenable.

A Question of Will

First, God has already created beings—angels—that *do His will and only His Will*. So why would He create humans to have the same restrictions. More decisively, God, being all powerful, can do anything He wants, and has everything He needs. And as He is beneficent, what would He gain by creating a species—humans—*just* to do His will. That doesn't seem like a very good God to me!

Indeed, in Psalm 50 God declares:

> Hear, Oh people, and I will speak.
> I need not take a bullock from your dwelling,
> Nor he-goats from your folds.
> For every beast of the forest is Mine;
> As are the cattle grazing on a thousand hills.

> Were I hungry, I would not tell you!
> For all the earth and its fullness is Mine.
> Shall I eat the flesh of bullocks
> Or drink the blood of he-goats?
> Rather, offer to God thanksgiving,
> And redeem your vows to the Most High.
> Call upon Me on the day of distress.
> I will deliver you, and you shall honor Me."
> Whoever appreciates My bounty, honors Me.
> And to him who orders his way,
> I will show the salvation of the Lord.[266]

As an analogy, imagine you are interviewed by a medium-sized company for your expertise: engineering, accounting, information services, perhaps marketing, and you meet with the CEO, who is ready to make you an offer. He says, "I understand you are very good at your profession and you can help our company. I am prepared to hire you, with an excellent salary, full health benefits, a 401K plan, three weeks vacation to start, and stock options, provided you agree to the following."

"What is that, sir?" you ask.

He hands you a document that states you will use your talent to carry out *his* will and direction. Whatever *he* deems best for the company, you will implement it. The document explicitly states you are to do *no* independent thinking or suggest proposals for new ways of doing business. There will be no arguments, discussions, or debates once you get your assignment. He impresses upon you that he has been successful for 25 years, and

---

[266] Psalm 50

everything needs to be done his way. You only carry out the details. "If that's agreeable, sign here and you can start Monday."

Would any sane person take that job? Sure, there is great pay and other benefits, but at what price—selling your soul to be a slave? Did you go to college, graduate school, and work very hard to learn your profession, only to discover the 35 years or so you will be working, you will simply be a robot following one man's whims? I don't think so. The CEO is not an especially a good person, nor has he wisdom. Indeed, he is a control freak!

But God is not a control freak!

And God has wisdom we cannot begin to fathom. It is inconceivable for God to have created humans with the same restrictions as the CEO—that they must do His Will. As already stated, that does not seem to be a beneficent God. Only humans—misinformed and without good reason—tell us we need to do God's will. But, in fact, God states quite the opposite.

Thus, after David committed adultery with Bathsheba and had her husband, Uriah, placed in the front lines where the chances were good he'd be killed, God sent the prophet, Nathan, to inform David that he was to be severely punished.

> "I anointed you king over Israel and delivered you from Saul's hand. I gave you his house, and all of Israel. If that was not enough, *I would have given you even more*! Then why have you despised the word of the Lord doing what is evil in My eyes? You have struck down Uriah the Hittite with the

sword and taken his wife as your own. What you did in secret will be done to you in public."[267]

Saving the World

Follow your dreams, but do so with clean hands and a pure heart; that is all God requires! God hates deceit or hypocrisy. To be sure, I am not remotely suggesting you give up your religion. The culture you grew up in is important to adhere to; it provides the comfort we all need. Only put religion in perspective. At best, it is a means to the end, not an end in-and-of itself. God created the world before religion. All was good. There was no death, famine, sickness, hurricanes, or war. The world was pure, and God could walk "softly" in His garden. Adam and Eve only had one commandment: not to eat from the Tree of the Knowledge of Good and Evil.

Alas, having free will, they failed to keep it, and since then, God's love for us has been on rocks. But that can change! Remember, history is not based on power, economics, or politics, but on the moral decisions individuals and nations make!

Let us all learn from the Book of Esther, when the king's minister Haman decreed that on a certain date, all the Jews in the Kingdom of Persia were to be destroyed and their possessions taken as spoils. The queen's uncle, Mordechai, appealed to Esther to intercede on behalf of her people:

---

[267] II Samuel 12:7

So [Mordechai] charged [Esther] that she should appeal to the king for her people. . . . And Esther [replied,] "All in the king's realm know that whoever shall approach the king in the inner court without being summoned shall be put to death, except such to whom the king shall hold out his golden scepter. But I have not been called into the king's court these thirty days."

Then Mordechai wrote to Esther, "Do not think that you shall escape because you are queen, any more than all the other Jews. For if you remain silent, then deliverance shall arise from another; but you and your father's house shall be destroyed. Besides, who knows whether you have become queen for such a time as this?"

So Esther answered, "Instruct all the Jews that are present in the Capitol to fast for me, and neither eat nor drink for three days. I and my maidens will fast likewise; and then I will approach the king—and if I die, I die."[268]

Esther interceded, the king held out his scepter, and she revealed what Haman had planned, enraging the king. Haman was hung, and the Jews saved.

Accordingly, it behooves us to concern ourselves with *each* and *every* ethical decision we make, however trivial it seems. At the same time, we should take great encouragement in that each of us, whether born into great poverty or great wealth, is capable of changing the world! On what basis can one make that statement? It is built upon an idea best echoed by Maimonides: "A person must see himself and the world as equally balanced on two ends of a scale. By doing one good deed, he tips the scale and brings for himself and the entire world redemption and

---

[268] Esther 4:8

salvation."[269] For who is to say that God did not long ago decide, that when the number of ethically "good" choices (helping one's neighbor) is one greater than the number of ethically "bad" choices (spurning a poor person), redemption and salvation would follow!

Your destiny is not fated or absolute. It all depends on you!

Do good, take God into consideration, and you will thrive!

And like Noah, you can save the world!

---

[269] Maimonides, *Laws of Repentance*: No. 3:4.
https://yeshua1blog.files.wordpress.com/2014/09/maimonides-the-laws-of-repentance.pdf

Epilogue

If you have gotten this far without skipping chapters, you might concede that some of your ideas, thoughts, and impressions of God need re-evaluating—whatever religion, if any, you may subscribe to. If so, the author sincerely hopes it will result in God becoming more personal to you—that you will establish a relationship with Him—so your life will be more meaningful, easier, less painful, and more joyous. *God may be ineffable, but He is not unreachable*!

For we have shown how to gain God's blessings. It is really not that hard. As the title, "Love on the Rocks" suggests, God created us out of His love, but we as humans have abrogated our responsibility, caused Him untold pain, and to a greater or lesser extent are estranged from Him. Isn't it time we re-evaluated our behavior and altered it? After all, God is not asking us to go to a mountain, eat berries and flagellate ourselves three times a day. Nor is He requiring us to sit and study the Talmud or the Koran from six in the morning to midnight, get some sleep, and do it again next day, while our spouses struggle with paying the bills and bringing up the children. Nor does God *not* want us to enjoy marital relations, watch a ballgame, enjoy a Bach concert, or see a Broadway play. He is only asking us to be righteous; to be compassionate; to have integrity; to be charitable. And imagine the bonus we would receive, if we heeded the many signs He provides to help us with our daily lives. Is that so difficult?

Appendix I
The Ten Commandments[270]

(1) I am the Lord your God, Who brought you out of the land of Egypt—the house of slavery. You shall have no other gods besides Me.

(2) You shall not make for yourself an idol, or any likeness of what is in heaven above, on the earth below, or in the seas. You shall not worship or serve them; for I, the Lord, am a jealous God, visiting the iniquity of the fathers upon the children of the third and fourth generations of those who hate Me, but showing favor to the thousandth generation of those who love Me and keep My commandments.

(3) You shall not take the Name of the Lord your God in vain, for the Lord will not hold him guiltless who takes His Name in vain.

(4) Remember the Sabbath to keep it holy. Six days you shall labor and do all your work, but the seventh day is a Sabbath of the Lord your God. You shall not do any work; neither you, nor your son, nor your daughter, nor your male nor your female servant, nor your cattle, nor the sojourner who stays with you. For in six days the Lord made the heavens and the earth, the sea and all that is in them, and rested on the seventh day. Therefore, the Lord blessed the Sabbath day and made it holy.

(5) Honor your father and your mother, that your days may be prolonged in the land which the Lord your God gives you.

(6) You shall not murder.

(7) You shall not commit adultery.

(8) You shall not steal.

(9) You shall not bear false witness against your neighbor.

(10) You shall not covet your neighbor's house. You shall not covet your neighbor's wife, nor his male servant, nor his female servant, nor his ox, his donkey, nor anything that belongs to him.

---

[270] Exodus 20:2

Appendix II
FAQs about God

1. What are the essential attributes of God?
   God is loving, righteous, truthful, compassionate, fair, forgiving, and faithful.

2. Does God have feelings?
   Yes!

3. Can you negotiate with God?
   Absolutely. Everything is negotiable—even with God. For examples, see Scripture relating to Cain, Abraham, and Moses.[271] God listens to man. How many times did He want to destroy the Children of Israel, but changed His mind because of Moses?

4. Does God have unlimited Power?
   Yes, except He can voluntarily give some of it up.

5. Is God Perfect?
   That is a meaningless question. Perfection is a **human** *concept and does not apply to God. Even humans do not agree on what it means. For example, if someone is tried for murder who actually committed it and is sentenced to death, many would say the law is imperfect, because they are against capital punishment. But that is only their opinion. Another example: In baseball, a pitcher retires all 27 batters in a row, and so is credited with a perfect game. But from the perspective of the team that lost, they were as imperfect as can be.*

6. Should or can we depend on God to perform miracles?
   No. Or, at least, not any more. God truly helps those that help themselves. Do not rely on miracles. We live in a material world, and God is committed to having His creation interact with His established laws. God provides us with knowledge; how we use it—for good or evil—is up to us.

---

[271] Genesis 4:5; Genesis 18.24; Exodus 33:13

7. Can God ever be deceitful?
   No. Deceit is a negation of truth.

8. What was God's first act of compassion?
   In gently asking Adam and Eve, "Where art thou?" Although God knew they sinned by eating from the tree, and knew where they were, He gave them a chance to catch their breath, perhaps admit their sin, and ask for forgiveness. Alas, Eve blamed the serpent, and Adam blamed Eve.

9. Is God involved in the daily lives of individuals?
   Absolutely. God is continually giving us taps on the shoulder, so to speak. But we must be open to them. As the sages of old declared, "Give God the eye of a needle and you will be able to drive a wagon through."[272]

10. Does God want us to be poor and constantly do penance?
    Not at all. To God, material wealth is absolutely acceptable. Abraham, Isaac, Jacob, Solomon, and Mohammed, to name a few, were quite wealthy. We only need to arrive at it honestly, and be charitable once we have it.

---

[272] See http://www.aish.com/h/hh/rh/ag/Let_Me_In.html

Appendix III
Ten Ways to Connect to God

There are easily dozens, if not hundreds, of ways in your everyday life that you can connect to God; little things you can do that will not only make God feel good, but make you feel good—and result in additional blessings for you. Following are ten simple things you can do on a daily basis. I have tried them all, and can personally testify to what follows.

I'm sure you can think of many more. What is common about them is that you desire to honor God by doing a good deed, refraining from evil, and/or appreciating His creation. Try to do one positive thing a day, and see if life doesn't become easier for you.

- *Don't pay cash to avoid sales tax.*
  When paying a large bill such as for auto repairs or furniture, and the proprietor tells you if you pay by cash or even write a check, he won't charge you sales tax. *Decline!* It is against the law (in most states), and while you may never be caught (and presumably he won't have to report your business as income), God knows and will be displeased.

- *Let busses or trucks have right of way.*
  If driving in the city streets and a bus or truck is signaling to pull out from the curb, don't speed up to get around them. Rather stop and let them go ahead of you. Soon you will notice that when you want to pull out from the curb, and there is a bus or truck behind you, *they* will stop for *you*.

- *If you are in the right lane of an expressway, and an entrance is ahead, move to center lane—if safe—so cars entering can do so safely.*
  As in the above, you will find that when *you* enter a highway, God will usually see to it that you have plenty of time to merge into the traffic flow.

- *Pick up litter, coffee cups, flyers, candy wrappers, etc., when seeing them on God's grass.*

  Picking up even one item a day tells God you are thinking of Him, and making up for someone who had the insensitivity to litter His creation.

- *Hold a door or the elevator for someone even if they are more than a few feet away.*

  While you might hold the door for an elderly person four steps behind you, when going into a building, look around and if it seems someone even 25 feet way is also going inside, be courteous and hold the door as well. You will feel good, the person will feel good, and God will feel good.

- *Don't gloat if you win a bet, or your team wins a sports event.*

  When doing anything competitive and you win, don't gloat and/or make fun of your opponent(s). When you hurt someone's feelings, God is extremely displeased.

- *Never embarrass someone, if at all possible. (Although if someone insults or disrespects you for no good reason, feel free to put him/her in his/her place.)*

- *Compliment a person—if sincere—when you can.*

  For example, a cashier with a pretty dress or hair style; a colleague wearing a nice suit or tie.

- *When you pass a homeless person, give him/her a dollar.*

  Don't judge someone less fortunate, and don't be callous. Have a little compassion for another, and, when you need it, God will have a lot of compassion for you,

- *When you are at the cashier with your cart full, let someone with a few items go ahead of you—especially if they are elderly or disabled*

  Again, God will be pleased by your compassion and reward you in kind.

Appendix IV
Psalms for Special Situations

Of all the books of the Old Testament, *The Psalms* can unlock the door to God. Equally valued by Jews and Christians, they constitute close to 50 percent of traditional Jewish liturgy. For Christians, they are, arguably, sung, recited, read, or used as a basis for a sermon more than any other text in Scripture.

Following are psalms suitable to recite for a number of special situations most of encounter during the course of our life. For a modern non-denomination translation of the psalms, *A Guide to the Psalms of David* by the author can be purchased at Amazon, or ordered at your local bookstore.

<u>DAYS OF OUR LIFE</u>
JOINING THE ARMY/GOING TO WAR
2...9...11...18...27...121...144

SEEKING EMPLOYMENT
20...104...112...113...141...145

SEEKING A MATE
1...20...128

BEFORE A WEDDING
67...112...133...134

FOR A BARREN COUPLE
112...113...127...128

DURING PREGNANCY/BEFORE GIVING BIRTH
127...128...145

310 Appendix IV

DURING A DIVORCE BREAKUP
16... 23...121...145...146

BEFORE SURGERY
24... 34...103...121

FOR A SERIOUS ILLNESS
16... 20...103...121...146

AT THE DEATH OF A LOVED ONE
8...23...33...117...150

NEEDING HELP
SUFFERING EMOTIONAL OR PHYSICAL ABUSE
3...5...6...52...55...64...70...140...142

AFTER A NATURAL DISASTER
32...46...49...91

WHEN IN DANGER
3...5...7...13...46...86...116...142

AFTER BEING RESCUED FROM DANGER
6...40...107...116...120

IF SUICIDAL
42...77...116...139

MISCELLANEOUS PETITIONS
GOING ON LONG TRIP (ESPECIALLY BY PLANE)
8...121...146

FEELING ALONE
23...120...121...123...130...142

IF NEEDY/POOR
34...49...112...113...146...147

UPON SEEING BEAUTIFUL SUNRISE/NATURAL PHENONEMA
8...19...104...111...136...148

Appendix V
An Irresistible Force vs. an Immovable Object

Have you ever thought what happens when an *irresistible force* and *immovable object* collide? Guess what? That is a logical impossibility! No universe can include *both*! If there is such a thing as an *irresistible force* and an *immovable object*, they must—by definition—be in *separate* universes.

But isn't God both? For is there anyone or anything that can resist Him?

> *Then the Lord answered Job out of the whirlwind, and said: "Who is this who darkens counsel by words without knowledge? Where were you when I laid the foundations of the earth? Who determined its measurements? To what were its foundations fastened? Or Who laid its cornerstone? Who shut in the sea with doors, when it burst forth and issued from the womb; When I made the clouds its garment, And thick darkness its swaddling band; When I fixed My limit for it, and set bars and doors; when I said, 'This far you may come, but no further; here your proud waves must stop! Tell Me, if you have understanding.'"*[273]

On the other hand, is there anyone or anything that can move Him?

> *Then the cloud covered the tent of meeting, and the glory of the Lord filled the tabernacle. And Moses was not able to enter the tent of meeting, because the cloud rested above it, and the glory of the Lord filled the tabernacle.*[274]

"Aha," you say. "God is in a *separate* universe from us."

But wait . . . Is that really the case? After all, doesn't Scripture tell us clearly that God is *here*, in *our* universe—the one *He* created for *us*?

---

[273] Job 38:1
[274] Exodus 40:38

"True," you say. "So our logic must be deficient."

But that doesn't seem right either, for *logic* comes from God; so our ability to reason *must* be perfect!

"You're stuck," you say?

No problem. If you think about it for a little while, it is really quite simple . . . God *transcends* logic and can accomplish what to us seems impossible! Now, is there anyone in our universe who has that power; i.e. is both an *irresistible force and an immovable object?*

NOT A CHANCE!

That being the case, I, for one, would want to hitch up my pants to His star. Wouldn't you? I mean, let's face it. To rise up the metaphorical *corporate ladder*, whatever our ambitions may be requires a "rabbi" of some sort; one who watches over us; mentors us; encourages us; goes to bat for us. And can there be any greater rabbi then God, Who is both an *irresistible force* and *immovable object*!

But if we want His help, we need to show we are worthy of it; that we deserve it. How does one figure *that* out? Ah. That is easy, it is in Scripture. His teachings and guidelines of ethical and compassionate behavior are usually pretty clear.

But even when they are not, if you are sincere and make a reasonable effort to understand what God desires from you, He will help you figure it out. *That I am absolutely convinced of*!

He will inform you in a myriad of ways, sometimes directly, sometimes guiding you to a rabbi or pastor, doctor or janitor, engineer, butcher, or plumber who will show you the way—whether directly or through associations that will have special meaning to you.

So let God guide you! But under no circumstances, let another human being *dictate* what you should do. After all, what makes you think they have any more *wisdom* than you? (I would assert neither *knowledge nor brilliance* equates to *wisdom*. Indeed, they are usually negatively correlated.)

Do *not put your trust in princes, in mere men in whom there is no help. When he is gone, he returns to the earth.*[275]

How do you know when someone is *dictating* to you?

*Every question should be so easy. It is a **no-brainer**!*

If what someone tells you does not feel right—goes against your *intuition or conscience*—do *not* listen! That is a human *dictating*. God, on the other hand, *guides* and *teaches*. Of course, there will be times when things are muddled; when you are at sea; when you are not sure whether to go right or left; whether to follow Route A or Route B. When that occurs, *pray* to God! Do not be afraid! Do not feel you are unworthy, for that alone makes you worthy! Ask God for guidance, *directly*; in whatever language you are most comfortable with.

HE will not let you down!

---

[275] Psalm 146:3

Appendix VI
Ten Truisms about God

- God helps those that help themselves.
- Your deeds—good or bad—will come back to you.
- God will almost always give you the benefit of the doubt.
- God will help you real-time—if you let Him.
- Kindness and compassion go a long way with God.
- God is reasonable. You can negotiate with Him.
- God gives His love and blessings to those deserving.
- If you sincerely repent of evil, God will forgive you.
- God does not want you to appease those who are evil.
- Follow your intuition—it comes directly from God.

Appendix VII
Psalm 37
by David.

[1] Do not compete with villains
Nor be envious of the workers of iniquity.
[2] For like grass, they shall soon be uprooted;
And like greenery they will wither.
[3] Rather trust in the Lord and do good.
Dwell in the land, and sustain yourself upon His faithfulness.
[4] Delight in the Lord,
And He shall bestow upon you your heart's desires.
[5] Give your allegiance to the Lord, and He shall reciprocate.
[6] He shall reveal your righteousness as light,
And your fair-mindedness as high-noon.
[7] Remain calm in the Lord's Presence, and maintain patience.
Do not be envious of him who prospers—
The man who succeeds because of subterfuge.
[8] Cease from anger and abandon wrath.
Do not agonize; it only results in harm.
[9] For evildoers shall be cut off;
But those who hope in the Lord shall inherit the earth.
[10] Just a moment longer and the wicked shall be no more.
You will seek him, but he will not be found.
[11] Rather, the meek shall inherit the earth
And shall delight in abundant tranquility.
[12] The wicked devise plots against the righteous. . . .
[13] My Master laughs for He knows that his day is approaching.
[14] The wicked have unsheathed their swords.
They have bent their bows
To discomfit the poor and downtrodden;
To slaughter those who are upright.
[15] Their swords shall pierce their own hearts.
Their bows shall be shattered.
[16] Preferable are a few with the righteous
Than an army of the wicked.
[17] For the arms of the wicked shall be broken,
While the Lord sustain the righteous.
[18] The Lord appreciates the efforts of the upright,
And their heritage will endure forever.
[19] They will not be disgraced in times of evil.
During days of famine they shall eat their fill.
[20] But the wicked shall perish; and the adversaries of the Lord—

Like the fullness of vineyards—shall be consumed.
Like smoke they shall leave no trace.
[21] The wicked borrow and do not repay.
But the righteous is generous and bestows.
[22] Therefore, His hallowed ones shall inherit the earth.
But His accursed ones shall be cut off.
[23] The footsteps of the sincere are watched over by the Lord;
For He delights in his way.
[24] Though he may fall, he shall not be utterly abandoned.
The Lord will support him with His hand.
[25] I have been a youth, and now I am old.
Yet I have never seen the righteous entirely forsaken,
Nor his children begging for bread.
[26] For he is continually gracious and lends.
In his merit, his descendants are blessed.
[27] Renounce evil, do good, and abide forever.
[28] For the Lord loves justice, and does not forsake His faithful.
They are watched over forever.
But the descendants of the wicked shall be cut off.
[29] The righteous shall inherit the land, and inhabit it forever.
[30] The mouth of the righteous speaks wisdom
And his tongue talks of justice.
[31] The law of his God is in his heart;
His convictions never vacillate.
[32] The wicked stalk the righteous, and seek his death.
[33] But the Lord will not abandon him to their treacheries,
Nor allow him to be condemned when judged.
[34] Hope to the Lord and follow His paths,
And He shall exalt you to inherit the land.
And you will behold the expulsion of the wicked.
[35] I have seen the wicked prosper;
Deeply rooted as an indigenous evergreen.
[36] But Lo, he vanished; behold, he was no more.
I sought him, but he could not be found.
[37] Observe a man of integrity and behold the upright.
For the destiny of that man is peace.
[38] The corrupt shall be destroyed altogether;
For the future of the wicked is extermination.
[39] But deliverance of the righteous is from the Lord.
He is their strength in times of distress.
[40] The Lord shall help them and liberate them.
He shall deliver them from evildoers and rescue them,
Because they sought refuge in Him.

CPSIA information can be obtained
at www.ICGtesting.com
Printed in the USA
FSHW01n0854310718